The Wives of Henry the Eighth
and the Parts They Played in History

The Wives of
Henry the Eighth
and the Parts They Played in History

Martin A.S. Hume

United Kingdom
1905

Contents

PREFACE 1

CHAPTER I 3

    1488-1501 3

    INTRODUCTORY—WHY KATHARINE CAME TO ENGLAND—POLITICAL MATRIMONY
    3

CHAPTER II... 17

    1501-1509 17

    KATHARINE'S WIDOWHOOD AND WHY SHE STAYED IN ENGLAND 17

CHAPTER III 44

    1509-1527 44

    KATHARINE THE QUEEN—A POLITICAL MARRIAGE AND A PERSONAL DIVORCE.... 44

CHAPTER IV 74

    1527-1530 74

    KATHARINE AND ANNE—THE DIVORCE 74

CHAPTER V 101

    1530-1534 101

    HENRY'S DEFIANCE—THE VICTORY OF ANNE 101

CHAPTER VI 129

    1534-1536 129

    A FLEETING TRIUMPH—POLITICAL INTRIGUE AND THE BETRAYAL OF ANNE 129

CHAPTER VII... 164

    1536-1540 164

    PLOT AND COUNTERPLOT—JANE SEYMOUR AND ANNE OF CLEVES.................... 164

CHAPTER VIII 198

    1540-1542 198

    THE KING'S "GOOD SISTER" AND THE KING'S BAD WIFE—THE LUTHERANS AND
    ENGLISH CATHOLICS... 198

CHAPTER IX 225

    1542-1547 225

    KATHARINE PARR—THE PROTESTANTS WIN THE LAST TRICK 225

PREFACE

Either by chance or by the peculiar working of our constitution, the Queen Consorts of England have as a rule been nationally important only in proportion to the influence exerted by the political tendencies which prompted their respective marriages. England has had no Catharine or Marie de Medici, no Elizabeth Farnese, no Catharine of Russia, no Caroline of Naples, no Maria Luisa of Spain, who, either through the minority of their sons or the weakness of their husbands, dominated the countries of their adoption; the Consorts of English Kings having been, in the great majority of cases, simply domestic helpmates of their husbands and children, with comparatively small political power or ambition for themselves. Only those whose elevation responded to tendencies of a nationally enduring character, or who represented temporarily the active forces in a great national struggle, can claim to be powerful political factors in the history of our country. The six Consorts of Henry VIII., whose successive rise and fall synchronised with the beginning and progress of the Reformation in England, are perhaps those whose fleeting prominence was most pregnant of good or evil for the nation and for civilisation at large, because they personified causes infinitely more important than themselves.

The careers of these unhappy women have almost invariably been considered, nevertheless, from a purely personal point of view. It is true that the many historians of the Reformation have dwelt upon the rivalry between Katharine of Aragon and Anne Boleyn, and their strenuous efforts to gain their respective ends; but even in their case their action has usually been regarded as individual in impulse, instead of being, as I believe it was, prompted or thwarted by political forces and considerations, of which the Queens themselves were only partially conscious. The lives of Henry's Consorts have been related as if each of the six was an isolated phenomenon that had by chance attracted the desire of a lascivious despot, and in her turn had been deposed when his eye had fallen, equally fortuitously, upon another woman who pleased his errant fancy better. This view I believe to be a superficial and misleading one. I regard Henry himself not as the far-seeing statesman he is so often depicted for us, sternly resolved from the first to free his country from the yoke of Rome, and pressing forward through a lifetime with his eyes firmly fixed upon the goal of England's religious freedom; but rather as a weak, vain, boastful man, the plaything of his passions, which were artfully made use of by rival parties to forward religious and political ends in the struggle of giants that ended in the Reformation. No influence that could be exercised over the King was neglected by those who sought to lead him, and least of all that which appealed to his uxoriousness; and I hope to show in the text of this book how each of his wives in turn was but an instrument of politicians, intended to sway the King on one side or the other. Regarded from this point of view, the lives of these six unhappy Queens assume an importance in national history which cannot be accorded to them if they are considered in the usual light as the victims of a strong, lustful tyrant, each one standing apart, and in her turn simply the darling solace of his hours of dalliance. Doubtless the latter point of view provides to the historian a wider scope for the description of picturesque ceremonial and gorgeous millinery, as well as for pathetic passages dealing with the personal sufferings of the Queens in their distress; but I can only hope that the absence of much of this sentimental and feminine interest from my pages will be compensated by the wider aspect in which the public and political significance of Henry's wives is presented; that a clearer understanding than usual may thus be gained of the tortuous process by which the Reformation in England was effected, and that the figure of the King in the picture may stand in a juster proportion to his environment than is often the case.

MARTIN HUME.

LONDON, *October* 1905.

CHAPTER I

1488~1501

INTRODUCTORY—WHY KATHARINE CAME TO ENGLAND—POLITICAL MATRIMONY

The history of modern Europe takes its start from an event which must have appeared insignificant to a generation that had witnessed the violent end of the English dominion in France, had been dinned by the clash of the Wars of the Roses, and watched with breathless fear the savage hosts of Islam striking at the heart of Christendom over the still smoking ruins of the Byzantine Empire.

Late one night, in the beginning of October 1469, a cavalcade of men in the guise of traders halted beneath the walls of the ancient city of Burgo de Osma in Old Castile. They had travelled for many days by little-used paths through the mountains of Soria from the Aragonese frontier town of Tarrazona; and, impatient to gain the safe shelter of the fortress of Osma, they banged at the gates demanding admittance. The country was in anarchy. Leagues of churchmen and nobles warred against each other and preyed upon society at large. An impotent king, deposed with ignominy by one faction, had been as ignominiously set up again by another, and royal pretenders to the succession were the puppets of rival parties whose object was to monopolise for themselves all the fruits of royalty, whilst the monarch fed upon the husks. So when the new-comers called peremptorily for admittance within the gates of Osma, the guards upon the city walls, taking them for enemies or freebooters, greeted them with a shower of missiles from the catapults. One murderous stone whizzed within a few inches of the head of a tall, fair-haired lad of good mien and handsome visage, who, dressed as a servant, accompanied the cavalcade. If the projectile had effectively hit instead of missed the stripling, the whole history of the world from that hour to this would have been changed, for this youth was Prince Ferdinand, the heir of Aragon, who was being conveyed secretly by a faction of Castilian nobles to marry the Princess Isabel, who had been set forward as a pretender to her brother's throne, to the

~ 3 ~

exclusion of the King's doubtful daughter, the hapless Beltraneja. A hurried cry of explanation went up from the travellers: a shouted password; the flashing of torches upon the walls, the joyful recognition of those within, and the gates swung open, the drawbridge dropped, and thenceforward Prince Ferdinand was safe, surrounded by the men-at-arms of Isabel's faction. Within a week the eighteen-years-old bridegroom greeted his bride, and before the end of the month Ferdinand and Isabel were married at Valladolid.

To most observers it may have seemed a small thing that a petty prince in the extreme corner of Europe had married the girl pretender to the distracted and divided realm of Castile; but there was one cunning, wicked old man in Barcelona who was fully conscious of the importance of the match that he had planned; and he, John II. of Aragon, had found an apt pupil in his son Ferdinand, crafty beyond his years. To some extent Isabel must have seen it too, for she was already a dreamer of great dreams which she meant to come true, and the strength of Aragon behind her claim would insure her the sovereignty that was to be the first step in their realisation.

This is not the place to tell how the nobles of Castile found to their dismay that in Ferdinand and Isabel they had raised a King Stork instead of King Log to the throne, and how the Queen, strong as a man, subtle as a woman, crushed and chicaned her realms into order and obedience. The aims of Ferdinand and his father in effecting the union of Aragon and Castile by marriage went far beyond the Peninsula in which they lived. For ages Aragon had found its ambitions checked by the consolidation of France. The vision of a great Romance empire, stretching from Valencia to Genoa, and governed from Barcelona or Saragossa, had been dissipated when Saint Louis wrung from James the Conqueror, in the thirteenth century, his recognition of French suzerainty over Provence.

But Aragonese eyes looked still towards the east, and saw a Frenchman ever in their way. The Christian outpost in the Mediterranean, Sicily, already belonged to Aragon; so did the Balearic isles: but an Aragonese dynasty held Naples only in alternation and constant rivalry with the French house of Anjou; and as the strength of the French monarchy grew it stretched forth its hands nearer, and ever nearer, to the weak and divided principalities of Italy with covetous intent. Unless Aragon could check the French expansion across the Alps its own power in the Mediterranean would be dwarfed, its vast hopes must be abandoned, and it must settle down to the inglorious life of a petty State, hemmed in on all sides by more powerful neighbours. But although too weak to vanquish France alone, a King of Aragon who could dispose of the resources of greater Castile might hope, in spite of French opposition, to dominate a united Italy, and thence look towards the illimitable east. This was the aspiration that Ferdinand inherited, and to which the efforts of his long and strenuous life were all directed. The conquest of Granada, the unification of Spain, the greed, the cruelty, the lying, the treachery, the political marriages of all his children, and the fires of the Inquisition, were all means to the end for which he fought.

But fate was unkind to him. The discovery of America diverted Castilian energy from Aragonese objects, and death stepped in and made grim sport of all his marriage jugglery. Before he died, beaten and broken-hearted, he knew that the little realm of his fathers, instead of using the strength of others for its aims, would itself be used for objects which concerned it not. But though he failed his plan was a masterly one. Treaties, he knew, were rarely binding, for the age was faithless, and he himself never kept an oath an hour longer than suited him; but mutual interests by kinship might hold sovereigns together against a common opponent. So, one after the other, from their earliest youth, the children of Ferdinand and Isabel were made political counters in their father's great marriage league. The eldest daughter, Isabel, was married to the heir of Portugal, and every haven into which French galleys might shelter in their passage from the Mediterranean to the Bay of Biscay was at Ferdinand's bidding. The only son, John, was married to the daughter of Maximilian, King of the Romans, and (from 1493) Emperor, whose interest also it was to check the French advance towards north Italy and his own dominions. The second daughter, Juana, was married to the Emperor's son, Philip, sovereign, in right of his mother, of the rich inheritance of Burgundy, Flanders, Holland, and the Franche Comté, and heir to Austria and the Empire, who from Flanders might be trusted to watch the French on their northern and eastern borders; and the youngest of Ferdinand's daughters, Katharine, was destined almost from her birth to secure the alliance of England, the rival of France in the Channel, and the opponent of its aggrandisement towards the north.

Ferdinand of Aragon and Henry Tudor, Henry VII., were well matched. Both were clever, unscrupulous, and greedy; each knew that the other would cheat him if he could, and tried to get the better of every deal, utterly regardless not only of truth and honesty but of common decency. But, though Ferdinand usually beat Henry at his shuffling game, fate finally beat Ferdinand, and a powerful modern England is the clearly traceable consequence. How the great result was brought about it is one of the principal objects of this book to tell. That Ferdinand had everything to gain by thus surrounding France by possible rivals in his own interests is obvious, for if his plans had not miscarried he could have diverted France whenever it suited him, and his way towards the east would have been clear; but at first sight the interest of Henry VII. in placing himself into a position of antagonism towards France for the benefit of the King of Spain is not so evident. The explanation must be found in the fact that he held the throne of England by very uncertain tenure, and sought to disarm those who would be most able and likely to injure him. The royal house of Castile had been closely allied to the Plantagenets, and both Edward IV. and his brother Richard had been suitors for the hand of Isabel. The Dowager-Duchess of Burgundy, moreover, was Margaret Plantagenet, their sister, who sheltered and cherished in Flanders the English adherents of her house; and Henry Tudor, half a Frenchman by birth and sympathies, was looked at askance by the powerful group of Spain, the Empire, and Burgundy when first he usurped the English throne. He knew that he had little or nothing to fear from France, and one of his earliest acts was in 1487 to bid for the friendship of Ferdinand by means of an offer of alliance, and the marriage of his son Arthur, Prince of Wales, then a year old, with the Infanta Katharine, who was a few months older. Ferdinand at the time was trying to bring about a match between his eldest daughter, Isabel, and the young King of France, Charles VIII., and was not very eager for a new English alliance which might alarm the French. Before the end of the year, however, it was evident that there was no chance of the Spanish Infanta's marriage with Charles VIII. coming to anything, and Ferdinand's plan for a great coalition against France was finally adopted.

In the first days of 1488 Ferdinand's two ambassadors arrived in London to negotiate the English match, and the long duel of diplomacy between the Kings of England and Spain began. Of one of the envoys it behoves us to say something, because of the influence his personal character exercised upon subsequent events. Rodrigo de Puebla was one of the most extraordinary diplomatists that can be imagined, and could only have been possible under such monarchs as Henry and Ferdinand, willing as both of them were to employ the basest instruments in their underhand policy. Puebla was a doctor of laws and a provincial mayor when he attracted the attention of Ferdinand, and his first diplomatic mission of importance was that to England. He was a poor, vain, greedy man, utterly corrupt, and Henry VII. was able to dominate him from the first. In the course of time he became more of an intimate English minister than a foreign ambassador, though he represented at Henry's court not only Castile and Aragon, but also the Pope and the Empire. He constantly sat in the English council, and was almost the only man admitted to Henry's personal confidence. That such an instrument would be trusted entirely by the wary Ferdinand, was not to be expected: and though Puebla remained in England as ambassador to the end of his life, he was, to his bitter jealousy, always associated with others when important negotiations had to be conducted. Isabel wrote to him often, sometimes threatening him with punishment if he failed in carrying out his instructions satisfactorily, sometimes flattering him and promising him rewards, which he never got. He was recognised by Ferdinand as an invaluable means of gaining knowledge of Henry's real intentions, and by Henry as a tool for betraying Ferdinand. It is hardly necessary to say that he alternately sold both and was never fully paid by either. Henry offered him an English bishopric which his own sovereigns would not allow him to accept, and a wealthy wife in England was denied him for a similar reason; for Ferdinand on principle kept his agents poor. On a wretched pittance allowed him by Henry, Puebla lived thus in London until he died almost simultaneously with his royal friend. When not spunging at the tables of the King or English nobles he lived in a house of ill-fame in London, paying only twopence a day for his board, and cheating the other inmates, in the interests of the proprietor, for the balance. He was, in short, a braggart, a liar, a flatterer, and a spy, who served two rogues roguishly and was fittingly rewarded by the scorn of honest men.

This was the ambassador who, with a colleague called Juan de Sepulveda, was occupied through the spring of 1488 in negotiating the marriage of the two babies— Arthur, Prince of Wales, and the Infanta Katharine. They found Henry, as Puebla says, singing *Te Deum Laudamus* about the alliance and marriage: but when the parties came to close quarters matters went less smoothly. What Henry had to gain by the alliance was the disarming of possible enemies of his own unstable throne, whilst Ferdinand needed England's active or passive support in a war against France, for the purpose of extorting the restoration to Aragon of the territory of Roussillon and Cerdagne, and of preventing the threatened absorption of the Duchy of Brittany into the French monarchy. The contest was keen and crafty. First the English commissioners demanded with the Infanta a dowry so large as quite to shock Puebla; it being, as he said, five times as much as had been mentioned by English agents in Spain. Puebla and Sepulveda offered a quarter of the sum demanded, and hinted with pretended jocosity that it was a great condescension on the part of the sovereigns of Spain to allow their daughter to marry at all into such a parvenu family as the Tudors. After infinite haggling, both as to the amount and the form of the dowry, it was agreed by the ambassadors that 200,000 gold crowns of 4s. 2d. each should be paid in cash with the bride on her marriage. But the marriage was the least part of Ferdinand's object, if indeed he then intended, which is doubtful, that it should take place at all. What he wanted was the assurance of Henry's help against France; and, of all things, peace was the first need for the English king. When the demand was made therefore that England should go to war with France whenever Ferdinand chose to do so, and should not make peace without its ally, baited though the demand was with the hollow suggestion of recovering for England the territories of Normandy and Guienne, Henry's duplicity was brought into play. He dared not consent to such terms, but he wanted the benevolent regards of Ferdinand's coalition: so his ministers flattered the Spanish king, and vaguely promised "mounts and marvels" in the way of warlike aid, as soon as the marriage treaty was signed and sealed. Even Puebla wanted something more definite than this; and the English commissioners (the Bishop of Exeter and Giles Daubeney), "took a missal in their hands and swore in the most solemn way before the crucifix that it is the will of the King of England first to conclude the alliance and the marriage, and afterwards to make war upon the King of France, according to the bidding of the Catholic kings." Nor was this all: for when Puebla and his colleagues later in the day saw the King himself, Henry smiled at and flattered the envoys, and flourishing his bonnet and bowing low each time the names of Ferdinand and Isabel passed his lips, confirmed the oath of his ministers, "which he said we must accept for plain truth, unmingled with double dealing or falsehood." Ferdinand's ambassadors were fairly dazzled. They were taken to see the infant bridegroom; and Puebla grew quite poetical in describing his bodily perfections, both dressed and *in puribus naturalibus*, and the beauty and magnificence of the child's mother were equally extolled. The object of all Henry's amiability, and, indeed, of Puebla's dithyrambics also, was to cajole Ferdinand into sending his baby daughter Katharine into England at once on the marriage treaty alone. With such a hostage in his hands, Henry knew that he might safely break his oath about going to war with France to please the Spanish king.

But Ferdinand was not a man easy to cajole, and when hapless, simple Sepulveda reached Spain with the draft treaty he found himself in the presence of two very angry sovereigns indeed. Two hundred thousand crowns dowry, indeed! One hundred was the most they would give, and that must be in Spanish gold, or the King of England would be sure to cheat them over the exchange; and they must have three years in which to pay the amount, for which moreover no security should be given but their own signatures. The cost of the bride's trousseau and jewels also must be deducted from the amount of the dowry. On the other hand, the Infanta's dowry and income from England must be fully guaranteed by land rents; and, above all, the King of England must bind himself at the same time— secretly if he likes, but by formal treaty— to go to war with France to recover for Ferdinand Roussillon and Cerdagne. Though Henry would not go quite so far as this, he conceded much for the sake of the alliances so necessary to him. The dowry from Spain was kept at 200,000 crowns, and England was pledged to a war with France whenever Ferdinand should find himself in the same position.

With much discussion and sharp practice on both sides the treaties in this sense were signed in March 1489, and the four-years-old Infanta Katharine became Princess of Wales. It is quite clear throughout this early negotiation that the marriage that should give to the powerful coalition of which Ferdinand was the head a family interest in the maintenance of the Tudor dynasty was Henry's object, to be gained on terms as easy as practicable to himself; whereas with Ferdinand the marriage was but the bait to secure the armed co-operation of England against France; and probably at the time neither of the kings had any intention of fulfilling that part of the bargain which did not specially interest him. As will be seen, however, the force of circumstances and the keenness of the contracting parties led eventually to a better fulfilment of the treaty than was probably intended.

For the next two years the political intrigues of Europe centered around the marriage of the young Duchess of Brittany. Though Roussillon and Cerdagne mattered nothing to Henry VII., the disposal of the rich duchy opposite his own shores was of importance to him. France, Spain, England, and the Empire were all trying to outbid one another for the marriage of the Duchess; and, as Charles VIII. of France was the most dangerous suitor, Henry was induced to send his troops across the Channel to Brittany to join those of Spain and the Empire, though neither of the latter troops came. From the first all the allies were false to each other, and hastened to make separate terms with France; Ferdinand and Maximilian endeavouring above all to leave Henry at war. When, at the end of 1491, Charles VIII. carried off the matrimonial prize of the Duchess of Brittany and peace ensued, none of the allies had gained anything by their tergiversation. Reasons were soon found by Ferdinand for regarding the marriage treaty between Arthur and Katharine as in abeyance, and once more pressure was put upon Henry to buy its fulfilment by another warlike coalition. The King of England stood out for a time, especially against an alliance with the King of the Romans, who had acted so badly about Brittany; but at length the English contingent was led against Boulogne by the King himself, as part of the allied action agreed upon. This time, however, it was Henry who, to prevent the betrayal he foresaw, scored off his allies, and without striking a blow he suddenly made a separate peace with France (November 1492). But yet he was the only party who had not gained what he had bid for. Roussillon and Cerdagne were restored to Ferdinand, in consequence of Henry's threat against Boulogne; France had been kept in check during the time that all the resources of Spain were strained in the supreme effort to capture the last Moorish foothold in the Peninsula, the peerless Granada; the King of France had married the Duchess of Brittany and had thus consolidated and strengthened his realm; whilst Henry, to his chagrin, found that not only had he not regained Normandy and Guienne, but that in the new treaty of peace between Spain and France, "Ferdinand and Isabel engage their loyal word and faith as Christians, not to conclude or permit any marriage of their children with any member of the royal family of England; and they bind themselves to assist the King of France against all his enemies, and *particularly against the English*." This was Henry's first experience of Ferdinand's diplomacy, and he found himself outwitted at every point. Katharine, all unconscious as she conned her childish lessons at Granada, ceased for a time to be called "Princess of Wales."

With the astute King of England thus cozened by Ferdinand, it is not wonderful that the vain and foolish young King of France should also have found himself no match for his new Spanish ally. Trusting upon his alliance, Charles VIII. determined to strike for the possession of the kingdom of Naples, which he claimed as representing the house of Anjou. Naples at the time was ruled by a close kinsman of Ferdinand, and it is not conceivable that the latter ever intended to allow the French to expel him for the purpose of ruling there themselves. But he smiled, not unkindly at first, upon Charles's Italian adventure, for he knew the French king was rash and incompetent, and that the march of a French army through Italy would arouse the hatred and fear of the Italian princes and make them easy tools in his hands. The King of

Naples, moreover, was extremely unpopular and of illegitimate descent: and Ferdinand doubtless saw that if the French seized Naples he could not only effect a powerful coalition to expel them, but in the scramble might keep Naples for himself; and this is exactly what happened. The first cry against the French was raised by the Pope Alexander VI., a Spanish Borgia. By the time Charles VIII. of France was crowned King of Naples (May 1495) all Italy was ablaze against the intruders, and Ferdinand formed the Holy League— of Rome, Spain, Austria, Venice, and Milan— to crush his enemies.

Then, as usual, he found it desirable to secure the benevolence of Henry VII. of England. Again Henry was delighted, for Perkin Warbeck had been received by Maximilian and his Flemish kinsmen as the rightful King of England, and the Yorkist nobles still found aid and sympathy in the dominions of Burgundy. But Henry had already been tricked once by the allies, and was far more difficult to deal with than before. He found himself, indeed, for the first time in the position which under his successors enabled England to rise to the world power she attained; namely, that of the balancing factor between France and Spain. This was the first result of Ferdinand's coalition against France for the purpose of forwarding Aragonese aims, and it remained the central point of European politics for the next hundred years. Henry was not the man to overlook his new advantage, with both of the great European powers bidding for his alliance; and this time he drove a hard bargain with Ferdinand. There was still much haggling about the Spanish dowry for Katharine, but Henry stood firm at the 200,000 gold crowns, though a quarter of the amount was to take the form of jewels belonging the bride. One stipulation was that the new marriage was to be kept a profound secret, in order that the King of Scots might not be alarmed; for Ferdinand was trying to draw even him away from France by hints of marriage with an Infanta. By the new treaty, which was signed in October 1497, the formal marriage of Arthur and Katharine *per verba de presenti* was to be celebrated when Arthur had completed his fourteenth year; and the bride's dowry in England was to consist of a third of the revenues of Wales, Cornwall, and Chester, with an increase of the income when she became Queen.

But it was not all plain sailing yet. Ferdinand considered that Henry had tricked him about the amount and form of the dowry, but the fear that the King of France might induce the English to enter into a new alliance with him kept Ferdinand ostensibly friendly. In the summer of 1598 two special Spanish ambassadors arrived in London, and saw the King for the purpose of confirming him in the alliance with their sovereigns, and, if we are to believe Puebla's account of the interview, both Henry and his Queen carried their expressions of veneration for Ferdinand and Isabel almost to a blasphemous extent. Henry, indeed, is said to have had a quarrel with his wife because she would not give him one of the letters from the Spanish sovereigns always to carry about with him, Elizabeth saying that she wished to send her letter to the Prince of Wales.

But for all Henry's blandishments and friendliness, his constant requests that Katharine should be sent to England met with never-failing excuses and procrastination. It is evident, indeed, throughout that, although the Infanta was used as the attraction that was to keep Henry and England in the Spanish, instead of the French, interest, there was much reluctance on the part of her parents, and particularly of Queen Isabel, to trust her child, to whom she was much attached, to the keeping of a stranger, whose only object in desiring her presence was, she knew, a political one. Some anxiety was shown by Henry and his wife, on the other hand, that the young Princess should be trained in a way that would fit her for her future position in England. The Princess Margaret of Austria, daughter of Maximilian, who had just married Ferdinand's heir, Prince John, was in Spain, and Puebla reports that the King and Queen of England were anxious that Katharine should take the opportunity of speaking French with her, in order to learn the language. "This is necessary, because the English ladies do not understand Latin, and much less Spanish. The King and Queen also wish that the Princess should accustom herself to drink wine. The water of England is not drinkable, and even if it were, the climate would not allow the drinking of it." The necessary Papal Bulls for the marriage of the Prince and Princess arrived in 1498, and Henry pressed continually for the coming of the bride, but Ferdinand and Isabel were in no hurry. "The manner in which the marriage is to be performed, and the Princess sent to England, must all be settled first." "You must negotiate these points," they wrote to Puebla, "*but make no haste.*" Spanish envoys of better character and greater impartiality than Puebla urged that Katharine should be sent "before she had become too much attached to Spanish life and institutions"; though the writer of this admits the grave inconvenience of subjecting so young a girl to the disadvantages of life in Henry's court.

Young Arthur himself, even, was prompted to use his influence to persuade his new wife to join him, writing to his "most entirely beloved spouse" from Ludlow in October 1499, dwelling upon his earnest desire to see her, as the delay in her coming is very grievous to him, and he begs it may be hastened. The final disappearance of Perkin Warbeck in 1499 greatly changed the position of Henry and made him a more desirable connection: and the death without issue of Ferdinand's only son and heir about the same time, also made it necessary for the Spanish king to draw his alliances closer, in view of the nearness to the succession of his second daughter, Juana, who had married Maximilian's son, the Archduke Philip, sovereign of Flanders, who, as well as his Spanish wife, were deeply distrusted by both Ferdinand and Isabel. In 1500, therefore, the Spanish sovereigns became more acquiescent about their daughter's coming to England. By Don Juan Manuel, their most skilful diplomatist, they sent a message to Henry in January 1500, saying that they had determined to send Katharine in the following spring without waiting until Arthur had completed his fourteenth year. The sums, they were told, that had already been spent in preparations for her reception in England were enormous, and when in March there was still no sign of the bride's coming, Henry VII. began to get restive. He and his country, he said, would suffer great loss if the arrival of the Princess were delayed. But just then Ferdinand found that the treaty was not so favourable for him as he had expected, and the whole of the conditions, particularly as to the payment of the dowry, and the valuation of the bride's jewels, had once more to be laboriously discussed; another Spanish ambassador being sent, to request fresh concessions. In vain Puebla told his master that when once the Princess arrived all England would be at his bidding, assured him of Henry's good faith, and his own ability as a diplomatist. Ferdinand always found some fresh subject to be wrangled over: the style to be given to the King of England, the number of servants to come in the train of Katharine, Henry desiring that they should be few and Ferdinand many, and one of the demands of the English king was, "that the ladies who came from Spain with the Princess should all be beautiful, or at least none of them should be ugly."

In the summer of 1500 there was a sudden panic in Ferdinand's court that Henry had broken off the match. He had gone to Calais to meet for the first time the young Archduke Philip, Ferdinand's son-in-law, and it was rumoured that the distrusted Fleming had persuaded Henry to marry the Prince of Wales to his sister the Arch duchess Margaret, the recently widowed daughter in-law of Ferdinand. It was not true, though it made Ferdinand very cordial for a time, and soon the relations between England and Spain resumed their usual course of smooth-tongued distrust and tergiversation. Still another ambassador was sent to England, and reported that people were saying they believed the Princess would never come, though great preparations for her reception continued to be made, and the English nobles were already arranging jousts and tournaments for her entertainment. Ferdinand, on the other hand, continued to send reassuring messages. He was, he said, probably with truth now, more desirous than ever that the marriage should take place when the bridegroom had completed his fourteenth year; but it was necessary that the marriage should be performed again by proxy in Spain before the bride embarked. Then there was a delay in obtaining the ships necessary for the passage, and the Spanish sovereigns changed their minds again, and preferred that the second marriage, after Arthur had attained his fifteenth year, should be performed in England. The stormy weather of August was then an excuse for another delay on the voyage, and a fresh quibble was raised about the value of the Princess's jewels being considered as part of the *first* instalment of the dowry. In December 1500 the marriage was once more performed at Ludlow, Arthur being again present and pledging himself as before to Puebla.

Whilst delaying the voyage of Katharine as much as possible, now probably in consequence of her youth, her parents took the greatest of care to convince Henry of the indissoluble character of the marriage as it stood. Knowing the King of England's weakness, Isabel wrote in March 1501 deprecating the great expense he was incurring in the preparations. She did not wish, she said, for her daughter to cause a loss to England, either in money or any other way; but to be a source of happiness to every one. When all was ready for the embarkation at Corunna in April 1501, an excuse for further delay was found in a rebellion of the Moors of Ronda, which prevented Ferdinand from escorting his daughter to the port; then both Isabel and Katharine had a fit of ague, which delayed the departure for another week or two. But at last the parting could be postponed no longer, and for the last time on earth Isabel the Catholic embraced her favourite daughter Katharine in the fairy palace of the Alhambra which for ever will be linked with the memories of her heroism.

The Queen was still weak with fever, and could not accompany her daughter on the way, but she stood stately in her sternly suppressed grief, sustained by the exalted religious mysticism, which in her descendants degenerated to neurotic mania. Grief unutterable had stricken the Queen. Her only son was dead, and her eldest daughter and her infant heir had also gone to untimely graves. The hopes founded upon the marriages of their children had all turned to ashes, and the King and Queen saw with gloomy foreboding that their daughter Juana and her foreign husband would rule in Spain as well as in Flanders and the Empire, to Spain's irreparable disaster; and, worst of all, Juana had dared to dally with the hated thing heresy. In the contest of divided interest which they foresaw, it was of the utmost importance now to the Catholic kings that England at least should be firmly attached to them; and they dared no longer delay the sacrifice of Katharine to the political needs of their country. Katharine, young as she was, understood that she was being sent to a far country amongst strangers as much an ambassador as a bride, but she from her birth had been brought up in the atmosphere of ecstatic devotion that surrounded her heroic mother, and the din of battle against the enemies of the Christian God had rarely been silent in her childish ears. So, with shining eyes and a look of proud martyrdom, Katharine bade the Queen a last farewell, turned her back upon lovely Granada, and through the torrid summer of 1501 slowly traversed the desolate bridle-roads of La Mancha and arid Castile to the green valleys of Galicia, where, in the harbour of Corunna, her little fleet lay at anchor awaiting her.

From the 21st of May, when she last looked upon the Alhambra, it took her nearly two months of hard travel to reach Corunna, and it was almost a month more before all was ready for the embarkation with the great train of courtiers and servants that accompanied her. On the 17th August 1501 the flotilla sailed from Corunna, only to be stricken the next day by a furious north-easterly gale and scattered; the Princess's ship, in dire danger, being driven into the little port of Laredo in the north of Spain. There Katharine was seriously ill, and another long delay occurred, the apprehension that some untoward accident had happened to the Princess at sea causing great anxiety to the King of England, who sent his best seamen to seek tidings of the bride. The season was late, and when, on the 26th September 1501, Katharine again left Laredo for England, even her stout heart failed at the prospect before her. A dangerous hurricane from the south accompanied her across the Channel and drove the ships finally into the safety of Plymouth harbour on Saturday the 2nd October 1501.

The Princess was but little expected at Plymouth, as Southampton or Bristol had been recommended as the best ports for her arrival; and great preparations had been made for her reception at both those ports. But the Plymouth folk were nothing backward in their loyal welcome of the new Princess of Wales; for one of the courtiers who accompanied her wrote to Queen Isabel that "she could not have been received with greater rejoicings if she had been the saviour of the world." As she went in solemn procession through the streets to the church of Plymouth to give thanks for her safety from the perils past, with foreign speech sounding in her ears and surrounded by a curious crowd of fair folk so different from the swarthy subjects of her mother that she had left behind at Granada, the girl of sixteen might well be appalled at the magnitude of the task before her. She knew that henceforward she had, by diplomacy and woman's wit, to keep the might and wealth of England and its king on the side of her father against France; to prevent any coalition between her new father-in-law and her brother-in-law Philip in Flanders in which Spain was not included; and, finally, to give an heir to the English throne, who, in time to come, should be Aragonese in blood and sympathy. Thenceforward Katharine must belong to England in appearance if her mission was to succeed; and though Spain was always in her heart as the exotic pomegranate of Granada was on her shield, England in future was the name she conjured by, and all England loved her, from the hour she first set foot on English soil to the day of the final consummation of her martyrdom.

CHAPTER II

1501~1509

KATHARINE'S WIDOWHOOD AND WHY SHE
STAYED IN ENGLAND

The arrival of Katharine in England as his son's affianced wife meant very much for Henry VII. and his house. He had already, by a master-stroke of diplomacy, betrothed his eldest daughter to the King of Scots, and was thus safe from French intrigue on his vulnerable northern border, whilst the new King of France was far too apprehensive of Ferdinand's coalition to arouse the active enmity of England. The presence of Ferdinand's daughter on English soil completed the security against attack upon Henry from abroad. It is true that the Yorkists and their friends were still plotting: "Solicited, allured and provoked, by that old venomous serpent, the Duchess of Burgundy, ever the sower of sedition and beginner of rebellion against the King of England;" but Henry knew well that with Katharine at his Court he could strike a death-blow, as he soon did, at his domestic enemies, without fear of reprisals from her brother-in-law Philip, the present sovereign of Burgundy and Flanders.

Messengers were sent galloping to London to carry to the King the great news of Katharine's arrival at Plymouth; but the roads were bad, and it was not Henry's way to spoil his market by a show of over-eagerness, and though he sent forward the Duchess of Norfolk and the Earl of Surrey to attend upon the Princess on her way towards London, the royal party did not set out from Shene Palace to meet her until the 4th November. Travelling through a drenching rain by short stages from one seat to another, Henry VII. and his daughter-in-law gradually approached each other with their splendid troops of followers, all muffled up, we are told, in heavy rain cloaks to shield their finery from the inclemency of an English winter. Young Arthur, coming from the seat of his government in Wales, met his father near Chertsey, and together they continued their journey towards the west. On the third day, as they rode over the Hampshire downs, they saw approaching them a group of horsemen, the leader of which dismounted and saluted the King in Latin with a message from Ferdinand and Isabel. Ladies in Spain were kept in strict seclusion until their marriage, and the messenger, who was the Protonotary Cañazares, sent with Katharine to England to see that Spanish etiquette was not violated, prayed in the name of his sovereigns that the Infanta should not be seen by the King, and especially by the bridegroom, until the public marriage was performed. This was a part of the bargain that the cautious Puebla had not mentioned, and Henry was puzzled at such a request in his own realm, where no such oriental regard for women was known. Hastily taking counsel of the nobles on horseback about him, he decided that, as the Infanta was in England, she must abide by English customs. Indeed the demand for seclusion seems to have aroused the King's curiosity, for, putting spurs to his horse, with but a small following, and leaving the boy bridegroom behind, he galloped on to Dogmersfield, at no great distance away, where the Infanta was awaiting his arrival. When he came to the house in which she lodged, he found a little group of horrified Spanish prelates and nobles, the Archbishop of Santiago, the Bishop of Majorca, and Count Cabra, at the door of the Infanta's apartments, barring entrance. The Princess had, they said, retired to her chamber and ought not to be disturbed. There was no restraining a king in his own realm, however, and Henry brushed the group aside. "Even if she were in bed," he said, "he meant to see and speak with her, for that was the whole intent of his coming."

Finding that Spanish etiquette would not be observed in England, Katharine made the best of matters and received Henry graciously, though evidently her Latin and French were different from his; for they were hardly intelligible to one another. Then, after the King had changed his travelling garb, he sent word that he had a present for the Princess; and led in the blushing Prince Arthur to the presence of his bride. The conversation now was more easily conducted, for the Latin-speaking bishops were close by to interpret. Once more, and for the fourth time, the young couple formally pledged their troth; and then after supper the Spanish minstrels played, and the ladies and gentlemen of Katharine's suite danced: young Arthur, though unable to dance in the Spanish way, trod an English measure with Lady Guildford to show that he was not unversed in courtly graces.

Arthur appears to have been a slight, fair, delicate lad, amiable and gentle, and not so tall as his bride, who was within a month of sixteen years, Arthur being just over fifteen. Katharine must have had at this time at least the grace of girlhood, though she never can have been a great beauty. Like most of her mother's house she had pale, rather hard, statuesque features and ruddy hair. As we trace her history we shall see that most of her mistakes in England, and she made many, were the natural result of the uncompromising rigidity of principle arising from the conviction of divine appointment which formed her mother's system. She had been brought up in the midst of a crusading war, in which the victors drew their inspiration, and ascribed their triumph, to the special intervention of the Almighty in their favour; and already Katharine's house had assumed as a basis of its family faith that the cause of God was indissolubly linked with that of the sovereigns of Castile and Leon. It was impossible that a woman brought up in such a school could be opportunist, or would bend to the petty subterfuges and small complaisances by which men are successfully managed; and Katharine suffered through life from the inflexibility born of self-conscious rectitude.

Slowly through the rain the united cavalcades travelled back by Chertsey; and the Spanish half then rode to Kingston, where the Duke of Buckingham, with four hundred retainers in black and scarlet, met the bride, and so to the palace at Kennington hard by Lambeth, where Katharine was lodged until the sumptuous preparations for the public marriage at St. Paul's were completed. To give a list of all the splendours that preceded the wedding would be as tedious as it is unnecessary; but a general impression of the festivities as they struck a contemporary will give us a far better idea than a close catalogue of the wonderful things the Princess saw as she rode her white palfrey on the 12th November through Southwark, over London Bridge, and by Cheapside to the Bishop of London's house adjoining St. Paul's. "And, because I will not be tedious to you, I pass over the wise devices, the prudent speeches, the costly works, the cunning portraitures, practised and set forth in seven beautiful pageants erected and set up in divers places of the city. I leave also the goodaly ballds, the sweet harmony, the musical instruments, which sounded with heavenly noise in every side of the street. I omit the costly apparel, both of goldsmith's work and embroidery, the rich jewels, the massy chains, the stirring horses, the beautiful bards, and the glittering trappers, both with bells and spangles of gold. I pretermit also the rich apparel of the Princess, the strange fashion of the Spanish nation, the beauty of the English ladies, the goodly demeanour of the young damosels, the amorous countenance of the lusty bachelors. I pass over the fine engrained clothes, the costly furs of the citizens, standing upon scaffolds, railed from Gracechurch to St. Paul's. What should I speak of the odoriferous scarlets, and fine velvet and pleasant furs, and rich chains, which the Mayor of London with the Senate, sitting on horseback at the little conduit in Chepe, ware upon their bodies and about their necks. I will not molest you with rehearsing the rich arras, the costly tapestry, the fine cloths of silver and of gold, the curious velvets and satins, the pleasant silks, which did hang in every street where she passed; the wine that ran out of the conduits, the gravelling and railing of the streets, and all else that needeth not remembring." In short, we may conclude that Katharine's passage through London before her wedding was as triumphal as the citizens could make it. Even the common people knew that her presence in England made for security and peace, and her Lancastrian descent from John of Gaunt seemed to add promise of legitimacy to future heirs to the crown.

A long raised gangway of timber handsomely draped ran from the great west door of St. Paul's to the entrance to the choir. Near the end of the gangway there was erected upon it a high platform, reached by steps on each side, with room on the top for eight persons to stand. On the north side of the platform sat the King and Queen incognito in a tribune supposed to be private; whilst the corporation of London were ranged on the opposite side. The day of the ceremony was the 14th November 1501, Sunday and the day of St. Erkenwald, and all London was agog to see the show. Nobles and knights from every corner of the realm, glittering and flashing in their new finery, had come to do honour to the heir of England and his bride. Both bride and bridegroom were dressed in white satin, and they stood together, a comely young pair, upon the high scarlet stage to be married for the fifth time, on this occasion by the Archbishop of Canterbury. Then, after mass had been celebrated at the high altar with Archbishops, and mitred prelates by the dozen, a procession was formed to lead the newly married couple to the Bishop of London's palace across the churchyard. The stately bride, looking older than her years, came first, followed by a hundred ladies; and whilst on her left hand there hobbled the disreputable, crippled old ambassador, Dr. Puebla, the greatest day of whose life this was, on the other side the Princess was led by the most engaging figure in all that vast assembly. It was that of a graceful little boy of ten years in white velvet and gold; his bearing so gallant and sturdy, his skin so dazzlingly fair, his golden hair so shining, his smile so frank, that a rain of blessings showered upon him as he passed. This was the bridegroom's brother, Henry, Duke of York, who in gay unconsciousness was leading his own fate by the hand.

Again the details of crowds of lords and ladies in their sumptuous garments, of banquets and dancing, of chivalric jousts and puerile maskings, may be left to the imagination of the reader. When magnificence at last grew palling, the young bride and bridegroom were escorted to their chamber in the Bishop of London's palace, with the broad suggestiveness then considered proper in all well-conducted weddings, and duly recorded in this case by the courtly chroniclers of the times. In the morning Arthur called at the door of the nuptial chamber to his attendants for a draught of liquor. To the bantering question of the chamberlain as to the cause of his unaccustomed thirst, it was not unnatural, considering the free manners of the day, that the Prince should reply in a vein of boyish boastfulness, with a suggestion which was probably untrue regarding the aridity of the Spanish climate and his own prowess as being the causes of his droughtiness. In any case this indelicate bit of youthful swagger of Arthur's was made, nearly thirty years afterwards, one of the principal pieces of evidence gravely brought forward to prove the illegality of Katharine's marriage with Henry.

On the day following the marriage the King and Queen came in full state to congratulate the newly married pair, and led them to the abode that had been elaborately prepared for them at Baynard's Castle, whose ancient keep frowned over the Thames, below Blackfriars. On the Thursday following the feast was continued at Westminster with greater magnificence than ever. In a splendid tribune extending from Westminster Hall right across what is now Parliament Square sat Katharine with all the royal family and the Court, whilst the citizens crowded the stands on the other side of the great space reserved for the tilters. Invention was exhausted by the greater nobles in the contrivances by which they sought to make their respective entries effective. One had borne over him a green erection representing a wooded mount, crowded with allegorical animals; another rode under a tent of cloth of gold, and yet another pranced into the lists mounted upon a stage dragon led by a fearsome giant; and so the pageantry that seems to us so trite, and was then considered so exquisite, unrolled itself before the enraptured eyes of the lieges who paid for it all. How gold plate beyond valuation was piled upon the sideboards at the great banquet after the tilt in Westminster Hall, how Katharine and one of her ladies danced Spanish dances and Arthur led out his aunt Cicely, how masques and devices innumerable were paraded before the hosts and guests, and, above all, how the debonair little Duke of York charmed all hearts by his dancing with his elder sister; and, warming to his work, cast off his coat and footed it in his doublet, cannot be told here, nor the ceremony in which Katharine distributed rich prizes a few days afterwards to the successful tilters. There was more feasting and mumming at Shene to follow, but at last the celebration wore itself out, and Arthur and his wife settled down for a time to married life in their palace at Baynard's Castle.

King Henry in his letter to the bride's parents, expresses himself as delighted with her "beauty and agreeable and dignified manners," and promises to be to her "a second father, who will ever watch over her, and never allow her to lack anything that he can procure for her." How he kept his promise we shall see later; but there is no doubt that her marriage with his son was a great relief to him, and enabled him, first to cast his net awide and sweep into its meshes all the gentry of England who might be presumed to wish him ill, and secondly to send Empson and Dudley abroad to wring from the well-to-do classes the last ducat that could be squeezed in order that he might buttress his throne with wealth. Probably Arthur's letter to Ferdinand and Isabel written at the same time (November 30, 1501) was drafted by other hands than his own, but the terms in which he expresses his satisfaction with his wife are so warm that they doubtless reflect the fact that he really found her pleasant. "He had never," he assured them, "felt so much joy in his life as when he beheld the sweet face of his bride, and no woman in the world could be more agreeable to him." The honeymoon was a short, and could hardly have been a merry, one; for Arthur was obviously a weakling, consumptive some chroniclers aver; and the grim old castle by the river was not a lively abode.

Before the marriage feast were well over, Henry's avarice began to make things unpleasant for Katharine. We have seen how persistent he had been in his demands that the dowry should be paid to him in gold, and how the bride's parents had pressed that the jewels and plate she took with her should be considered as part of the dowry. On Katharine's wedding the first instalment of 100,000 crowns had been handed to Henry by the Archbishop of Santiago, and there is no doubt that in the negotiations Puebla had, as usual with him, thought to smooth matters by concealing from both sovereigns the inconvenient conditions insisted by each of them. Henry therefore imagined— he said that he was led to believe it by Puebla— that the jewels and plate were to be surrendered to him on a valuation as part of the second instalment; whereas the bride's parents were allowed to suppose that Katharine would still have the enjoyment of them. In the middle of December, therefore, Henry sent for Juan de Cuero, Katharine's chamberlain, and demanded the valuables as an instalment of the remaining 100,000 crowns of the dowry. Cuero, astounded at such a request, replied that it would be his duty to have them weighed and valued and a list given to the King in exchange for a receipt for their value, but that he had not to give them up. The King, highly irate at what he considered an evasion of his due, pressed his demand, but without avail, and afterwards saw Katharine herself at Baynard's Castle in the presence of Doña Elvira Manuel, her principal lady in waiting.

What was the meaning of it, he asked, as he told her of Cuero's refusal to surrender her valuables in fulfilment of the promise, and further exposed Puebla's double-dealing. Puebla, it appears, had gone to the King, and had suggested that if his advice was followed the jewels would remain in England, whilst their value would be paid to Henry in money as well. He had, he assured the King, already gained over Katharine to the plan, which briefly was to allow the Princess to use the jewels and plate for the present, so that when the time came for demanding their surrender her father and mother would be ashamed of her being deprived of them, and would pay their value in money. Henry explained to Katharine that he was quite shocked at such a dishonest suggestion, which he refused, he said, to entertain. He had therefore asked for the valuables at once as he saw that there was craft at work, and he would be no party to it. He acknowledged, however, that the jewels were not due to be delivered until the last payment on account of the dowry had to be made. It was all Puebla's fault, he assured his daughter-in-law, which was probably true, though it will be observed that the course pursued allowed Henry to assert his eventual claim to the surrender of the jewels, and his many professions of disinterestedness cloaked the crudeness of his demand.

The next day Henry sent for Bishop Ayala, who was Puebla's colleague and bitter enemy, and told him that Prince Arthur must be sent to Wales soon, and that much difference of opinion existed as to whether Katharine should accompany him. What did Ayala advise? The Spaniard thought that the Princess should remain with the King and Queen in London for the present, rather than go to Wales where the Prince must necessarily be absent from her a good deal, and she would be lonely. When Katharine herself was consulted by Henry she would express no decided opinion; and Arthur was worked upon by his father to persuade her to say that she wished to go to Wales. Finding that Katharine still avoided the expression of an opinion, Henry, with a great show of sorrow, decided that she should accompany Arthur. Then came the question of the maintenance of the Princess's household. Puebla had again tried to please every one by saying that Henry would provide a handsome dotation for the purpose, but when Doña Elvira Manuel, on the eve of the journey to Wales, asked the King what provision he was going to make, he feigned the utmost surprise at the question. He knew nothing about it, he said. The Prince would of course maintain his wife and her necessary servants, but no special separate grant could be made to the Princess. When Puebla was brought to book he threw the blame upon the members of Katharine's household, and was publicly rebuked by Henry for his shiftiness. But the Spaniards believed, probably with reason, that the whole comedy was agreed upon between the King and Puebla to obtain possession of the plate and jewels or their value: the sending of the Princess to Wales being for the purpose of making it necessary that she should use the objects, and so give good grounds for a demand for their value in money on the part of Henry. In any case Katharine found herself, only five weeks after her marriage, with an unpaid and inharmonious household, dependent entirely upon her husband for her needs, and conscious that an artful trick was in full execution with the object of either depriving her of her personal jewels, and everything of value, with which she had furnished her husband's table as well as her own, or else of extorting a large sum of money from her parents. Embittered already with such knowledge as this, Katharine rode by her husband's side out of Baynard's Castle on the 21st December 1501 to continue on the long journey to Wales, after passing their Christmas at Oxford.

The plague was rife throughout England, and on the 2nd April 1502 Arthur, Prince of Wales, fell a victim to it at Ludlow. Here was an unforeseen blow that threatened to deprive both Henry and Ferdinand of the result of their diplomacy. For Ferdinand the matter was of the utmost importance; for an approachment of England and Scotland to France would upset the balance of power he had so laboriously constructed, already threatened, as it was, by the prospect that his Flemish son-in-law Philip and his wife would wear the crowns of the Empire, Flanders, and Burgundy, as well as those of Spain and its possessions; in which case, he thought, Spanish interests would be the last considered. The news of the unexpected catastrophe was greeted in London with real sorrow, for Arthur was promising and popular, and both Henry and his queen were naturally attached to their elder son, just approaching manhood, upon whose training they had lavished so much care. Though Henry's grief at his loss may have been as sincere as that of Elizabeth of York certainly was, his natural inclinations soon asserted themselves. Ludlow was unhealthy, and after the pompous funeral of Arthur at Worcester, Katharine and her household prayed earnestly to be allowed to approach London, but for some weeks without success, and by the time she arrived at her new abode at Croydon, the political intrigues of which she was the tool were in full swing again.

When Ferdinand and Isabel first heard the news of their daughter's bereavement at the beginning of May they were at Toledo, and lost no time in sending off post haste to England a fresh ambassador with special instructions from themselves. The man they chose was the Duke de Estrada, whose only recommendation seems to have been his rank, for Puebla was soon able to twist him round his finger. His mission, as we now know, was an extraordinary and delicate one. Ostensibly he was to demand the immediate return of the 100,000 crowns paid to Henry on account of dowry, and the firm settlement upon Katharine of the manors and rents, securing to her the revenue assigned to her in England, and at the same time he was to urge Henry to send Katharine back to Spain at once. But these things were really the last that Ferdinand desired. He knew full well that Henry would go to any length to avoid disgorging the dowry, and secret instructions were given to Estrada to effect a betrothal between the ten-years-old Henry, Duke of York, and his brother's widow of sixteen. Strict orders also were sent to Puebla of a character to forward the secret design, although he was not fully informed of the latter. He was to press amongst other things that Katharine might receive her English revenue punctually— Katharine, it appears, had written to her parents, saying that she had been advised to borrow money for the support of her household; and the King and Queen of Spain were indignant at such an idea. Not a farthing, they said, must she be allowed to borrow, and none of her jewels sold: the King of England must provide for her promptly and handsomely, in accordance with his obligations. This course, as the writers well knew, would soon bring Henry VII. himself to propose the marriage for which Ferdinand was so anxious. Henry professed himself very ready to make the settlement of the English income as requested, but in such case, he claimed that the whole of the Spanish dowry in gold must be paid to him. Ferdinand could not see it in this light at all, and insisted that the death of Arthur had dissolved the marriage. This fencing went on for some time, neither party wishing to be the first to propose the indecorous marriage with Henry that both desired. It is evident that Puebla and the chaplain Alexander opposed the match secretly, and endeavoured to thwart it, either from an idea of its illegality or, more probably, with a view of afterwards bringing it about themselves. In the midst of this intrigue the King of France suddenly attacked Ferdinand both in Italy and on the Catalonian frontier, and made approaches to Henry for the marriage of his son with a French princess. This hurried the pace in Spain, and Queen Isabel ordered Estrada to carry through the betrothal of Katharine and her brother-in-law without loss of time, "for any delay would be dangerous." So anxious were the Spanish sovereigns that nothing should stand in the way, that they were willing to let the old arrangement about the dowry stand, Henry retaining the 100,000 crowns already paid, and receiving, when the marriage was consummated, the remaining 100,000; on condition that in the meanwhile Katharine was properly maintained in England. Even the incestuous nature of the union was to be no bar to its being effected, though no Papal dispensation had been yet obtained. Isabel sought salve for her conscience in this respect by repeating Doña Elvira Manuel's assurance that Katharine still remained intact; her marriage with Arthur not having been consummated. To lure Henry into an armed alliance against France once more, the old bait of the recovery of Normandy and Guienne was dangled before him. But the King of England played with a firmer hand now. He knew his worth as a balancing factor, his accumulated treasure made him powerful, and he held all the cards in his hand; for the King of Scots was his son-in-law, and the French were as anxious for his smiles as were the Spanish sovereigns. So he stood off and refused to pledge himself to a hostile alliance.

In view of this Ferdinand and Isabel's tone changed, and they developed a greater desire than ever to have their daughter— and above all her dowry— returned to them. "We cannot endure," wrote Isabel to Estrada on the 10th August 1502, "that a daughter whom we love should be so far away from us in her trouble.... You shall ... tell the King of England that you have our orders to freight vessels for her voyage. To this end you must make such a show of giving directions and preparing for the voyage that the members of the Princess's household may believe that it is true. Send also some of her household on board with the captain I am now sending you ... and show all signs of departure." If in consequence the English spoke of the betrothal with young Henry, the ambassador was to show no desire for it; but was to listen keenly to all that was proposed, and if the terms were acceptable he might clinch the matter at once without further reference. And then the saintly Queen concludes thus: "The one object of this business is to bring the betrothal to a conclusion as soon as possible in conformity with your instructions. For then all our anxiety will cease and we shall be able to seek the aid of England against France, for this is the most efficient aid we can have." Henry was not for the moment to be frightened by fresh demands for his armed alliance against France. The betrothal was to be forwarded first, and then the rest would follow. Puebla, who was quite confident that he alone could carry on the marriage negotiation successfully, was also urged by mingled flattery and threats by his sovereign to do his utmost with that end.

Whilst this diplomatic haggling was going on in London for the disposal of the widowed Katharine to the best advantage, a blow fell that for a moment changed the aspect of affairs. Elizabeth of York, the wife of Henry VII., died on the 11th February 1503, in the Tower of London, a week after giving birth to her seventh child. She had been a good and submissive wife to the King, whose claim to the throne she had fortified by her own greater right; and we are told that the bereaved husband was "heavy and dolorous" with his loss when he retired to a solitary place to pass his sorrow; but before many weeks were over he and his crony Puebla put their crafty heads together, and agreed that the King might marry his widowed daughter-in-law himself. The idea was cynically repulsive but it gives us the measure of Henry's unscrupulousness. Puebla conveyed the hint to Isabel and Ferdinand, who, to do them justice, appeared to be really shocked at the suggestion. This time (April 1503) the Spanish sovereigns spoke with more sincerity than before. They were, they told their ambassador, tired of Henry's shiftiness, and of their daughter's equivocal and undignified position in England, now that the Queen was dead and the betrothal still hung fire. The Princess was really to come to Spain in a fleet that should be sent for her, unless the marriage with the young Prince of Wales was agreed to at once. As for a wife for King Henry there was the widowed Queen of Naples, Ferdinand's niece, who lived in Valencia, and he might have her with the blessing of the Spanish sovereigns. The suggestion was a tempting one to Henry, for the Queen of Naples was well dowered, and the vigour of Isabel's refusal to listen to his marriage with her daughter, made it evident that that was out of the question. So Henry at last made up his mind at least to execute the treaty which was to betroth his surviving son to Katharine. In the treaty, which was signed on the 23rd June 1503, it is set forth that, inasmuch as the bride and bridegroom were related in the first degree of affinity, a Papal dispensation would be necessary for the marriage; and it is distinctly stated that the marriage with Arthur had been consummated. This may have been a diplomatic form considered at the time unimportant in view of the ease with which a dispensation could be obtained, but it is at direct variance with Doña Elvira Manuel's assurance to Isabel at the time of

Arthur's death, and with Katharine's assertion, uncontradicted by Henry, to the end of her life.

Henry, Prince of Wales, was at this time twelve years old; and, if we are to believe Erasmus, a prodigy of precocious scholarship. Though his learning was superficial and carefully made the most of, he was, in effect, an apt and diligent student. From the first his mother and father had determined that their children should enjoy better educational advantages than had fallen to them, and as Henry had been until Arthur's death intended for the Church, his learning was far in advance of that of most princes and nobles of his age. The bride, who thus became unwillingly affianced to a boy more than five years her junior, was now a young woman in her prime, experienced already in the chicane and falsity of the atmosphere in which she lived. She knew, none better, that in the juggle for her marriage she had been regarded as a mere chattel, and her own inclinations hardly taken into account, and she faced her responsibilities bravely in her mother's exalted spirit of duty and sacrifice when she found herself once more Princess of Wales.

When Ferdinand, in accordance with his pledge in the treaty, instructed his ambassador in Rome to ask for the Pope's dispensation, he took care to correct the statement embodied in the document to the effect that the marriage of Arthur and Katharine had been consummated; though the question might pertinently be asked, why, if it had not been, a dispensation was needed at all? The King himself answered the question by saying that "as the English are so much inclined to cavil, it appeared prudent to provide for the case as if the previous marriage had been completed; and the dispensation must be worded in accordance with the treaty, since the succession to the Crown depends on the undoubted legitimacy of the marriage." No sooner was the ratification of the betrothal conveyed to Ferdinand than he demanded the aid of Henry against France, and Estrada was instructed to "make use of" Katharine to obtain the favour demanded. If Henry hesitated to provide the money for raising the 2000 English troops required, Katharine herself was to be asked by her kind father to pawn her plate and jewels for the purpose. Henry, however, had no intention to be hurried now that the betrothal had been signed. There were several things he wanted on his side first. The Earl of Suffolk and his brother Richard Pole were still in Flanders; and the greatest wish of Henry's life was that they should be handed over to his tender mercies. So the armed coalition against France still hung fire, whilst a French ambassador was as busy courting the King of England as Ferdinand himself. In the meanwhile Katharine for a time lived in apparent amity with Henry and his family, especially with the young Princess Mary, who was her constant companion. In the autumn of 1504 she passed a fortnight with them at Windsor and Richmond, hunting every day; but just as the King was leaving Greenwich for a progress through Kent the Princess fell seriously ill, and the letters written by Henry during his absence to his daughter-in-law are worded as if he were the most affectionate of fathers. On this progress the Prince of Wales accompanied his father for the first time, as the King had previously been loath to disturb his studies. "It is quite wonderful," wrote an observer, "how much the King loves the Prince. He has good reason to do so, for he deserves all his love." Already the crafty and politic King was indoctrinating his son in the system he had made his own: that the command of ready money, gained no matter how, meant power, and that to hold the balance between two greater rivals was to have them both at his bidding. And young Henry, though of different nature from his father, made good use of his lesson.

Katharine's greatest trouble at this time (the autumn of 1504) was the bickering, and worse, of her Spanish household. We have already seen how Puebla had set them by the ears with his jealousy of his colleagues and his dodging diplomacy. Katharine appealed to Henry to bring her servants to order, but he refused to interfere, as they were not his subjects. Doña Elvira Manuel, the governess, was a great lady, and resented any interference with her domain. There is no doubt that her rule, so far as regarded the Princess herself, was a wise one; but, as we shall see directly, she, Castilian that she was and sister of the famous diplomatist Juan Manuel, took up a position inimical to Ferdinand after Isabel's death, and innocently led Katharine into grave political trouble.

In November 1504 the death of Isabel, Queen of Castile, long threatened after her strenuous life, changed the whole aspect for Ferdinand. The heiress of the principal crown of Spain was now Katharine's sister Juana, who had lived for years in the latitudinarian court of Brussels with her consort Philip. The last time she had gone to Spain, her freedom towards the strict religious observances considered necessary in her mother's court had led to violent scenes between Isabel and Juana. Even then the scandalised Spanish churchmen who flocked around Isabel whispered that the heiress of Castile must be mad: and her foreign husband, the heir of the empire, was hated and distrusted by the "Catholic kings." Isabel by her will had left her husband guardian of her realms for Juana; and from the moment the Queen breathed her last the struggle between Ferdinand and his son-in-law never ceased, until Philip the Handsome, who thought he had beaten wily old Ferdinand, himself was beaten by poison. The death of her mother not only threw Katharine into natural grief for her loss, which truly was a great one; for, at least, Isabel deeply loved her youngest child, whilst Ferdinand loved nothing but himself and Aragon; but it greatly altered for the worse her position in England. Philip of Austria and his father the Emperor had begun to play false to Ferdinand long before the Queen's death; and now that the crown of Castile had fallen to poor weak Juana, and a struggle was seen to be impending for the regency, Henry VII. found himself as usual courted by both sides in the dispute. The widowed Archduchess Margaret, who had married as a first husband Ferdinand's heir, was offered to Henry as a bride by Philip and Maximilian and a close alliance between them proposed; and Ferdinand, whilst denouncing his son-in-law's ingratitude, also bade high for the King of England's countenance. Henry listened to both parties, but it was clear to him that he had now more to hope for from Philip and Maximilian, who were friendly with France, than from Ferdinand; and the unfortunate Katharine was again reduced to the utmost neglect and penury, unable to buy food for her own table, except by pawning her jewels.

In the ensuing intrigues Doña Elvira Manuel was on the side of the Queen of Castile, as against her father; and Katharine lost the impartial advice of her best counsellor, and involved herself in a very net of trouble. In the summer of 1505 it was already understood that Philip and Juana on their way to Spain by sea might possibly trust themselves in an English port; and Henry, in order to be ready for any matrimonial combinations that might be suggested, caused young Henry to make solemn protest before the Bishop of Winchester at Richmond against his marriage with Katharine. Of this, at the time, of course the Spanish agents were ignorant; and so completely was even Puebla hoodwinked, that almost to the arrival of Philip and his wife in England he believed that Henry was in favour of Ferdinand against Philip and Maximilian. Early in August 1505, Puebla went to Richmond to see Katharine, and as he entered one of the household told him that an ambassador from the Archduke Philip, King of Castile, had just arrived and was waiting to see her. Puebla at once himself conveyed the news to Katharine; and to his glee served as interpreter between the ambassador and the Princess. On his knees before her the Fleming related that he had come to propose a marriage between the Duchess of Savoy (*i.e.* the widowed Archduchess Margaret) and Henry VII., and showed the Princess two portraits of the Archduchess. Furthermore, he said that Philip and his wife were going by overland through France to Spain, and he was to ask Henry what he thought of the plan. Puebla's eyes were thus partially opened: and when a few days later he found that Doña Elvira had not only contrived frequent private meetings between Katharine and the Flemish ambassador, but had persuaded the Princess to propose a meeting between Philip, Juana, and the King of England, he at once sounded a note of alarm. Katharine, it must be recollected, was yet young; and probably did not fully understand the deadly antagonism that existed between her father and her brother-in-law. She was much under the influence of Doña Elvira, and doubtless yearned to see her unhappy sister Juana. So she was induced to write a letter to Philip, and to propose a meeting with Henry at Calais. When a prompt affirmative reply came, the Princess innocently showed it to Puebla at Durham House before sending it to Henry VII. The ambassador was aghast, and soundly rated Katharine for going against the interests of her father. He would take the letter to the King, he said. But this Katharine would not allow, and Doña Elvira was appealed to. She promised to retain the letter for the present, but just as Puebla was sitting down to dinner an hour afterwards, he learnt that she had broken her word and sent Philip's letter to Henry VII. Starting up, he rushed to Katharine's apartments, and with tears streaming down his face at his failure, told the Princess, under pledge of secrecy, that the proposed interview was a plot of the Manuels to injure both her father and sister. She must at once write a letter to Henry which he, Puebla, would dictate; and, whilst still feigning a desire for the meeting, she must try to prevent it with all her might, and beware of Doña Elvira in future. Poor Katharine, alarmed at his vehemence, did as she was told; and the letter was sent flying to Henry, apologising for the proposal of the interview. Henry must have smiled when he saw how eager they all were to court him. Nothing would please him better than the close alliance with Philip, which was already being secretly negotiated, though he was effusively assuring Ferdinand at the same time of the inviolability of their friendship; promising that the marriage— which he had secretly denounced— between his son and Katharine, should be celebrated on the very day provided by the treaty, and approving of some secret plot of Ferdinand against Philip which had been communicated to him.

Amidst such falsity as this it is most difficult to pick one's way, though it is evident through it all that Henry had now gained the upper hand, and was fully a match for Ferdinand in his altered circumstances. But as things improved for Henry they became worse for Katharine. In December 1505 she wrote bitterly to her father from Richmond, complaining of her fate, the unhappiness of which, she said, was all Puebla's fault. "Every day," she wrote, "my troubles increase. Since my arrival in England I have not received a farthing except for food, and I and my household have not even garments to wear." She had asked Puebla to pray the King to appoint an English dueña for her whilst Doña Elvira was in Flanders, but instead of doing so he had arranged with Henry that her household should be dismissed altogether, and that she should reside at Court. Her letter throughout shows that at the time she was in deep despondency and anger at her treatment; and especially resentful of Puebla, whom she disliked and distrusted profoundly, as did Doña Elvira Manuel. The very elements seemed to fight on the side of the King of England. Ferdinand was, in sheer desperation, struggling to prevent his paternal realms from being merged in Castile and the empire, and with that end was negotiating his marriage with the French king's niece, Germaine de Foix, and a close alliance with France, in which England should be included, when Philip of Austria and his wife, Juana of Aragon, Queen of Castile, sailed from Flanders to claim their kingdom at Ferdinand's hands. They too had made friends with France some time before, but the marriage of Ferdinand with a French princess had now drawn them strongly to the side of England; and as we have seen, they were already in full negotiation with Henry for his marriage with the doubly widowed and heavily dowered Archduchess Margaret.

The King and Queen of Castile were overtaken by a furious south-west gale in the Channel and their fine fleet dispersed. The ship that carried Philip and Juana was driven by the storm into Melcombe Regis, on the Dorset coast, on the 17th January 1506, and lay there weather-bound for some time. Philip the Handsome was a poor sailor, and was, we are told by an eye-witness, "fatigate and unquyeted in mynde and bodie." He doubtless yearned to tread dry land again, and, against the advice of his Council, had himself rowed ashore. Only in the previous year he had as unguardedly put himself into the power of the King of France; and his boldness had succeeded well, as it had resulted in the treaty with the French king that had so much alarmed and shocked Ferdinand, but it is unlikely that Philip on this occasion intended to make any stay in England or to go beyond Weymouth. The news of his coming brought together all the neighbouring gentry to oppose or welcome him, according to his demeanour, and, finding him friendly, Sir John Trenchard prevailed upon him to take up his residence in his manor-house hard by until the weather mended. In the meanwhile formidable English forces mustered in the country around, and Philip began to grow uneasy; but Trenchard's hospitality was pressing, and to all hints from the visitor that he wanted to be gone the reply was given that he really must wait until the King of England could bid him welcome. When at last Philip was given to understand that he was practically a prisoner, he made the best of the position, and with seeming cordiality awaited King Henry's message. No wonder, as a chronicler says, that Henry when he heard the news "was replenyshed with an exceeding gladnes ... for that he trusted his landing in England should turn to his profit and commoditie." This it certainly did. Philip and Juana were brought to Windsor in great state, and met by Henry and his son and a splendid train of nobles. Then the visitors were led through London in state to Richmond, and Philip, amidst all the festivity, was soon convinced that he would not be allowed to leave England until the rebel Plantagenet Earl of Suffolk was handed to Henry. And so the pact was made that bound England to Philip and Flanders against Ferdinand; the Archduchess Margaret with her vast fortune being promised, with unheard-of guarantees, to the widowed Henry. When the treaty had been solemnly ratified on oath, taken upon a fragment of the true Cross in St. George's Chapel, Windsor, Philip was allowed to go his way on the 2nd March to join his ship at Falmouth, whither Juana had preceded him a fortnight before.

This new treaty made poor Katharine of little value as a political asset in England; since it was clear now that Ferdinand's hold over anything but his paternal heritage in the Mediterranean was powerless. Flanders and Castile were a far more advantageous ally to England than the King of Aragon, and Katharine was promptly made to feel the fact. Dr. Puebla was certainly either kept quite out of the way or his compliance bought, or he would have been able to devise means for Katharine to inform her sister Juana of the real object of Henry's treaty with Philip; for Ferdinand always insisted that Juana was a dutiful daughter, and was not personally opposed to him. As it was, Katharine was allowed to see her sister but for an hour just before Juana's departure, and then in the presence of witnesses in the interests of Philip. Only a few weeks after the visitors had departed Katharine wrote to her father, in fear lest her letter should be intercepted, begging him to have pity upon her. She is deep in debt, not for extravagant things but for food. "The King of England refuses to pay anything, though she implores him with tears to do so. He says he has been cheated about the marriage portion. In the meanwhile she is in the deepest anguish, her servants almost begging for alms, and she herself nearly naked. She has been at death's door for months, and prays earnestly for a Spanish confessor, as she cannot speak English."

How false Ferdinand met his "dear children," and made with his daughter's husband that hellish secret compact in the church of Villafafila, that seemed to renounce everything to Philip whilst Ferdinand went humbly to his realm of Naples, and his ill-used daughter Juana to life-long confinement, cannot be told here, nor the sudden death of Philip the Handsome, which brought back Ferdinand triumphant. If Juana was sane before, she certainly became more or less mad after her husband's death, and moreover was morbidly devoted to his memory. But what mattered madness or a widow's devotion to Henry VII. when he had political objects to serve? All through the summer and autumn of 1506 Katharine had been ill with fever and ague, unhappy at the neglect and poverty she suffered. Ferdinand threw upon Castile the duty of paying the rest of her dowry; the Castilians retorted that Ferdinand ought to pay it himself: and Katharine, in the depth of despondency, in October 1506 learnt of her brother-in-law Philip's death. Like magic Henry VII. became amiable again to his daughter-in-law. He deplored her illness now, and cordially granted her the change of residence from Eltham to Fulham that she had so long prayed for in vain. The reason was soon evident; for before Juana had completed her dreary pilgrimage through Spain to Granada with her husband's dead body, Henry had cajoled Katharine to ask her father for the distraught widow for his wife. Katharine must have fulfilled the task with repulsion, though she seems to have advocated the match warmly; and Ferdinand, though he knew, or rather said, that Juana was mad, was quite ready to take advantage of such an opportunity for again getting into touch with Henry. The letter in which Ferdinand gently dallied with Henry's offer was written in Naples, after months of shifty excuses for not sending the rest of Katharine's dowry to England, and doubtless the time he gained by postponing the answer about Juana's marriage until he returned to Spain was of value to him; for he was determined, now that a special providence carefully prepared had removed Philip from his path, that once more all Spain should bear his sway whilst he lived, and then should be divided, rather than his dear Aragon should be rendered subordinate to other interests.

The encouraging talk of Henry's marriage with Juana, with which both Katharine and Puebla were instructed to beguile him, was all very well in its way, and the King of England became quite joyously sentimental at the prospect of the new tie of relationship between the houses of Tudor and Aragon; but, really, business was business: if that long overdue dowry for Katharine was not sent soon, young Henry would listen to some of the many other eligible princesses, better dowered than Katharine, who were offered to him. With much demur Henry at length consented to wait for five months longer for the dowry; that is to say, until Michaelmas 1507, and in the meanwhile drove a bargain as hard as that of a Jew huckster in the valuation of Katharine's jewels and plate, which were to be brought into the account. It is easy to see that this concession of five months' delay was granted by Henry in the hope that his marriage with Juana would take place. The plan was hideously wicked, and Puebla made no secret of it in writing to Ferdinand. "No king in the world would make so good a husband to the Queen of Castile, whether she be sane or insane. She might recover her reason when wedded to such a husband, but even in that case King Ferdinand would at all events be sure to retain the regency of Castile. On the other hand, if the insanity of the Queen should prove incurable it would perhaps be not inconvenient that she should live in England. The English do not seem to mind her insanity much; especially since it is asserted that her mental malady would not prevent her from childbearing." Could anything be more repulsive than this pretty arrangement, which had been concocted by Henry and Puebla at Richmond during a time when the former was seriously ill with quinsy and inaccessible to any one but the Spanish ambassador?

In the meanwhile Katharine felt keenly the wretched position in which she found herself. The plate, about which so much haggling was taking place, was being pawned or sold by her bit by bit to provide the most necessary things for her own use; her servants were in rags, and she herself was contemned and neglected; forbidden even to see her betrothed husband for months together, though living in the same palace with him. The more confident Henry grew of his own marriage with the Archduchess Margaret, or with Queen Juana, the less inclined he was to wed his son to Katharine. A French princess for the Prince of Wales, and the Queen of Castile for Henry, would indeed have served England on all sides. On one occasion, in April 1507, Henry frankly told Katharine that he considered himself no longer bound by her marriage treaty, since her dowry was overdue, and all the poor Princess could do was to weep and pray her father to fulfil his part of the compact by paying the rest of her portion, whilst she, serving as Ferdinand's ambassador, tried to retain Henry's good graces by her hopeful assurances about the marriage of the latter with Juana.

In all Katharine's lamentations of her own sufferings and privation, she never forgot to bewail the misery of her servants. Whilst she herself, she said, had been worse treated than any woman in England, her five women servants, all she had retained, had never received a farthing since their arrival in England six years before, and had spent everything they possessed. Katharine at this time of trial (August 1507) was living alone at Ewelme, whilst Henry was hunting at various seats in the midlands. At length the King made some stay at Woodstock, where Katharine saw him. With suspicious alacrity he consented to a further postponement of the overdue dowry; and showed himself more eager than ever to marry Juana, no matter how mad she might be. Katharine was quite acute enough to understand his motives, and wrote to her father that so long as the money due of her dowry remained unpaid the King considered himself free, so far as regarded her marriage with the Prince of Wales. "Mine is always the worst part," she wrote. "The King of England prides himself upon his magnanimity in waiting so long for the payment.... His words are kind but his deeds are as bad as ever." She bitterly complained that Puebla himself was doing his utmost to frustrate her marriage in the interests of the King of England; and it is clear to see in her passionate letter to her father (4th October 1507) that she half distrusted even him, as she had been told that he was listening to overtures from the King of France for a marriage between Juana and a French prince. She failed in this to understand the political position fully. If Juana had married a Frenchman it is certain that Henry would have been only too eager to complete the marriage of his son with Katharine. But she was evidently in fear that, unless Henry was allowed to marry her sister, evil might befall her. Speaking of the marriage she says: "I bait him with this ... and his words and professions have changed for the better, although his acts remain the same.... They fancy that I have no more in me than what outwardly appears, or that I shall not be able to fathom his (Puebla's) design." Under stress of her circumstances Katharine was developing rapidly. She was no longer a girl dependent upon others. Doña Elvira had gone for good; Puebla she hated and distrusted as much as she did Henry; and there was no one by her to whom she could look for help. Her position was a terribly difficult one, pitted alone, as she was, against the most unscrupulous politicians in Europe, in whose hands she knew she was only one of the pieces in a game. Juana was still carrying about with her the unburied corpse of her husband, and falling into paroxysms of fury when a second marriage was suggested to her; and yet Katharine considered it necessary to keep up the pretence to Henry that his suit was prospering. She knew that though the Archduchess Margaret had firmly refused to tempt providence again by a third marriage with the

King of England, the boy sovereign of Castile and Flanders, the Arch-duke Charles, had been securely betrothed to golden-haired little Mary Tudor, Henry's younger daughter; and that the close alliance thus sealed was as dangerous to her father King Ferdinand's interests as to her own. And yet she was either forced, or forced herself, to paint Henry, who was still treating her vilely, in the brightest colours as a chivalrous, virtuous gentleman, really and desperately in love with poor crazy Juana. Katharine's letters to her sister on behalf of Henry's suit are nauseous, in view of the circumstances as we know them; and show that the Princess of Wales was already prepared to sacrifice every human feeling to political expediency.

This miserable position could not continue indefinitely, for the extension of time for the payment of the dowry was fast running out. Juana was more intractable than ever. Katharine, in rage and despair at the contumely with which she was treated, insisted at length that her father should send an ambassador to England, who could speak as the mouthpiece of a great sovereign rather than like a fawning menial of Henry as Puebla was. The new ambassador was Gomez de Fuensalida, Knight Commander of Haro and Membrilla, a man as haughty as Puebla had been servile, and he went far beyond even Katharine's desires in his plain speaking to Henry and his ministers. Ferdinand, indeed, by this time had once more gained the upper hand in Europe, and could afford to speak his mind. Henry was no longer so vigorous or so bold as he had been, and his desire to grasp everything whilst risking nothing had enabled his rivals to form a great coalition from which he was excluded— the League of Cambrai. Fuensalida offended Henry almost as soon as he arrived, and was roughly refused permission to enter the English Court. He could only storm, as he did, to Henry's ministers that unless the Princess of Wales was at once sent home to Spain with her dowry, King Ferdinand and his allies would wreak vengeance upon England. But Henry knew that with such a hostage as Katharine in his hands he was safe from attack, and held the Princess in defiance of it all. But he was already a waning force. Whilst Fuensalida had no good word for the King, he, like all other Spanish agents, turned to the rising sun and sang persistently the praises of the Prince of Wales. His gigantic stature and sturdy limbs, his fair skin and golden hair, his manliness, his prudence, and his wisdom were their constant theme: and even Katharine, unhappy as she was, with her marriage still in the balance, seems to have liked and admired the gallant youth whom she was allowed to see so seldom.

It has become so much the fashion to speak of Katharine not only as an unfortunate woman, but as a blameless saint in all her relations, that an historian who regards her as a fallible and even in many respects a blameworthy woman, who was to a large extent the cause of her own troubles, must be content to differ from the majority of his predecessors. We have already seen, by the earnest attempts she made to drag her afflicted sister into marriage with a man whom she herself considered false, cruel, and unscrupulous, that Katharine was no better than those around her in moral principle: the passion and animosity shown in her letters to her father about Puebla, Fuensalida, and others whom she distrusted, show her to have been anything but a meek martyr. She was, indeed, at this time (1508-9) a self-willed, ambitious girl of strong passion, impatient of control, domineering and proud. Her position in England had been a humiliating and a hateful one for years. She was the sport of the selfish ambitions of others, which she herself was unable to control; surrounded by people whom she disliked and suspected, lonely and unhappy; it is not wonderful that when Henry VII. was gradually sinking to his grave, and her marriage with his son was still in doubt, this ardent Southern young woman in her prime should be tempted to cast to the wind considerations of dignity and prudence for the sake of her love for a man.

She was friendless in a foreign land; and when her father was in Naples in 1506, she wrote to him praying him to send her a Spanish confessor to solace her. Before he could do so she informed him (April 1507) that she had obtained a very good Spanish confessor for herself. This was a young, lusty, dissolute Franciscan monk called Diego Fernandez, who then became a member of Katharine's household. When the new outspoken ambassador, Fuensalida, arrived in England in the autumn of 1508, he, of course, had frequent conference with the Princess, and could not for long shut his eyes to the state of affairs in her establishment. He first sounded the alarm cautiously to Ferdinand in a letter of 4th March 1509. He had hoped against hope, he said, that the marriage of Katharine and Prince Henry might be effected soon; and the scandal might remedy itself without his worrying Ferdinand about it. But he must speak out now, for he has been silent too long. It is high time, he says, that some person of sufficient authority in the confidence of Ferdinand should be put in charge of Katharine's household and command respect: "for at present the Princess's house is governed by a young friar, whom her Highness has taken for her confessor, though he is, in my opinion, and that of others, utterly unworthy of such a position. He makes the Princess commit many errors; and as she is so good and conscientious, this confessor makes a mortal sin of everything that does not please him, and so causes her to commit many faults." The ambassador continues that he dare not write all he would because the bearer (a servant of Katharine's) is being sent by those who wish to injure him; but he begs the King to interrogate the man who takes the letter as to what had been going on in the Princess's house in the last two months. "The root of all the trouble is this young friar, who is flighty, and vain, and extremely scandalous. He has spoken to the Princess very roughly about the King of England; and because I told the Princess something of what I thought of this friar, and he learnt it, he has disgraced me with her worse than if I had been a traitor.... That your Highness may judge what sort of person he is, I will repeat exactly without exaggeration the very words he used to me. 'I know,' he said, 'that they have been telling you evil tales of me.' 'I can assure you, father,' I replied, 'that no one has said anything about you to me.' 'I know,' he replied; 'the same person who told you told me himself.' 'Well,' I said, 'any one can bear false witness, and I swear by the Holy Body that, so far as I can recollect, nothing has been said to me about you.' 'Ah,' he said, 'there are scandal-mongers in this house who have defamed me, and not with the lowest either, but with the highest, and that is no disgrace to me. If it were not for contradicting them I should be gone already.'" Proud Fuensalida tells the King that it was only with the greatest difficulty he kept his hands off the insolent priest at this. "His constant presence with the Princess and amongst her women is shocking the King of England and his Court dreadfully;" and then the ambassador hints strongly that Henry is only allowing the scandal to go on, so as to furnish him with a good excuse for still keeping Katharine's marriage in abeyance.

With this letter to Spain went another from Katharine to her father, railing bitterly against the ambassador. She can no longer endure her troubles, and a settlement of some sort must be arrived at. The King of England treats her worse than ever since his daughter Mary was betrothed to the young Archduke Charles, sovereign of Castile and Flanders. She had sold everything she possessed for food and raiment; and only a few days before she wrote, Henry had again told her that he was not bound to feed her servants. Her own people, she says, are insolent and turn against her; but what afflicts her most is that she is too poor to maintain fittingly her confessor, "the best that ever woman had." It is plain to see that the whole household was in rebellion against the confessor who had captured Katharine's heart, and that the ambassador was on the side of the household. The Princess and Fuensalida had quarrelled about it, and she wished that the ambassador should be reproved. With vehement passion she begged her father that the confessor might not be taken away from her. "I implore your Highness to prevent him from leaving me; and to write to the King of England that you have ordered this Father to stay with me; and beg him for your sake to have him well treated and humoured. Tell the prelates also that you wish him to stay here. The greatest comfort in my trouble is the consolation he gives me. Almost in despair I send this servant to implore you not to forget that I am still your daughter, and how much I have suffered for your sake.... Do not let me perish like this, but write at once deciding what is to be done. Otherwise in my present state I am afraid I may do something that neither the King of England nor your Highness could prevent, unless you send for me and let me pass the few remaining days of my life in God's service."

That the Princess's household and the ambassador were shocked at the insolent familiarity of the licentious young priest with their mistress, and that she herself perfectly understood that the suspicions and rumours were against her honour, is clear. On one occasion Henry VII. had asked Katharine and his daughter Mary to go to Richmond, to meet him. When the two princesses were dressed and ready to set out on their journey from Hampton Court to Richmond, the confessor entered the room and told Katharine she was not to go that day as she had been unwell. The Princess protested that she was then quite well and able to bear the short journey. "I tell you," replied Father Diego, "that, on pain of mortal sin, you shall not go to-day;" and so Princess Mary set out alone, leaving Katharine with the young priest of notorious evil life and a few inferior servants. When the next day she was allowed to go to Richmond, accompanied amongst others by the priest, King Henry took not the slightest notice of her, and for the next few weeks refused to speak to her. The ambassador even confessed to Ferdinand that, since he had witnessed what was going on in the Princess's household, he acquitted Henry of most of the blame for his treatment of his Spanish daughter-in-law. Whilst the Princess was in the direst distress, her household in want of food, and she obliged to sell her gowns to send messengers to her father, she went to the length of pawning the plate that formed part of her dowry to "satisfy the follies of the friar."

Deaf to all remonstrances both from King Henry and her own old servants, Katharine obstinately had her way, and the chances of her marriage in England grew smaller and smaller. It is not to be supposed that the ambassador would have dared to say so much as he did to the lady's own father if he had not taken the gravest view of Katharine's conduct and its probable political result. But his hints to Ferdinand's ministers were much stronger still. "The Princess," he said, "was guilty of things a thousand times worse" than those he had mentioned; and the "parables" that he had written to the King might be made clear by the examination of Katharine's own servant, who carried her letters. "The devil take me," he continues, "if I can see anything in this friar for her to be so fond of him; for he has neither learning, nor good looks, nor breeding, nor capacity, nor authority; but if he takes it into his head to preach a new gospel, they have to believe it." By two letters still extant, written by Friar Diego himself, we see that the ambassador in no wise exaggerated his coarseness and indelicacy, and it is almost incredible that Katharine, an experienced and disillusioned woman of nearly twenty-four, can have been ready to jeopardise everything political and personal, and face the opposition of the world, for the sake alone of the spiritual comfort to be derived from the ministrations of such a man. How far, if at all, the connection was actually immoral we shall probably never know, but the case as it stands shows Katharine to have been passionate, self-willed, and utterly tactless. Even after her marriage with young Henry Friar Diego retained his ascendency over her for several years, and ruled her with a rod of iron until he was publicly convicted of fornication, and deprived of his office as Chancellor of the Queen. We shall have later to consider the question of his relationship with Katharine after her marriage; but it is almost certain that the ostentatious intimacy of the pair during the last months of Henry VII. had reduced Katharine's chance of marriage with the Prince of Wales almost to vanishing point, when the death of the King suddenly changed the political position and rendered it necessary that the powerful coalition of which Ferdinand was the head should be conciliated by England.

Henry VII. died at Richmond on the 22nd April 1509, making a better and more generous end than could have been expected from his life. He, like his rival Ferdinand, had been avaricious by deliberate policy; and his avarice was largely instrumental in founding England's coming greatness, for the overflowing coffers he left to his son lent force to the new position assumed by England as the balancing power, courted by both the great continental rivals. Ferdinand's ambition had o'erleaped itself, and the possession of Flanders by the King of Castile had made England's friendship more than ever necessary thenceforward, for France was opposed to Spain now, not in Italy alone, but on long conterminous frontiers in the north, south, and east as well.

Henry VIII. at the age of eighteen was well fitting to succeed his father. All contemporary observers agree that his grace and personal beauty as a youth were as remarkable as his quickness of intellect and his true Tudor desire to stand well in the eyes of his people. Fully aware of the power his father's wealth gave him politically, he was determined to share no part of the onus for the oppression with which the wealth had been collected; and on the day following his father's death, before himself retiring to mourning reclusion in the Tower of London, the unpopular financial instruments of Henry VII., Empson and Dudley and others, were laid by the heels to sate the vengeance of the people. The Spanish match for the young king was by far more popular in England than any other; and the alacrity of Henry himself and his ministers to carry it into effect without further delay, now that his father with his personal ambitions and enmities was dead, was also indicative of his desire to begin his reign by pleasing his subjects.

The death of Henry VII. had indeed cleared away many obstacles. Ferdinand had profoundly distrusted him. His evident desire to obtain control of Castile, either by his marriage with Juana or by that of his daughter Mary with the nine-year-old Archduke Charles, had finally hardened Ferdinand's heart against him, whilst Henry's fear and suspicion of Ferdinand had, as we have seen, effectually stood in the way of the completion of Katharine's marriage. With young Henry as king affairs stood differently. Even before his father's death Ferdinand had taken pains to assure him of his love, and had treated him as a sovereign over the dying old king's head. Before the breath was out of Henry VII., Ferdinand's letters were speeding to London to make all things smooth. There would be no opposition now to Ferdinand's ratification of his Flemish grandson's marriage with Henry's sister Mary. The clever old Aragonese knew there was still plenty of time to stop that later; and certainly young Henry could not interfere in Castile, as his father might have done, on the strength of Mary Tudor's betrothal. So all went merry as a marriage bell. Ferdinand, for once in his life, was liberal with his money. He implored his daughter to make no unpleasantness or complaint, and to raise no question that might obstruct her marriage. The ambassador, Fuensalida, was warned that if the bickering between himself and the Princess, or between the confessor and the household, was allowed to interfere with the match, disgrace and ruin should be his lot, and Katharine was admonished that she must be civil to Fuensalida, and to the Italian banker who was to pay the balance of her dowry. The King of Aragon need have had no anxiety. Young Henry and his councillors were as eager for the popular marriage as he was, and dreaded the idea of disgorging the 100,000 crowns dowry already paid and the English settlements upon Katharine. On the 6th May, accordingly, three days before the body of Henry VII. was borne in gloomy pomp to its last resting-place at Westminster, Katharine wrote to her delighted father that her marriage with Henry was finally settled.

CHAPTER III

1509~1527

KATHARINE THE QUEEN—A POLITICAL MAR-RIAGE AND A PERSONAL DIVORCE

"Long live King Henry VIII.!" cried Garter King of Arms in French as the great officers of state broke their staves of office and cast them into the open grave of the first Tudor king. Through England, like the blast of a trumpet, the cry was echoed from the hearts of a whole people, full of hope that the niggardliness and suspicion which for years had stood between the sovereign and his people were at last banished. The young king, expansive and hearty in manner, handsome and strong as a pagan god in person, was well calculated to captivate the love of the crowd. His prodigious personal vanity, which led him to delight in sumptuous raiment and gorgeous shows; the state and ceremony with which he surrounded himself and his skill in manly exercises, were all points in his favour with a pleasure-yearning populace which had been squeezed of its substance without seeing any return for it: whilst his ardent admiration for the learning which had during his lifetime become the fashion made grave scholars lose their judgment and write like flattering slaves about the youth of eighteen who now became unquestioned King of England and master of his father's hoarded treasures.

As we shall see in the course of this history, Henry was but a whited sepulchre. Young, light-hearted, with every one about him praising him as a paragon, and his smallest whim indulged as a divine command, there was no incitement for the exhibition of the baser qualities that underlay the big, popular manner, the flamboyant patriotism, and, it must be added, the real ability which appealed alike to the gentle and simple over whom he was called to rule. Like many men of his peculiar physique, he was never a strong man morally, and his will grew weaker as his body increased in gross flabbiness. The obstinate self-assertion and violence that impressed most observers as strength, hid behind them a spirit that forever needed direction and support from a stronger soul. So long as he was allowed in appearance to have his own way and his policy was showy, he was, as one of his wisest ministers said in his last days, the easiest man in the world to manage. His sensuality, which was all his own, and his personal vanity, were the qualities by means of which one able councillor after another used him for the ends they had in view, until the bridle chafed him, and his temporary master was made to feel the vengeance of a weak despot who discovers that he has been ruled instead of ruling. In Henry's personal character as sketched above we shall be able to find the key of the tremendous political events that made his reign the most important in our annals; and we shall see that his successive marriages were the outcome of subtle intrigues in which representatives of various parties took advantage of the King's vanity and lasciviousness to promote their own political or religious views. That the emancipation of England from Rome was the ultimate result cannot fairly be placed to Henry's personal credit. If he could have had his own way without breaking with the Papacy he would have preferred to maintain the connection; but the Reformation was in the air, and craftier brains than Henry's led the King step by step by his ruling passions until he had gone too far to retreat. To what extent his various matrimonial adventures served these intrigues we shall see in the course of this book.

That Henry's marriage with Katharine soon after his accession was politically expedient has been shown in the aforegoing pages; and the King's Council were strongly in favour of it, with the exception of the Archbishop of Canterbury, Lord Chancellor Warham, who was more purely ecclesiastical than his colleagues, and appears to have had doubts as to the canonical validity of the union. As we have seen, the Pope had given a dispensation for the marriage years before, in terms that covered the case of the union with Arthur having been duly consummated, though Katharine strenuously denied that it had been, or that she knew how the dispensation was worded. The Spanish confessor also appears to have suggested to Fuensalida some doubts as to the propriety of the marriage, but King Ferdinand promptly put his veto upon any such scruples. Had not the Pope given his dispensation? he asked; and did not the peace of England and Spain depend upon the marriage? The sin would be not the marriage, but the failure to effect it after the pledges that had been given. So the few doubters were silenced; young Henry himself, all eager for his marriage, was not one of them, nor was Katharine, for to her the match was a triumph for which she had worked and suffered for years: and on the 11th June 1509 the pair were married privately by Warham at Henry's palace of Greenwich.

Rarely in its long history has London seen so brave a pageant as the bride and bridegroom's triumphal passage through the city on Saturday the 21st June from the Tower to Westminster for their coronation. Rich tapestries, and hangings of cloth of gold, decked the streets through which they passed. The city companies lined the way from Gracechurch Street to Bread Street, where the Lord Mayor and the senior guild stood in bright array, whilst the goldsmiths' shops in Chepe had each to adorn it a figure of the Holy Virgin in white with many wax tapers around it. The Queen rode in a litter of white and gold tissue drawn by two snowy palfreys, she herself being garbed in white satin and gold, with a dazzling coronet of precious stones upon her head, from which fell almost to her feet her dark russet hair. She was twenty-four years of age, and in the full flush of womanhood; her regular classical features and fair skin bore yet the curves of gracious youth; and there need be no doubt of the sincerity of the ardent affection for her borne by the pink and white young giant who rode before her, a dazzling vision of crimson velvet, cloth of gold, and flashing precious stones. "God save your Grace," was the cry that rattled like platoon firing along the crowded ways, as the splendid cavalcade passed on.

The next day, Sunday, 24th June, the pair were crowned in the Abbey with all the tedious pomp of the times. Then the Gargantuan feast in Westminster Hall, of which the chronicler spares us no detail, and the endless jousts and devices, in which roses and pomegranates, castles and leopards jostled each other in endless magnificence, until a mere catalogue of the splendour grows meaningless. The death of the King's wise old grandmother, the Countess of Richmond, interrupted for a time the round of festivities; but Henry was too new to the unchecked indulgence of his taste for splendour and pleasure to abandon them easily, and his English councillors, as well as the watchful Spanish agents, began before many weeks were over to hint gravely that the young king was neglecting his business. Katharine appears to have entered fully into the life of pleasure led by her husband. Writing to her father on the 29th July, she is enthusiastic in her praise. "We are all so happy," she says; "our time passes in continual feasting." But in her case, at least, we see that mixed with the frivolous pleasure there was the personal triumph of the politician who had succeeded. "One of the principal reasons why I love my husband the King, is because he is so true a son to your Majesty. I have obeyed your orders and have acted as your ambassador. My husband places himself entirely in your hands. This country of England is truly your own now, and is tranquil and deeply loyal to the King and to me." What more could wife or stateswoman ask? Katharine had her reward. Henry was hers and England was at the bidding of Ferdinand, and her sufferings had not been in vain. Henry, for his part, was, if we are to believe his letters to his father-in-law, as much enamoured of his wife as she was satisfied with him.

And so, amidst magnificent shows, and what seems to our taste puerile trifling, the pair began their married life highly contented with each other and the world. The inevitable black shadows were to come later. In reality they were an entirely ill-matched couple, even apart from the six years' disparity in their ages. Henry, a bluff bully, a coward morally, and also perhaps physically, a liar, who deceived himself as well as others, in order to keep up appearances in his favour, he was just the man that a clever, tactful woman could have managed perfectly, beginning early in his life as Katharine did. Katharine, for all her goodness of heart and exalted piety, was, as we have seen, none too scrupulous herself; and if her ability and dexterity had been equal to her opportunities she might have kept Henry in bondage for life. But, even before her growing age and fading charms had made her distasteful to her husband, her lack of prudence and management towards him had caused him to turn to others for the guidance that she might still have exercised.

The first rift of which we hear came less than a year after the marriage. Friar Diego, who was now Katharine's chancellor, wrote an extraordinary letter to King Ferdinand in May 1510, telling him of a miscarriage that Katharine had had at the end of January; the affair he says having been so secret that no one knew it but the King, two Spanish women, the physician, and himself; and the details he furnishes show him to have been as ignorant as he was impudent. Incidentally, however, he says: "Her Highness is very healthy and the most beautiful creature in the world, with the greatest gaiety and contentment that ever was. The King adores her, and her Highness him." But with this letter to the King went another to his secretary, Almazan, from the new Spanish ambassador, Carroz, who complains bitterly that the friar monopolises the Queen entirely, and prevents his access to her. He then proceeds to tell of Henry and Katharine's first matrimonial tiff. The two married sisters of the Duke of Buckingham were at Court, one being a close friend of Katharine whilst the other was said to be carrying on an intrigue with the King through his favourite, Sir William Compton. This lady's family, and especially her brother the Duke, who had a violent altercation with Compton, and her sister the Queen's friend, shocked at the scandal, carried her away to a convent in the country. In revenge for this the King sent the Queen's favourite away, and quarrelled with Katharine. Carroz was all for counselling prudence and diplomacy to the Queen; but he complains that Friar Diego was advising her badly and putting her on bad terms with her husband.

Many false alarms, mostly, it would seem, set afloat by the meddling friar, and dwelt upon by him in his letters with quite unbecoming minuteness, kept the Court agog as to the possibility of an heir to the crown being born. Henry himself, who was always fond of children, was desperately anxious for a son; and when, on New Year's Day 1511, the looked-for heir was born at Richmond, the King's unrestrained rejoicing again took his favourite form of sumptuous entertainments, after he had ridden to the shrine of Our Lady at Walsingham in Norfolk to give thanks for the favour vouchsafed to him. Once again Westminster glittered with cloth of gold and gems and velvet. Once again courtiers came to the lists disguised as hermits, to kneel before Katharine, and then to cast off their gowns and stand in full panoply before her, craving for leave to tilt in her honour. Once again fairy bowers of gold and artificial flowers sheltered sylvan beauties richly bedizened, the King and his favourites standing by in purple satin garments with the solid gold initials of himself and his wife sewn upon them. Whilst the dazzling company was dancing the "scenery" was rolled back. It came too near the crowd of lieges at the end of the hall, and pilfering fingers began to pluck the golden ornaments from the bowers. Emboldened by their immunity for this, people broke the bounds, swarmed into the central space, and in the twinkling of an eye all the lords and ladies, even the King himself, found themselves stripped of their finery to their very shirts, the golden letters and precious tissues intended as presents for fine ladies being plunder now in grimy hands that turned them doubtless to better account. Henry in his bluff fashion made the best of it, and called the booty largesse. Little recked he, if the tiny heir whose existence fed his vanity throve. But the babe died soon after this costly celebration of his birth.

During the ascendency that the anticipated coming of a son gave to Katharine, Ferdinand was able to beguile Henry into an offensive league against France, by using the same bait that had so often served a similar purpose with Henry VII.; namely, the reconquest for England of Guienne and Normandy. Spain, the Empire, the Papacy, and England formed a coalition that boded ill for the French cause in Italy. As usual the showy but barren part fell to Henry. Ferdinand promised him soldiers to conquer Normandy, but they never came. All Ferdinand wanted was to keep as many Frenchmen as possible from his own battle-grounds, and he found plenty of opportunities for evading all his pledges. Henry was flattered to the top of his bent. The Pope sent him the blessed golden rose, and saluted him as head of the Italian league; and the young king, fired with martial ardour, allowed himself to be dragged into war by his wife's connections, in opposition to the opinion of the wiser heads in his Council. A war with France involved hostilities with Scotland, but Henry was, in the autumn of 1512, cajoled into depleting his realm of troops and sending an army to Spain to attack France over the Pyrenees, whilst another force under Poynings went to help the allies against the Duke of Gueldres. The former host under the Marquis of Dorset was kept idle by its commander because it was found that Ferdinand really required them to reduce the Spanish kingdom of Navarre, and after months of inactivity and much mortality from sickness, they returned ingloriously home to England. This was Henry's first experience of armed alliances, but he learned nothing by experience, and to the end of his life the results of such coalitions to him were always the same.

But his ambition was still unappeased, and in June 1513 he in person led his army across the Channel to conquer France. His conduct in the campaign was puerile in its vanity and folly, and ended lamely with the capture of two (to him) unimportant fortresses in the north, Therouenne and Tournai, and the panic flight of the French at the Battle of the Spurs or Guingate. Our business with this foolish and fruitless campaign, in which Henry was every one's tool, is confined to the part that Katharine played at the time. On the King's ostentatious departure from Dover he left Katharine regent of the realm, with the Earl of Surrey— afterwards Duke of Norfolk— to command the army in the north. Katharine, we are told, rode back from Dover to London full of dolour for her lord's departure; but we see her in her element during the subsequent months of her regency. Bold and spirited, and it must be added utterly tactless, she revelled in the independent domination which she enjoyed. James IV. of Scotland had threatened that an English invasion of France would be followed by his own invasion of England. "Let him do it in God's name," shouted Henry; and Katharine when the threat was made good delivered a splendid oration in English to the officers who were going north to fight the Scots. "Remember," she said, "that the Lord smiled upon those who stood in defence of their own. Remember that the English courage excels that of all other nations upon earth." Her letters to Wolsey, who accompanied Henry as almoner, or rather secretary, are full of courage, and as full of womanly anxiety for her husband. "She was troubled," she wrote, "to learn that the King was so near the siege of Therouenne," until Wolsey's letter assured her of the heed he takes to avoid all manner of dangers. "With his life and health nothing can come amiss with him, without them I see no manner of good thing that shall fall after it." But her tactlessness even in this letter shows clearly when she boasts that the King in France is not so busy with war as she is in England against the Scots. "My heart is very good of it, and I am horribly busy making standards, banners, and badges." After congratulating Henry effusively upon the capture of Therouenne and his meeting with the Emperor, Katharine herself set forth with reinforcements towards Scotland, but before she had travelled a hundred miles (to Woburn) she met the couriers galloping south to bring her the great news of Surrey's victory at Flodden Field. Turning aside to thank Our Lady of Walsingham for the destruction of the Scottish power, Katharine on the way sent the jubilant news to Henry. James IV. in his defeat had been left dead upon the field, clad in his check surcoat, and a fragment of this coat soaked with blood the Queen sent to her husband in France, with a heartless gibe at his dead brother-in-law. We are told that in another of her letters first giving the news of Flodden, and referring to Henry's capture of the Duke of Longueville at Therouenne, she vaingloriously compared her victory with his. "It was no great thing for one armed man to take another, but she was sending three captured by a woman; if he (Henry) sent her a captive Duke she would send him a prisoner king." For a wife and *locum tenens* to write thus in such circumstances to a supremely vain man like Henry, whose martial ambition was still unassuaged, was to invite his jealousy and dislike. His people saw, as he with all his boastfulness cannot fail to have done, that Flodden was the real English victory, not Therouenne, and that Katharine and Surrey, not Henry, were the heroes. Such knowledge was gall and wormwood to the King; and especially when the smoke of battle had blown away, and he saw how he had been "sold" by his wife's relations, who kept the fruit of victory whilst he was put off with the shell.

From that time Katharine's influence over her husband weakened, though with occasional intermission, and he looked for guidance to a subtler mind than hers. With Henry to France had gone Thomas Wolsey, one of the clergy of the royal chapel, recently appointed almoner by the patronage of Fox, Bishop of Winchester, Henry's leading councillor in foreign affairs. The English nobles, strong as they still were territorially, could not be trusted with the guidance of affairs by a comparatively new dynasty depending upon parliament and the towns for its power; and an official class, raised at the will of the sovereign, had been created by Henry VII., to be used as ministers and administrators. Such a class, dependent entirely upon the crown, were certain to be distasteful to the noble families, and the rivalry between these two governing elements provided the germ of party divisions which subsequently hardened into the English constitutional tradition: the officials usually being favourable to the strengthening of the royal prerogative, and the nobles desiring to maintain the check which the armed power of feudalism had formerly exercised. For reasons which will be obvious, the choice of both Henry VII. and his son of their diplomatists and ministers fell to a great extent upon clergymen; and Wolsey's brilliant talents and facile adaptiveness during his close attendance upon Henry in France captivated his master, who needed for a minister and guide one that could never become a rival either in the field or the ladies' chamber, where the King most desired distinction.

Henry came home in October 1513, bitterly enraged against Katharine's kin, and ripe for the close alliance with France which the prisoner Duke of Longueville soon managed to bring about. What mattered it that lovely young Mary Tudor was sacrificed in marriage to the decrepit old King Louis XII., notwithstanding her previous solemn betrothal to Katharine's nephew, young Charles of Austria, and her secret love for Henry's bosom friend, Sir Charles Brandon? Princesses were but pieces in the great political game, and must perforce take the rough with the smooth. Henry, in any case, could thus show to the Spaniard that he could defy him by a French connection. It must have been with a sad heart that Katharine took part in the triumphal doings that celebrated the peace directed against her father. The French agents, then in London, in describing her say that she was lively and gracious, quite the opposite of her gloomy sister: and doubtless she did her best to appear so, for she was proud and schooled to disappointment; but with the exception of the fact that she was again with child, all around her looked black. Her husband openly taunted her with her father's ill faith; Henry was carrying on now an open intrigue with Lady Tailebois, whom he had brought from Calais with him; Ferdinand the Catholic at last was slowly dying, all his dreams and hopes frustrated; and on the 13th August 1514, in the palace of Greenwich, Katharine's dear friend and sister-in-law, Mary Tudor, was married by proxy to Louis XII. Katharine, led by the Duke of Longueville, attended the festivity. She was dressed in ash-coloured satin, covered with raised gold embroidery, costly chains and necklaces of gems covered her neck and bust, and a coif trimmed with precious stones was on her head. The King at the ball in the evening charmed every one by his graceful dancing, and the scene was so gay that the grave Venetian ambassador says that had it not been for his age and office he would have cast off his gown and have footed it with the rest.

But already sinister whispers were rife, and we may be sure they were not unknown to Katharine. She had been married five years, and no child of hers had lived; and, though she was again pregnant, it was said that the Pope would be asked to authorise Henry to put her aside, and to marry a French bride. Had not his new French brother-in-law done the like years ago? To what extent this idea had really entered Henry's head at the time it is difficult to say; but courtiers and diplomatists have keen eyes, and they must have known which way the wind was blowing before they talked thus. In October 1514 Katharine was borne slowly in a litter to Dover, with the great concourse that went to speed Mary Tudor on her loveless two months' marriage; and a few weeks afterwards Katharine gave birth prematurely to a dead child. Once more the hopes of Henry were dashed, and though Peter Martyr ascribed the misfortune to Henry's unkindness, the superstitious time-servers of the King, and those in favour of the French alliance, began to hint that Katharine's offspring was accursed, and that to get an heir the King must take another wife. The doings at Court were still as brilliant and as frivolous as ever; the King's great delight being in adopting some magnificent, and, of course, perfectly transparent disguise in masque or ball, and then to disclose himself when every one, the Queen included, was supposed to be lost in wonder at the grace and agility of the pretended unknown. Those who take pleasure in the details of such puerility may be referred to Hall's *Chronicle* for them: we here have more to do with the hearts beneath the finery, than with the trappings themselves.

That Katharine was striving desperately at this time to retain her influence over her husband, and her popularity in England, is certain from the letter of Ferdinand's ambassador (6th December 1514). He complains that on the recommendation of Friar Diego Katharine had thrown over her father's interests in order to keep the love of Henry and his people. The Castilian interest and the Manuels have captured her, wrote the ambassador, and if Ferdinand did not promptly "put a bridle on this colt" (*i.e.* Henry) and bring Katharine to her bearings as her father's daughter, England would be for ever lost to Aragon. There is no doubt that at this time Katharine felt that her only chance of keeping her footing was to please Henry, and "forget Spain," as Friar Diego advised her to do.

When the King of France died on New Year's Day, 1515, and his young widow— Katharine's friend, Mary Tudor— clandestinely married her lover, Charles Brandon, Katharine's efforts to reconcile her husband to the peccant pair are evidence, if no other existed, that Henry's anger was more assumed than real, and that his vanity was pleased by the submissive prayers for his forgiveness. As no doubt the Queen, and Wolsey, who had joined his efforts with hers, foresaw, not only were Mary and Brandon pardoned, but taken into high favour. At the public marriage of Mary and Brandon at Greenwich at Easter 1515 more tournaments, masques and balls, enabled the King to show off his gallantry and agility in competition with his new brother-in-law; and on the subsequent May Day at Shooter's Hill, Katharine and Mary, who were inseparable, took part in elaborate and costly *al fresco* entertainments in which Robin Hood, several pagan deities, and the various attributes of spring, were paraded for their delectation. It all sounds very gay, though somewhat silly, as we read the endless catalogues of bedizenment, of tilts and races, feasting, dancing, and music that delighted Henry and his friends; but before Katharine there ever hovered the spectre of her childlessness, and Henry, after the ceremonial gaiety and overdone gallantry to his wife, would too frequently put spurs to his courser and gallop off to New Hall in Essex, where Lady Tailebois lived.

A gleam of hope and happiness came to her late in 1515 when she was again expecting to become a mother. By liberal gifts— "the greatest presents ever brought to England," said Henry himself— and by flattery unlimited, Ferdinand, almost on his death-bed, managed to "bridle" his son-in-law, to borrow a large sum of money from him and draw him anew into a coalition against France. But the hope was soon dashed; King Ferdinand died almost simultaneously with the birth of a girl-child to his daughter Katharine. It is true the babe was like to live, but a son, not a daughter, was what Henry wanted. Yet he put the best face on the matter publicly. The Venetian ambassador purposely delayed his congratulations, because the child was of the wrong sex; and when finally he coldly offered them, he pointedly told the King that they would have been much more hearty if the child had been a son. "We are both young," replied Henry. "If it is a daughter this time, by the grace of God sons will follow." The desire of the King for a male heir was perfectly natural. No Queen had reigned independently over England; and for the perpetuation of a new dynasty like the Tudors the succession in the male line was of the highest importance. In addition to this, Henry was above all things proud of his manliness, and he looked upon the absence of a son as in some sort reflecting a humiliation upon him.

Katharine's health had never been robust; and at the age of thirty-three, after four confinements, she had lost her bloom. Disappointment and suffering, added to her constitutional weakness, was telling upon her, and her influence grew daily smaller. The gorgeous shows and frivolous amusements in which her husband so much delighted palled upon her, and she now took little pains to feign enjoyment in them, giving up much of her time to religious exercises, fasting rigidly twice a week and saints' days throughout the year, in addition to the Lenten observances, and wearing beneath her silks and satins a rough Franciscan nun's gown of serge. As in the case of so many of her kindred, mystical devotion was weaving its grey web about her, and saintliness of the peculiar Spanish type was covering her as with a garment. Henry, on the contrary, was a full-blooded young man of twenty-eight, with a physique like that of a butcher, held by no earthly control or check upon his appetites, overflowing with vitality and the joy of life; and it is not to be wondered at that he found his disillusioned and consciously saintly wife a somewhat uncomfortable companion.

The death of Louis XII., Maximilian, and Ferdinand, and the peaceful accession of young Charles to the throne of Spain and the prospective imperial crown, entirely altered the political aspect of Europe. Francis I. needed peace in the first years of his reign; and to Charles it was also desirable, in order that his rule over turbulent Spain could be firmly established and his imperial succession secured. All the English ministers and councillors were heavily bribed by France, Wolsey himself was strongly in favour of the French connection, and everybody entered into a conspiracy to flatter Henry. The natural result was a league first of England and France, and subsequently a general peace to which all the principal Christian potentates subscribed, and men thought that the millennium had come. Katharine's international importance had disappeared with the death of her father and the accession of Charles to the throne of Aragon as well as to that of Castile. Wolsey was now Henry's sole adviser in matters of state and managed his master dexterously, whilst endeavouring not entirely to offend the Queen. Glimpses of his harmonious relations with Katharine at this time (1516-1520) are numerous. At the splendid christening of the Princess Mary, Wolsey was one of the sponsors, and he was "gossip" with Katharine at the baptism of Mary Tudor Duchess of Suffolk's son.

Nor can the Queen's famous action after the evil May Day (1517) have been opposed or discountenanced by the Cardinal. The universal

peace had brought to London hosts of foreigners, especially Frenchmen, and the alien question was acute. Wolsey, whose sudden rise and
insolence had deeply angered the nobles, had, as principal promoter of
the unpopular peace with France, to bear a full share of the detestation
in which his friends the aliens were held. Late in April there were rumours that a general attack upon foreigners by the younger citizens
would be made, and at Wolsey's instance the civic authorities ordered
that all the Londoners should keep indoors. Some lads in Chepe disregarded the command, and the Alderman of the Ward attempted to arrest one of them. Then rose the cry of "'Prentices and Clubs! Death to
the Cardinal!" and forth there poured from lane and alley riotous
youngsters by the hundred, to wreak vengeance on the insolent foreigners who took the bread out of worthy Englishmen's mouths. Sack
and pillage reigned for a few hours, but the guard quelled the boys with
blood, the King rode hastily from Richmond, the Lieutenant of the
Tower dropped a few casual cannon-balls into the city, and before sun-
set all was quiet. The gibbets rose at the street corners and a bloody
vengeance fell upon the rioters. Dozens were hanged, drawn, and quartered with atrocious cruelty; and under the ruthless Duke of Norfolk
four hundred more were condemned to death for treason to the King,
who, it was bitterly said in London, loved outlanders better than his
own folk. It is unlikely that Henry really meant to plunge all his capital
in mourning by hanging the flower of its youth, but he loved, for vanity's sake, that his clemency should be publicly sought, and to act the
part of a deity in restoring to life those legally dead. In any case,
Katharine's spontaneous and determined intercession for the 'prentice
lads would take no denial, and she pleaded with effect. Her intercession, nevertheless, could hardly have been so successful as it was if
Wolsey had been opposed to it; and the subsequent comedy in the great
Hall at Westminster on the 22nd May was doubtless planned to afford
Henry an opportunity of appearing in his favourite character. Seated
upon a canopied throne high upon a daïs of brocade, surrounded by
his prelates and nobles and with Wolsey by his side, Henry frowned in
crimson velvet whilst the "poore younglings and olde false knaves"
trooped in, a sorry procession, stripped to their shirts, with halters
around their necks. Wolsey in stern words rebuked their crime, and
scolded the Lord Mayor and Aldermen for their laxity; ending by saying
they all deserved to hang. "Mercy! gracious lord, mercy!" cried the terrified boys and their distracted mothers behind; and the Cardinal and
the peers knelt before the throne to beg the life of the offenders, which
the King granted, and with a great shout of joy halters were stripped

from many a callow neck, and cast into the rafters of the Hall for very joy. But all men knew, and the mothers too, that Wolsey's intercession was only make-believe, and that what they saw was but the ceremonial act of grace. The Queen they thanked in their hearts and not the haughty Cardinal, for the King had pardoned the 'prentices privately days before, when Katharine and her two sisters-in-law, the widowed Queens of France and Scotland, had knelt before the King in unfeigned tears, and had clamoured for the lives of the Londoners. To the day of the Queen's unhappy death this debt was never forgotten by the citizens, who loved her faithfully to the end far better than any of her successors.

The sweating sickness in the autumn of 1517 sent Henry and his wife as far away from contagion as possible, for sickness always frightened the big bully into a panic. During his absence from London, Wolsey was busy negotiating a still closer alliance with France, by the marriage of the baby Princess Mary to the newly born Dauphin. It can hardly have been the match that Katharine would have chosen for her cherished only child, but she was a cypher by the side of Wolsey now, and made no open move against it at the time. Early in the spring of 1518 the plague broke out again, and Henry in dire fear started upon a progress in the midlands. Richard Pace, who accompanied him, wrote to Wolsey on the 12th April telling him as a secret that the Queen was again pregnant. "I pray God heartily," he continued, "that it may be a prince to the surety and universal comfort of the realm;" and he begs the Cardinal to write a kind letter to the Queen. In June the glad tidings were further confirmed, as likely to result in "an event most earnestly desired by the whole kingdom." Still dodging the contagion, the King almost fled from one place to another, and when at Woodstock in July Henry himself wrote a letter to Wolsey which tells in every line how anxious he was that the coming event should be the fulfilment of his ardent hope. Katharine had awaited him at Woodstock, and he had been rejoiced at the confident hope she gave him. He tells Wolsey the news formally, and says that he will remove the Queen as little and as quietly as may be to avoid risk. Soon all the diplomatists were speculating at the great things that would happen when the looked-for prince was born; and it was probably the confident hope that this time Henry would not be disappointed, that made possible the success of Wolsey's policy and the marriage of the Princess Mary with the infant Dauphin. Of Wolsey's magnificent feasts that accompanied the ratification of peace and the betrothal on the 5th October, feasts more splendid, says the Venetian ambassador, than ever were given by Caligula or

Cleopatra, no account can be given here. It was Wolsey's great triumph, and he surpassed all the records of luxury in England in its celebration. The sweet little bride dressed in cloth of gold stood before the thrones upon which her father and mother sat in the great Hall of Greenwich, and then, carried in the arms of a prelate, was held up whilst the Cardinal slipped the diamond wedding-ring upon her finger and blessed her nuptials with the baby bridegroom. That the heir of France should marry the heiress of England was a danger to the balance of Europe, and especially a blow to Spain. It was, moreover, not a match which England could regard with equanimity; for a French King Consort would have been repugnant to the whole nation, and Henry could never have meant to conclude the marriage finally, unless the expected heir was born. But alas! for human hopes. On the night of 10th November 1518, Katharine was delivered of a daughter, "to the vexation of as many as knew it," and King and nation mourned together, now that, after all, a Frenchman might reign over England.

To Katharine this last disappointment was bitter indeed. Her husband, wounded and irritated, first in his pride, and now in his national interests, avoided her; her own country and kin had lost the English tie that meant so much to them, and she herself, in poor health and waning attractions, could only mourn her misfortunes, and cling more closely than ever to her one darling child, Mary, for the new undesired infant girl had died as soon as it was born. The ceaseless round of masking, mummery, and dancing, which so much captivated Henry, went on without abatement, and Katharine perforce had to take her part in it; but all the King's tenderness was now shown not to his wife but to his little daughter, whom he carried about in his arms and praised inordinately. So frivolous and familiar indeed had Henry's behaviour grown that his Council took fright, and, under the thin veil of complaints against the behaviour of his boon companions, Carew, Peachy, Wingfield, and Brian, who were banished from Court, they took Henry himself seriously to task. The four French hostages, held for the payment of the war indemnity, were also feasted and entertained so familiarly by Henry, under Wolsey's influence, as to cause deep discontent to the lieges, who had always looked upon France as an enemy, and knew that the unpopular Cardinal's overwhelming display was paid for by French bribes. At one such entertainment Katharine was made to act as hostess at her dower-house of Havering in Essex, where, in the summer of 1519, we are told that, "for their welcomyng she purveyed all thynges in the most liberalist manner; and especially she made to the Kyng suche a sumpteous banket that he thanked her hartely, and the strangers gave it great praise." Later in the same year Katharine was present at a grand series of entertainments given by the King in the splendid new manor-house which he had built for Lady Tailebois, who had just rejoiced him by giving birth to a son. We have no record of Katharine's thoughts as she took part here in the tedious foolery so minutely described by Hall. She plucked off the masks, we are told, of eight disguised dancers in long dominos of blue satin and gold, "who danced with the ladies sadly, and communed not with them after the fashion of maskers." Of course the masqueraders were the Duke of Suffolk (Brandon) and other great nobles, as the poor Queen must well have known; but when she thought that all this mummery was to entertain Frenchmen, and the house in which it passed was devoted to the use of Henry's mistress, she must have covered her own heart with a more impenetrable mask than those of Suffolk and his companions, if her face was attuned to the gay sights and sounds around her.

KATHARINE OF ARAGON
From a portrait by HOLBEIN *in the National Portrait Gallery*

Katharine had now almost ceased to strive for the objects to which her life had been sacrificed, namely, the binding together of England and Spain to the detriment of France. Wolsey had believed that his own interests would be better served by a close French alliance, and he had had his way. Henry himself was but the vainglorious figure in the international pageant; the motive power was the Cardinal. But a greater than Wolsey, Charles of Austria and Spain, though he was as yet only a lad of nineteen, had appeared upon the scene, and soon was to make his power felt throughout the world. Wolsey's close union with France and the marriage of the Princess Mary with the Dauphin had been meant as a blow to Spain, to lead if possible to the election of Henry to the imperial crown, in succession to Maximilian, instead of the latter's grandson Charles. If the King of England were made Emperor, the way of the Cardinal of York to the throne of St. Peter was clear. Henry was flattered at the idea, and was ready to follow his minister anywhere to gain such a showy prize. But quite early in the struggle it was seen that the unpopular French alliance which had already cost England the surrender of the King's conquests in the war was powerless to bring about the result desired. Francis I., as vain and turbulent as Henry, and perhaps more able, was bidding high for the Empire himself. His success in the election would have been disastrous both to Spain and England, and yet the French alliance was too dear to Wolsey to be easily relinquished, and Francis was assured that all the interest of his dear brother of England should be cast in his favour, whilst, with much more truth, the Spanish candidate was plied with good wishes for his success, and underhand attempts were made at the same time to gain the electors for the King of England. Wolsey hoped thus to win in any case; and up to a certain point he did so; for he gave to Charles the encouragement he needed for the masterly move which soon after revolutionised political relations.

Charles at this time (1519), young as he was, had already developed his marvellous mental and physical powers. Patient and self-centred, with all his Aragonese grandfather's subtlety, he possessed infinitely greater boldness and width of view. He knew well that the seven prince electors who chose the Emperor might, like other men, be bought, if enough money could be found. To provide it and give to him the dominant power of the world, he was ready to crush the ancient liberties of Castile, to squeeze his Italian and Flemish dominions of their last obtainable ducat, for he knew that his success in the election would dazzle his subjects until they forgot what they had paid for it. And so it happened. Where Francis bribed in hundreds Charles bribed in thousands, and England in the conflict of money-bags and great territorial interests hardly counted at all. When Charles was elected Emperor in June 1519, Henry professed himself delighted; but it meant that the universal peace that had been proclaimed with such a flourish of trumpets only three years before was already tottering, and that England must soon make a choice as to which of the two great rivals should be her friend, and which her enemy.

Francis nursed his wrath to keep it warm, and did his best to retain Henry and Wolsey on his side. Bribes and pensions flowed freely from France upon English councillors, the inviolable love of Henry and Francis, alike in gallantry and age, was insisted upon again and again; the three-year-old Princess Mary was referred to always as Dauphiness and future Queen of France, though when the little Dauphin was spoken of as future King of England, Henry's subjects pulled a wry face and cursed all Frenchmen. A meeting between the two allies, which for its splendour should surpass all other regal displays, was constantly urged by the French hostages in England by order of Francis, as a means of showing to the world that he could count upon Henry. To the latter the meeting was agreeable as a tribute to his power, and as a satisfaction to his love of show, and to Wolsey it was useful as enhancing his sale value in the eyes of two lavish bidders. To Charles, who shared none of the frivolous tastes of his rival sovereigns, it only appealed as a design against him to be forestalled and defeated. When, therefore, the preparations for the Field of the Cloth of Gold were in full swing early in the year 1520, Charles, by a brilliant though risky move such as his father Philip would have loved, took the first step to win England to his side in the now inevitable struggle for supremacy between the Empire and France. Whilst he was still wrangling with his indignant Castilian parliament in March, Charles sent envoys to England to propose a friendly meeting with Henry whilst on his way by sea from Spain to Flanders. It was Katharine's chance and she made the most of it. She had suffered long and patiently whilst the French friendship was paramount; but if God would vouchsafe her the boon of seeing her nephew in England it would, she said to his envoys, be the measure of her desires. Wolsey, too, smiled upon the suggestion, for failing Francis the new Emperor in time might help him to the Papacy. So, with all secrecy, a solemn treaty was signed on the 11th April 1520, settling, down to the smallest details, the reception of Charles by Henry and Katharine at Sandwich and Canterbury, on his voyage or else at a subsequent meeting of the monarchs between Calais and Gravelines.

It was late in May when news came from the west that the Spanish fleet was sailing up the Channel; and Henry was riding towards the sea from London ostensibly to embark for France when he learnt that the Emperor's ships were becalmed off Dover. Wolsey was despatched post-haste to greet the imperial visitor and invite him to land; and Charles, surrounded by a gorgeous suite of lords and ladies, with the black eagle of Austria on cloth of gold fluttering over and around him, was conducted to Dover Castle, where before dawn next morning, the 27th May, Henry arrived and welcomed his nephew. There was no mistaking the cordiality of the English cheers that rang in peals from Dover to Canterbury and through the ancient city, as the two monarchs rode side by side in gorgeous array. They meant, as clearly as tone could speak, that the enemy of France and Queen Katharine's nephew was the friend for the English people, whatever the Cardinal of York might think. To Katharine it was a period of rejoicing, and her thoughts were high as she welcomed her sister's son; the sallow young man with yellow hair, already in title the greatest monarch in the world, though beset with difficulties. By her stood beautiful Mary Tudor, Duchess of Suffolk, twice married since she had, as a child, been betrothed under such heavy guarantees to Charles himself; and, holding her mother's hand, was the other Mary Tudor, a prim, quaint little maid of four, with big brown eyes. Already great plans for her filled her mother's brain. True, she was betrothed to the Dauphin; but what if the hateful French match fell through, and the Emperor, he of her own kin, were to seal a national alliance by marrying the daughter of England? Charles feasted for four days at Canterbury, and then went on his way amidst loving plaudits to his ships at Sandwich; but before he sailed he whispered that to Wolsey which made the Cardinal his servant; for the Emperor, suzerain of Italy and King of Naples, Sicily, and Spain, might do more than a King of France in future towards making a Pope.

By the time that Henry and Francis met early in June on the ever-memorable field between Ardres and Guisnes, the riot of splendour which surrounded the sovereigns and Wolsey, though it dazzled the crowd and left its mark upon history as a pageant, was known to the principal actors of the scene to be but hollow mockery. The glittering baubles that the two kings loved, the courtly dallying, the pompous ceremony, the masques and devices to symbolise eternal amity, were not more evanescent than the love they were supposed to perpetuate. Katharine went through her ceremonial part of the show as a duty, and graciously received the visit of Francis in the wonderful flimsy palace of wood, drapery, and glass at Guisnes; but her heart was across the Flemish frontier a few miles away, where her nephew awaited the coming of the King of England to greet him as his kinsman and future ally. Gravelines was a poor place, but Charles had other ways of influencing people than by piling up gewgaws before them. A single day of rough, hearty feasting was an agreeable relief to Henry after the glittering insincerity of Guisnes; and the four days following, in which Charles was entertained at Calais as the guest of Henry and Katharine, made up in prodigality for the coarseness of the Flemish fare; whilst Wolsey, who was already posing as the arbitrator between all Christian potentates, was secured to the side of the Emperor in future by a grant of the bulk of the income from two Spanish bishoprics, Badajoz and Palencia.

Already the two great rivals were bidding against each other for allies, and Charles, though his resources were less concentrated than those of Francis, could promise most. Leo X. for his own territorial ambition, and in fear of Luther, rallied to the side of the Emperor, the German princes seconded their suzerain, and the great struggle for the supremacy of Christendom began in March 1521. England by treaty was bound to assist France, but this did not suit Wolsey or Henry in their new mood, and the Cardinal pressed his arbitration on the combatants. Francis reluctantly consented to negotiate; but minds were aflame with a subject that added fierceness to the political rivalry between Charles and Francis. The young Emperor, when he had met the German princes at Worms (April 1521), had thrown down the gage to Luther, and thenceforward it was war to the knife between the old faith and the new spirit. Henry, we may be certain to the delight of Katharine, violently attacked Luther in his famous book, and was flattered by the fulsome praises of the Pope and the Emperor. In the circumstances Wolsey's voyage to Calais for the furtherance of arbitration was turned into one to conclude an armed alliance with Charles and the Pope. The Cardinal, who had bent all others to his will, was himself bent by the Emperor; and the arbitrator between two monarchs became the servant of one. By the treaty signed at Bruges by Wolsey for Henry, Charles contracted an engagement to marry his little cousin, Princess Mary, and to visit England for a formal betrothal in the following year.

How completely Wolsey had at this time surrendered himself to the Emperor, is evident from Katharine's new attitude towards him. During his period of French sympathy she had been, as we have seen, practically alienated from state affairs, but now in Henry's letters to Wolsey her name is frequently mentioned and her advice was evidently welcome. During his absence in Flanders, for instance, Wolsey received a letter from Henry, in which the King says: "The Queen, my wife, hath desired me to make her most hearty recommendation unto you, as to him that she loveth very well; and both she and I would fain know when you would repair unto us." Great news came that the Emperor and his allies were brilliantly successful in the war, but in the midst of victory the great Medici, Pope Leo X., though still a man in his prime, died. There is no doubt that a secret promise had been made by Charles to Wolsey of his support in case a vacancy in the Papacy arose, but no one had dreamed of its occurring so quickly, and Charles found his hand forced. He needed for his purpose a far more pliable instrument in the pontifical chair than the haughty Cardinal of York. So, whilst pretending to work strenuously to promote Wolsey's elevation, and thus to gain the goodwill of Henry and his minister, he took care secretly that some humbler candidate, such as the one ultimately chosen by the Conclave, his old schoolmaster, Cardinal Adrian, should be the new Pope. Wolsey was somewhat sulky at the result of the election, and thenceforward looked with more distrust on the imperial connection; but, withal, he put as good a face on the matter as possible; and when, at the end of May 1522, he again welcomed the Emperor in Henry's name as he set foot on English soil at Dover, the Cardinal, though watchful, was still favourable to the alliance. This visit of the young Emperor was the most splendid royal sojourn ever made in England; and Henry revelled in the ceremonies wherein he was the host of the greatest monarch upon earth.

Charles came with a train of a thousand horse and two thousand courtiers; and to feed and house such a multitude, the guilds of London, and even the principal citizens, were obliged to make return of all their spare beds and stocks of provisions in order to provide for the strangers. The journey of the monarchs was a triumphal progress from Dover through Canterbury, Sittingbourne, and Rochester to Gravesend. On the downs between Dover and Canterbury, Henry and a great train of nobles was to have met his nephew; but the more to do him honour the King rode into Dover itself, and with pride showed his visitor his new great ship the *Harry Grace à Dieu*, and the rest of the English fleet; whereupon, "the Emperor and his lords much praised the making of the ships, and especially the artillery: they said they had never seen ships so armed." From Gravesend the gallant company rowed in the royal barges amidst salvoes of guns to Greenwich. There at the hall door of the palace stood Katharine surrounded by her ladies, and holding her tiny daughter by the hand. Sinking upon one knee the Emperor craved his aunt's blessing, which was given, and thenceforward for five weeks the feasting and glorious shows went on without intermission.

On the second day after the arrival at Greenwich, whilst Henry was arming for a joust, a courier, all travel-stained and weary, demanded prompt audience, to hand the King a letter from his ambassador in France. The King read the despatch with knitted brows, and, turning to his friend Sir William Compton, said: "Go and tell the Emperor I have news for him." When Charles came the letter was handed to him, and it must have rejoiced his heart as he read it. Francis bade defiance to the King of England, and thenceforward Henry and the Emperor were allies in arms against a common enemy. Glittering pageants followed in London and Windsor, where Charles sat as Knight of the Garter under triumphant Henry's presidency; masques and dances, banquets and hunting, delighted the host and surprised the guests with the unrestrained lavishness of the welcome; but we may be certain that what chiefly interested Katharine and her nephew was not this costly trifling, but the eternal friendship between England and Spain solemnly sworn upon the sacrament in St. George's Chapel, Windsor, by the Emperor and Henry, and the binding alliance between them in peace and war, cemented by the pledge that Charles should marry his cousin Mary Tudor and no one else in the world. It was Katharine's final and greatest triumph, and the shadows fell thick and fast thereafter.

Henry promptly took his usual showy and unprofitable part in the war. Only a few weeks after the Emperor bade his new ally farewell, an English force invaded Picardy, and the Earl of Surrey's fleet threatened all French shipping in the Channel. Coerced by the King of England too, Venice deserted France and joined forces with the allies; the new Pope and the Italian princes did the same, and the Emperor's arms carried all before them in Italy. Henry was kept faithful to his ally by the vain hope of a dismemberment of France, in which he should be the principal gainer; the Pope Clement VII., the ambitious Medici, who succeeded Adrian in September 1523, hungered for fresh territory which Charles alone could give him; the rebel De Bourbon, the greatest soldier of France, was fighting against his own king; and in February 1525 the crushing blow of Pavia fell, and Francis, "all lost except honour," was a prisoner in the hands of his enemy, who looking over Christendom saw none to say him nay but the bold monk at Wittemberg.

Three years of costly war for interests not primarily their own had already disillusioned the English people. By methods more violent and tyrannical than ever had been adopted by any previous king, Henry had wrung from parliament supplies so oppressive and extortionate for the purposes of the war as to disgust and incense the whole country. Wolsey, too, had been for the second time beguiled about the Papacy he coveted, and knew now that he could not trust the Emperor to serve any interests but his own. The French collapse at Pavia, moreover, and pity for the captive Francis languishing at Madrid, had caused in England and elsewhere a reaction in his favour. Henry himself was, as was his wont, violently angry at the cynical way in which his own hopes in France were shelved by Charles; and the Pope, alarmed now at the Emperor's unchecked dominion in Italy, and the insufficient share of the spoil offered to him, also began to look askance at his ally. So, notwithstanding the official rejoicings in England when the news of Pavia came, and the revived plan of Henry and Wolsey to join Bourbon in his intention to dismember France, with or without the aid of Charles, the Archbishop of Canterbury, Warham, correctly interpreted the prevailing opinion in England in his letter to Wolsey (quoted by Hallam), saying that the people had "more cause to weep than to rejoice" at the French defeat. The renewed extortionate demands for money aroused in England discontent so dangerous as to reach rebellion against the King's officers. Risings in Kent and the eastern counties, and the outspoken remonstrances of the leaders of the middle and working classes at length convinced Wolsey, and through him the King, that a change of policy was inevitable. England once more had been made the cat's-paw of Spain; and now, with an empty exchequer and a profoundly discontented people, was obliged again to shift its balance to the side which promised the best hopes for peace, and to redress the equilibrium in Europe upon which the English power depended. France was still rich in resources, and was made to pay or rather promise the vast sum of two million crowns in instalments, and an annuity of a hundred thousand a year to the King for England's friendship, whilst Francis was forced to abandon all his claims on Italy and Burgundy (January 1526), and marry the Emperor's sister Leonora, before he was permitted to return to France, at peace once more. It is true that every party to the treaties endeavoured to evade the fulfilment of his pledges; but that was the custom of the times. The point that interests us here is that the new policy now actively pursued by Wolsey of close friendship with France, necessarily meant the ruin of Katharine, unless she was dexterous and adaptable enough either to reverse the policy or openly espouse it. Unfortunately she did neither. She was now forty-one years of age, and had ceased for nearly two years to cohabit with her husband. Her health was bad; she had grown stout, and her comeliness had departed; all hopes of her giving to the King the son and heir for whom he so ardently craved had quite vanished, and with them much of her personal hold upon her husband. To her alarm and chagrin, Henry, as if in despair of being succeeded by a legitimate heir, in 1525, before signing the new alliance with France, had created his dearly loved natural son, Henry Fitzroy, a duke under the royal title of Duke of Richmond, which had been borne by his father; and Katharine, not without reason, feared the King's intention to depose her daughter, the betrothed of the Emperor, in favour of an English bastard. We have in previous pages noticed the peculiar absence of tact and flexibility in Katharine's character; and Wolsey's ostentatious French leanings after 1525 were met by the Queen with open opposition and acrimonious reproach, instead of by temporising wiliness. The Emperor's off-hand treatment of his betrothed bride, Mary Tudor, further embittered

Katharine, who was thus surrounded on every side by disillusionment and disappointment. Charles sent commissioners to England just before the battle of Pavia to demand, amongst other unamiable requirements, the prompt sending of Mary, who was only nine years old, to Flanders with an increased dowry. This was no part of the agreement, and was, as no doubt Charles foresaw and desired, certain to be refused. The envoys received from Henry and Katharine, and more emphatically from Wolsey, a negative answer to the request, Mary being, as they said, the greatest treasure they had, for whom no hostages would be sufficient. Katharine would not let her nephew slip out of his engagement without a struggle. Mary herself was made soon after to send a fine emerald to her betrothed with a grand message to the effect that when they came together she would be able to know (*i.e.* by the clearness or otherwise of the gem) "whether his Majesty do keep himself as continent and chaste as, with God's grace, she will." As at this time the Emperor was a man of twenty-five, whilst his bride had not reached ten years, the cases were hardly parallel; and within three months (in July 1525) Charles had betrothed himself to his cousin of Portugal. The treaty that had been so solemnly sworn to on the high altar at Windsor only three years before, had thus become so much waste-paper, and Katharine's best hopes for her child and herself were finally defeated. A still greater trial for her followed; for whilst Wolsey was drawing nearer and nearer to France, and the King himself was becoming more distant from his wife every day, the little Princess was taken from the loving care of her mother, and sent to reside in her principality of Wales. Thenceforward the life of Katharine was a painful martyrdom without one break in the monotony of misfortune.

Katharine appears never to have been unduly jealous of Henry's various mistresses. She, one of the proudest princesses in Christendom, probably considered them quite beneath her notice, and as usual adjuncts to a sovereign's establishment. Henry, moreover, was far from being a generous or complaisant lover; and allowed his lady favourites no great social and political power, such as that wielded by the mistresses of Francis I. Lady Tailebois (Eleanor Blount) made no figure at Court, and Mary Boleyn, the wife of William Carey, a quite undistinguished courtier, who had been Henry's mistress from about 1521, was always impecunious and sometimes disreputable, though her greedy father reaped a rich harvest from his daughter's attractions. Katharine evidently troubled herself very little about such infidelity on the part of her husband, and certainly Wolsey had no objection. The real anxiety of the Queen arose from Henry's ardent desire for a legitimate son, which she could not hope to give him; and Wolsey, with his eyes constantly fixed on the Papacy, decided to make political capital and influence for himself by binding France and England so close together both dynastically and politically as to have both kings at his bidding before the next Pope was elected. The first idea was the betrothal of the jilted Princess Mary of ten to the middle-aged widower who sat upon the throne of France. An embassy came to London from the Queen Regent of France, whilst Francis was still a prisoner in Madrid in 1525, to smooth the way for a closer intimacy. Special instructions were given to the ambassador to dwell upon the complete recovery of Francis from his illness, and to make the most of the Emperor's unfaithfulness to his English betrothed for the purpose of marrying the richly dowered Portuguese. Francis eventually regained his liberty on hard conditions that included his marriage with Charles's widowed sister Leonora, Queen Dowager of Portugal; and his sons were to remain in Spain as hostages for his fulfilment of the terms. But from the first Francis intended to violate the treaty of Madrid, wherever possible; and early in 1527 a stately train of French nobles, headed by De Grammont, Bishop of Tarbes, came with a formal demand for the hand of young Mary Tudor for the already much-married Francis. Again the palace of Greenwich was a blaze of splendour for the third nuptials of the little princess; and the elaborate mummery that Henry loved was re-enacted. On the journeys to and from their lodgings in Merchant Taylors' Hall, the Bishop of Tarbes and Viscount de Turenne heard nothing but muttered curses, saw nothing but frowning faces of the London people; for Mary was in the eyes of Henry's subjects the heiress of England, and they would have, said they, no Frenchman to reign over them when their own king should die. Katharine took little part in the betrothal festivities, for she was a mere shadow now. Her little daughter was made to show off her accomplishments to the Frenchmen, speaking to them in French and Latin, playing on the harpsichord, and dancing with the Viscount de Turenne, whilst the poor Queen looked sadly on. Stiff with gems and cloth of gold, the girl, appearing, we are told, "like an angel," gravely played her part to her proud father's delight, and the Bishop of Tarbes took back with him to his master enthusiastic praises of this "pearl of the world," the backward little girl of eleven, who was destined, as Francis said, to be the "cornerstone of the new covenant" between France and England, either by her marriage with himself, or, failing that, with his second son, the Duke of Orleans, which in every respect would have been a most suitable match.

No sooner had the treaty of betrothal been signed than there came (2nd June 1527) the tremendous news that the Emperor's troops under Bourbon had entered and sacked Rome with ruthless fury, and that Pope Clement was a prisoner in the castle of St. Angelo, clamouring for aid from all Christian princes against his impious assailants. All those kings who looked with distrust upon the rapidly growing power of Charles drew closer together. When the news came, Wolsey was in France on his embassy of surpassing magnificence, whilst public discontent in England at what was considered his warlike policy was already swelling into fierce denunciations against him, his pride, his greed, and his French proclivities. English people cared little for the troubles of the Italian Pope; or indeed for anything else, so long as they were allowed to live and trade in peace; and they knew full well that war with the Emperor would mean the closing of the rich Flemish and Spanish markets to them, as well as the seizure of their ships and goods. But to Wolsey's ambition the imprisonment of Clement VII. seemed to open a prospect of unlimited power. If Francis and Henry were closely allied, with the support of the Papacy behind them, Wolsey might be commissioned to exercise the Papal authority until he relieved the Pontiff from duress, and in due course might succeed to the chair of St. Peter. So, deaf to the murmuring of the English people, he pressed on; his goal being to bind France and England closely together that he might use them both.

The marriage treaty of Mary with the Duke of Orleans, instead of with his father, was agreed upon by Francis and the Cardinal at Amiens in August 1527. But Wolsey knew that the marriage of the children could not be completed for some years yet, and he was impatient to forge an immediately effective bond. Francis had a sister and a sister-in-law of full age, either of whom might marry Henry. But Katharine stood in the way, and she was the personification of the imperial connection. Wolsey had no scruples: he knew how earnestly his master wished for a son to inherit his realm, and how weak of will that master was if only he kept up the appearance of omnipotence. He knew that Katharine, disappointed, glum, and austere, had lost the charm by which women rule men, and the plan, that for many months he had been slowly and stealthily devising, was boldly brought out to light of day. Divorce was easy, and it would finally isolate the Emperor if Katharine were set aside. The Pope would do anything for his liberators: why not dissolve the unfruitful marriage, and give to England a new French consort in the person of either the widowed Margaret Duchess of Alençon, or of Princess Renée? It is true that the former indignantly refused the suggestion, and dynastic reasons prevented Francis from favouring that of a marriage of Renée of France and Brittany with the King of England; but women, and indeed men, were for Wolsey but puppets to be moved, not creatures to be consulted, and the Cardinal went back to England exultant, and hopeful that, at last, he would compass his aspiration, and make himself ruler of the princes of Christendom. Never was hope more fallacious or fortune's irony more bitter. With a strong master Wolsey would have won; with a flabby sensualist as his stalking-horse he was bound to lose, unless he remained always at his side. The Cardinal's absence in France was the turning-point of his fortunes; whilst he was glorying abroad, his enemies at home dealt him a death-blow through a woman.

At exactly what period, or by whom, the idea of divorcing Katharine at this time had been broached to Henry, it is difficult to say; but it was no unpardonable or uncommon thing for monarchs, for reasons of dynastic expediency, to put aside their wedded wives. Popes, usually in a hurry to enrich their families, could be bribed or coerced; and the interests of the individual, even of a queen-consort, were as nothing in comparison of those of the State, as represented by the sovereign. If the question of religious reform had not complicated the situation and Henry had married a Catholic princess of one of the great royal houses, as Wolsey intended, instead of a mere upstart like Anne Boleyn, there would probably have been little difficulty about the divorce from Katharine: and the first hint of the repudiation of a wife who could give the King no heir, for the sake of his marrying another princess who might do so, and at the same time consolidate a new international combination, would doubtless be considered by those who made it as quite an ordinary political move.

It is probable that the Bishop of Tarbes, when he was in England in the spring of 1527 for the betrothal of Mary, conferred with Wolsey as to the possibility of Henry's marriage to a French princess, which of course would involve the repudiation of Katharine. In any case the King and Wolsey— whether truly or not— asserted that the Bishop had first started the question of the validity of Henry's marriage with his wife, with special reference to the legitimacy of the Princess Mary, who was to be betrothed to Francis I. or his son. It may be accepted as certain, however, that the matter had been secretly fermenting ever since Wolsey began to shift the centre of gravity from the Emperor towards France. Katharine may have suspected it, though as yet no word reached her. But she was angry at the intimate hobnobbing with France, at her daughter's betrothal to the enemy of her house, and at the elevation of Henry's bastard son to a royal dukedom. She was deeply incensed, too, at her alienation from State affairs, and had formed around her a cabal of Wolsey's enemies, for the most part members of the older nobility traditionally in favour of the Spanish alliance and against France, in order, if possible, to obstruct the Cardinal's policy.

The King, no doubt fully aware of Wolsey's plan, was as usual willing to wound, but yet afraid to strike; not caring how much wrong he did if he could only gloze it over to appear right and save his own responsibility before the world. The first formal step, which was taken in April 1527, was carefully devised with this end. Henry, representing that his conscience was assailed by doubts, secretly consulted certain of his councillors as to the legality of his union with his deceased brother's widow. It is true that he had lived with her for eighteen years, and that any impediment to the marriage on the ground of affinity had been dispensed with to the satisfaction of all parties at the time by the Pope's bull. But trifles such as these could never stand in the way of so tender a conscience as that of Henry Tudor, or so overpowering an ambition as that of his minister. The councillors— most of those chosen were of course French partisans— thought the case was very doubtful, and were favourable to an inquiry.

On the 17th May 1527, Warham, Archbishop of Canterbury, who, it will be recollected, had always been against the marriage; with Wolsey, Stephen Gardiner, and certain doctors-of-law, held a private sitting at the York House, Westminster, at which the King had been cited to appear and answer the charge of having lived in incest with his sister-in-law. The Court was adjourned twice, to the 20th and 31st May, during which time the sham pleadings for and against the King were carefully directed to the desired end. But before the first sitting was well over the plot got wind and reached Katharine. The Queen and the imperial connection were popular, Wolsey and the French were feared and detested. The old nobility and the populace were on the Queen's side; the mere rumour of what was intended by the prelates at York House set people growling ominously, and the friends of the Spanish-Flemish alliance became threateningly active. The King and Wolsey saw that for a decree of nullity to be pronounced by Warham and Wolsey alone, after a secret inquiry at which the Queen was not represented, would be too scandalous and dangerous in the state of public feeling, and an attempt was made to get the bishops generally to decide, in answer to a leading question, that such a marriage as that of the King and Katharine was incestuous. But the bishops were faithful sons of the Papacy, and most of them shied at the idea of ignoring the Pope's bull allowing the marriage. Henry had also learnt during the proceedings of the sacking of Rome and the imprisonment of Clement, which was another obstacle to his desires, for though the Pope would doubtless have been quite ready to oblige his English and French friends to the detriment of the Emperor when he was free, it was out of the question that he should do so now that he and his dominions were at the mercy of the imperial troops.

The King seems to have had an idea that he might by his personal persuasion bring his unaccommodating wife to a more reasonable frame of mind. He and Wolsey had been intensely annoyed that she had learnt so promptly of the plot against her, but since some spy had told her, it was as well, thought Henry, that she should see things in their proper light. With a sanctimonious face he saw her on the 22nd June 1527, and told her how deeply his conscience was touched at the idea that they had been living in mortal sin for so many years. In future, he said, he must abstain from her company, and requested that she would remove far away from Court. She was a haughty princess— no angel in temper, notwithstanding her devout piety; and she gave Henry the vigorous answer that might have been expected. They were man and wife, as they had always been, she said, with the full sanction of the Church and the world, and she would stay where she was, strong in her rights as an honest woman and a queen. It was not Henry's way to face a strong opponent, unless he had some one else to support him and bear the brunt of the fight, and, in accordance with his character, he whined that he never meant any harm: he only wished to discover the truth, to set at rest the scruples raised by the Bishop of Tarbes. All would be for the best, he assured his angry wife; but pray keep the matter secret.

Henry did not love to be thwarted, and Wolsey, busy making ready for his ostentatious voyage to France, had to bear as best he might his master's ill-humour. The famous ecclesiastical lawyer, Sampson, had told the Cardinal that the marriage with Arthur had never been consummated; and consequently that, even apart from the Pope's dispensation, the present union was unimpeachable. The Queen would fight the matter to the end, he said; and though Wolsey did his best to answer Sampson's arguments, he was obliged to transmit them to the King, and recommend him to handle his wife gently; "until it was shown what the Pope and Francis would do." Henry acted on the advice, as we have seen, but Wolsey was scolded by the King as if he himself had advanced Sampson's arguments instead of answering them. Katharine did not content herself with sitting down and weeping. She despatched her faithful Spanish chamberlain, Francisco Felipe, on a pretended voyage to a sick mother in Spain, in order that he might beg the aid of the Emperor to prevent the injustice intended against the Queen; and Wolsey's spies made every effort to catch the man, and lay him by the heels. She sent to her confessor, Fisher, Bishop of Rochester, begging for his counsel, he being one of the bishops who held that her marriage was valid; she "desired," said Wolsey to the King, "counsel, as well of strangers as of English," and generally showed a spirit the very opposite of that of the patient Griselda in similar circumstances. How entirely upset were the King and Wolsey by the unexpected force of the opposition is seen in the Cardinal's letter to his master a day or two after he had left London at the beginning of July to proceed on his French embassy. Writing from Faversham, he relates how he had met Archbishop Warham, and had told him in dismay that the Queen had discovered their plan, and how irritated she was; and how the King, as arranged with Wolsey, had tried to pacify and reassure her. To Wolsey's delight, Warham persisted that, whether the Queen liked it or not, "truth and law must prevail." On his way through Rochester, Wolsey tackled Fisher, who was known to favour the Queen. He admitted under Wolsey's pressure that she had sent to him, though he pretended not to know why, and "greatly blamed the Queen, and thought that if he might speak to her he might bring her to submission." But Wolsey considered this would be dangerous, and bade the bishop stay where he was. And so, with the iniquitous plot temporarily shelved by the unforeseen opposition, personal and political, Wolsey and his great train, more splendid than that of any king, went on his way to Dover, and to Amiens, whilst in his absence that happened in England which in due time brought all his dignity and pride to dust and ashes.

CHAPTER IV

1527~1530

KATHARINE AND ANNE—THE DIVORCE

Enough has been said in the aforegoing pages to show that Henry was no more a model of marital fidelity than other contemporary monarchs. It was not to be expected that he should be. The marriages of such men were usually prompted by political reasons alone; and for the indulgence of affairs of the heart kings were forced to look elsewhere than towards the princesses they had taken in fulfilment of treaties. Mary, the younger daughter of Sir Thomas Boleyn and wife of William Carey, was the King's mistress for some years after her marriage in 1521, with the result that her father had received many rich grants from the crown; and in 1525 was created Lord Rochford. As treasurer of the household Lord Rochford was much at Court, and his relationship with the Howards, St. Legers, and other great families through his marriage with Lady Elizabeth, daughter of the Duke of Norfolk, naturally allied him with the party of nobles whose traditions ran counter to those of the bureaucrats in Henry's Council. His elder daughter Anne, who was born early in 1503, probably at Hever Castle in Kent, had been carefully educated in the learning and accomplishments considered necessary for a lady of birth at Court, and she accompanied Mary Tudor to France in 1514 for her fleeting marriage with the valetudinarian Louis XII., related in an earlier chapter. On Queen Mary's return to England a few months afterwards with her second husband, Charles Brandon, the youthful Anne Boleyn remained to complete her courtly education in France, under the care of the new Queen of France, Claude, first wife of Francis I.

When the alliance of the Emperor and England was negotiated in 1521, and war with France threatened, Anne was recalled home; and in 1522 began her life in the English Court and with her family in their various residences. Her six years in the gay Court of Francis I. during her most impressionable age, had made her in manner more French than English. She can never have been beautiful. Her face was long and thin, her chin pointed, and her mouth hypocritically prim; but her eyes were dark and very fine, her brows arched and high, and her complexion dazzling. Above all, she was supremely vain and fond of admiration. Similar qualities to these might have been, and doubtless were, possessed by a dozen other high-born ladies at Henry's Court; but circumstances, partly political and partly personal, gave to them in Anne's case a national importance that produced enduring consequences upon the world. We have already glanced at the mixture of tedious masquerading, hunting, and amorous intrigue which formed the principal occupations of the ladies and gentlemen who surrounded Henry and Katharine in their daily life; and from her arrival in England, Anne appears to have entered to the full into the enjoyment of such pastimes. There was some negotiation for her marriage, even before she arrived in England, with Sir Piers Butler, an Irish cousin of hers, but it fell through on the question of settlements, and in 1526, when she was already about twenty-three, she took matters in her own hands, and captivated an extremely eligible suitor, in the person of a silly, flighty young noble, Henry Percy, eldest son and heir to the Earl of Northumberland.

Percy was one of the Court butterflies who attached themselves to Wolsey's household, and when angrily taken to task by the Cardinal for flirting with Anne, notwithstanding his previous formal betrothal to another lady, the daughter of the Earl of Shrewsbury, the young man said that, as he loved Anne best, he would rather marry her. The Cardinal did not mince words with his follower, but Percy stood stoutly to his choice, and the Earl of Northumberland was hastily summoned to London to exercise his authority over his recalcitrant son. Cavendish gives an amusing account of the interview between them, at which he was present. The Earl seems to have screwed up his courage by a generous draught of wine when he left Wolsey's presence to await his son in the hall of York House. When the youth did come in, the scolding he got was vituperative in its violence, with the result that Percy was reluctantly forced to abandon the sweetheart to whom he had plighted his troth. Wolsey's interference in their love affair deeply angered both Anne and her sweetheart. Percy was a poor creature, and could do Wolsey little harm; but Anne did not forget, swearing "that if ever it lay in her power she would do the Cardinal some displeasure, which indeed she afterwards did."

The reason for Wolsey's strong opposition to a match which appeared a perfectly fitting one for both the lovers, is not far to seek. Cavendish himself gives us the clue when he says that when the King first heard that Anne had become engaged to Percy, "he was much moved thereat, for he had a private affection for her himself which was not yet discovered to any": and the faithful usher in telling the story excuses Wolsey by saying that "he did nothing but what the King commanded." This affair marks the beginning of Henry's infatuation for Anne. There was no reason for Wolsey to object to a flirtation between the girl and her royal admirer; indeed the devotion of the King to a new mistress would doubtless make him the more ready to consent to contract another entirely political marriage, if he could get rid of Katharine; and the Cardinal smiled complaisantly at the prospect that all was going well for his plans. Anne, for the look of the thing, was sent away from Court for a short time after the Percy affair had been broken off; but before many weeks were over she was back again as one of Katharine's maids of honour, and the King's admiration for her was evident to all observers.

It is more than questionable whether up to this time (1526) Anne ever dreamed of becoming Henry's wife; but in any case she was too clever to let herself go cheaply. She knew well the difference in the positions held by the King's mistresses in the French Court and that which had been occupied by her sister and Lady Tailebois in England, and she coyly held her royal lover at arm's length, with the idea of enhancing her value at last. Henry, as we have seen, was utterly tired of, and estranged from, Katharine; and his new flame, with her natural ability and acquired French arts, flattered and pleased his vanity better than any woman had done before. It is quite probable that she began to aim secretly at the higher prize in the spring of 1527, when the idea of the divorce from Katharine had taken shape in the King's mind under the sedulous prompting of Wolsey for his personal and political ends; but if such was the case she was careful not to show her hand prematurely. Her only hope of winning such a game was to keep imperious Henry in a fever of love, whilst declining all his illicit advances. It was a difficult and a dangerous thing to do, for her quarry might break away at any moment, whereas if such a word as marriage between the King and her reached the ears of the cardinal, she and her family would inevitably be destroyed.

Such was the condition of affairs when Wolsey started for France in July 1527. He went, determined to leave no stone unturned to set Henry free from Katharine. He knew that there was no time to be lost, for the letters from Mendoza, the Spanish ambassador in London, and Katharine's messenger Felipe, were on their way to tell the story to the Emperor in Spain; and Clement VII., a prisoner in the hands of the imperialists, would not dare to dissolve the marriage after Charles had had time to command him not to do so. It was a stiff race who should get to the Pope first. Wolsey's alternative plan in the circumstances was a clever one. It was to send to Rome the Bishop of Worcester (the Italian Ghinucci), Henry's ambassador in Spain, then on his way home, to obtain, with the support of the cardinals of French sympathies, a "general faculty" from Clement VII. for Wolsey to exercise all the Papal functions during the Pope's captivity: "by which, without informing the Pope of your (*i.e.* Henry's) purpose, I may delegate such judges as the Queen will not refuse; and if she does the cognisance of the cause shall be devolved upon me, and by a clause to be inserted in the general commission no appeal be allowed from my decision to the Pope."

How unscrupulous Wolsey and Henry were in the matter is seen in a letter dated shortly before the above was written, in which Wolsey says to Ghinucci (Bishop of Worcester) and Dr. Lee, Henry's ambassador with the Emperor, that "a rumour has, somehow or other, sprung up in England that proceedings are being taken for a divorce between the King and the Queen, which is entirely without foundation, yet not altogether causeless, for there has been some discussion about the Papal dispensation; not with any view to a divorce, but to satisfy the French, who raised the objection on proposing a marriage between the Princess (Mary Tudor) and their sovereign. The proceedings which took place on this dispute gave rise to the rumour, and reached the ears of the Queen, who expressed some resentment but was satisfied after explanation; and no suspicion exists, except, perchance, the Queen may have communicated with the Emperor." Charles had, indeed, heard the whole story, as far as Katharine knew it, from the lips of Felipe before this was written, and was not to be put off with such smooth lies. He wrote indignantly to his ambassador Mendoza in London, directing him to see Henry and point out to him, in diplomatic language veiling many a threat, the danger, as well as the turpitude, of repudiating his lawful wife with no valid excuse; and more vigorously still he let the Pope know that there must be no underhand work to his detriment or that of his family. Whilst the arrogant Cardinal of York was thus playing for his own hand first, and for Henry secondly, in France, his jealous enemies in England might put their heads together and plot against him undeterred by the paralysing fear of his frown. His pride and insolence, as well as his French political leanings, had caused the populace to hate him; the commercial classes, who suffered most by the wars with their best customers, the Flemings and Spaniards, were strongly opposed to him; whilst the territorial and noble party, which had usually been friendly with Katharine, and were traditionally against bureaucratic or ecclesiastical ministers of the crown, suffered with impatience the galling yoke of the Ipswich butcher's son, who drove them as he listed.

Anne was in the circumstances a more powerful ally for them than Katharine. She was the niece of the Duke of Norfolk, the leader of the party of nobles, and her ambition would make her an apt and eager instrument. The infatuation of the King for her grew more violent as she repelled his advances, and, doubtless at the prompting of Wolsey's foes, it soon began to be whispered that if Henry could get rid of his wife he might marry his English favourite. Before the Cardinal had been in France a month, Mendoza, the Spanish ambassador, first sounded the new note of alarm to the Emperor, by telling him that Anne might become the King's wife. It is hardly possible that no hint of the danger can have reached Wolsey, but if it did he was confident of his power over his master when he should return to England. Unfortunately for him his ideas for the King's divorce were hampered by the plans for his own advancement; and the proposals he wrote to Henry were all founded on the idea of exerting international pressure, either for the liberation of the Pope, or to obtain from the Pontiff the decree of divorce. It was evident that this process must be a slow one, and Anne as well as Henry was in a hurry. Unlike Charles, who, though he was falsity itself to his rivals, never deceived his own ministers, Henry constantly showed the moral cowardice of his character by misleading those who were supposed to direct his policy, and at this juncture he conceived a plan of his own which promised more rapidity than that of Wolsey. Without informing Wolsey of the real object of his mission, old Dr. Knight, the King's confidential secretary, was sent to endeavour to see the Pope in St. Angelo, and by personal appeal from the King persuade him to grant a dispensation for Henry's marriage either before his marriage with Katharine was dissolved formally (*constante matrimonio*), or else, if that was refused, a dispensation to marry after the declaration had been made nullifying the previous union (*soluto matrimonio*); but in either case the strange demand was to be made that the dispensation was to cover the case of the bride and bridegroom being connected within the prohibited degrees of affinity.

Knight saw Wolsey on his way through France and hoodwinked him as to his true mission by means of a bogus set of instructions, though the Cardinal was evidently suspicious and ill at ease. This was on the 12th September 1527, and less than a fortnight later Wolsey hurried homeward. When he had set forth from England three months before he seemed to hold the King in the hollow of his hand. Private audience for him was always ready, and all doors flew open at his bidding. But when he appeared on the 30th September at the palace of Richmond, and sent one of his gentlemen to inquire of the King where he would receive him, Anne sat in the great hall by Henry's side, as was usual now. Before the King could answer the question of Wolsey's messenger, the favourite, with a petulance that Katharine would have considered undignified, snapped, "Where else should the Cardinal come but where the King is?" For the King to receive his ministers at private audience in a hall full of people was quite opposed to the usual etiquette of Henry's Court, and Wolsey's man still stood awaiting the King's reply. But it only came in the form of a nod that confirmed the favourite's decision. This must have struck the proud Cardinal to the heart, and when he entered the hall and bowed before his sovereign, who was toying now with his lady-love, and joking with his favourites, the minister must have known that his empire over Henry had for the time vanished. He was clever and crafty: he had often conquered difficulties before, and was not dismayed now that a young woman had supplanted him, for he still held confidence in himself. So he made no sign of annoyance, but he promptly tried to checkmate Knight's mission when he heard of it, whilst pretending approval of the King's attachment to Anne. The latter was deceived. She could not help seeing that with Wolsey's help she would attain her object infinitely more easily than without it, and she in her turn smiled upon the Cardinal, though her final success would have boded ill for him, as he well knew.

His plan, doubtless, was to let the divorce question drag on as long as possible, in the hope that Henry would tire of his new flame. First he persuaded the King to send fresh instructions to Knight, on the ground that the Pope would certainly not give him a dispensation to commit bigamy in order that he might marry Anne, and that it would be easier to obtain from the Pontiff a decree leaving the validity of the marriage with Katharine to the decision of the Legates in England, Wolsey and another Cardinal. Henry having once loosened the bridle, did not entirely return to his submission to Wolsey. Like most weak men, he found it easier to rebel against the absent than against those who faced him; but he was not, if he and Anne could prevent it, again going to put his neck under the Cardinal's yoke completely, and in a secret letter to Knight he ordered him to ask Clement for a dispensation couched in the curious terms already referred to, allowing him to marry again, even within the degrees of affinity, as soon as the union with Katharine was dissolved. Knight had found it impossible to get near the Pope in Rome, for the imperialists had been fully forewarned by this time; but at length Clement was partially released and went to Orvieto in December, whither Knight followed him before the new instructions came from England. Knight was no match for the subtle churchmen. Clement dared not, moreover, mortally offend the Emperor, whose men-at-arms still held Rome; and the dispensation that Knight sent so triumphantly to England giving the Legate's Court in London power to decide the validity of the King's marriage, had a clause slipped into it which destroyed its efficacy, because it left the final decision to the Pontiff after all.

It may be asked, if Henry believed, as he now pretended, that his first marriage had never been legal in consequence of Katharine being his brother's widow, why he needed a Papal dispensation to break it. The Papal brief that had been previously given allowing the marriage, was asserted by Henry's ecclesiastical friends to be *ultra vires* in England, because marriage with a brother's widow was prohibited under the common law of the land, with which the Pope could not dispense. But the matter was complicated with all manner of side issues: the legitimacy of the Princess Mary, the susceptibilities of the powerful confederation that obeyed the Emperor, the sentiment of the English people, and, above all, the invariable desire of Henry to appear a saint whilst he acted like a sinner and to avoid personal responsibility; and so Henry still strove with the ostensible, but none too hearty, aid of Wolsey, to gain from the Pope the nullification of a marriage which he said was no marriage at all. Wolsey's position had become a most delicate and dangerous one. As soon as the Emperor learned of Anne's rise, he had written to Mendoza (30th September 1527), saying that the Cardinal must be bought at any price. All his arrears of pension (45,000 ducats) were to be paid, 6000 ducats a year more from a Spanish bishopric were to be granted, and a Milanese marquisate was to be conferred upon him with a revenue of 15,000 ducats a year, if he would only serve the Emperor's interests. But he dared not do it quickly or openly, dearly as he loved money, for Anne was watchful and Henry suspicious of him. His only hope was that the King's infatuation for this long-faced woman with the prude's mouth and the blazing eyes might pall. Then his chance would come again.

Far from growing weaker, however, Henry's passion grew as Anne's virtue became more rigid. She had not always been so austere, for gossip had already been busy with her good name. Percy and Sir Thomas Wyatt had both been her lovers, and with either or both of them she had in some way compromised herself. But she played her game cleverly, for the stake was a big one, and her fascination must have been great. She was often away from Court, feigning to prefer the rural delights of Hever to the splendours of Greenwich or Richmond, or offended at the significant tittle-tattle about herself and the King. She was thus absent when in July 1527 Wolsey had gone to France, but took care to keep herself in Henry's memory by sending him a splendid jewel of gold and diamonds representing a damsel in a boat on a troubled sea. The lovesick King replied in the first of those extraordinary love-letters of his which have so often been printed. "Henceforward," he says, "my heart shall be devoted to you only. I wish my body also could be. God can do it if He pleases, to whom I pray once a day that it may be, and hope at length to be heard:" and he signs *Escripte de la main du secretaire, que en cœur, corps, et volonté, est vostre loiall et plus assuré serviteure, H. (autre cœur ne cherche) R.* Soon afterwards, when Wolsey was well on his way, the King writes to his lady-love again. "The time seems so long since I heard of your good health and of you that I send the bearer to be better ascertained of your health and your purpose: for since my last parting from you I have been told you have quite abandoned the intention of coming to Court, either with your mother or otherwise. If so I cannot wonder sufficiently; for I have committed no offence against you, and it is very little return for the great love I bear you to deny me the presence of the woman I esteem most of all the world. If you love me, as I hope you do, our separation should be painful to you. I trust your absence is not wilful; for if so I can but lament my ill fortune and by degrees abate my great folly." This was the tone to bring Anne to her lover again, and before many days were over they were together, and in Wolsey's absence the marriage rumours spread apace.

The fiasco of Knight's mission had convinced Henry and Anne that they must proceed through the ordinary diplomatic channels and with the aid of Wolsey in their future approaches to the Pope; and early in 1528 Stephen Gardiner and Edward Fox, two ecclesiastics attached to the Cardinal, were despatched on a fresh mission to Orvieto to urge Clement to grant to Wolsey and another Legate power to pronounce finally on the validity of Henry's marriage. The Pope was to be plied with sanctimonious assurances that no carnal love for Anne prompted Henry's desire to marry her, as the Pope had been informed, but solely her "approved excellent, virtuous qualities— the purity of her life, her constant virginity, her maidenly and womanly pudicity, her soberness, her chasteness, meekness, humility, wisdom, descent right noble and high through royal blood, education in all good and laudable qualities and manners, apparent aptness to procreation of children, with her other infinite good qualities." Gardiner and Fox on their way to Dover called at Hever, and showed to Anne this panegyric penned by Wolsey upon her, and thenceforward for a time all went trippingly.

Gardiner was a far different negotiator from Knight, and was able, though with infinite difficulty, to induce Clement to grant the new bull demanded, relegating the cause finally to the Legatine Court in London. The Pope would have preferred that Wolsey should have sat alone as Legate, but Wolsey was so unpopular in England, and the war into which he had again dragged the country against the Emperor was so detested, whilst Queen Katharine had so many sympathisers, that it was considered necessary that a foreign Legate should add his authority to that of Wolsey to do the evil deed. Campeggio, who had been in England before, and was a pensioner of Henry as Bishop of Hereford, was the Cardinal selected by Wolsey; and at last Clement consented to send him. Every one concerned appears to have endeavoured to avoid responsibility for what they knew was a shabby business. The Pope, crafty and shifty, was in a most difficult position, and blew hot and cold. The first commission given to Gardiner and Fox, which was received with such delight by Anne and Henry when Fox brought it to London in April 1528, was found on examination still to leave the question open to Papal veto. It is true that it gave permission to the Legates to pronounce for the King, but the responsibility for the ruling was left to them, and their decision might be impugned. When, at the urgent demand of Gardiner, the Pope with many tears gave a decretal laying down that the King's marriage with Katharine was bad by canon law if the facts were as represented, he gave secret orders to the Legate Campeggio that the decretal was to be burnt and not to be acted upon.

Whilst the Pope was thus between the devil and the deep sea, trying to please the Emperor on the one hand and the Kings of France and England on the other, and deceiving both, the influence of Anne over her royal lover grew stronger every day. Wolsey was in the toils and he knew it. When Charles had answered the English declaration of war (January 1528), it was the Cardinal's rapacity, pride, and ambition against which he thundered as the cause of the strife and of the insult offered to the imperial house. To the Emperor the Cardinal could not again turn. Henry, moreover, was no longer the obedient tool he had been before Anne was by his side to stiffen his courage; and Wolsey knew that, notwithstanding the favourite's feline civilities and feigned dependence upon him, it would be the turn of his enemies to rule when once she became the King's wedded wife. He was, indeed, hoist with his own petard. The divorce had been mainly promoted, if not originated, by him, and the divorce in the present circumstances would crush him. But he had pledged himself too deeply to draw back openly; and he still had to smile upon those who were planning his ruin, and himself urge forward the policy by which it was to be effected.

In the meanwhile Katharine stood firm, living under the same roof as her husband, sitting at the same table with him with a serene countenance in public, and to all appearance unchanged in her relations to him. But though her pride stood her in good stead she was perplexed and lonely. Henry's intention to divorce her, and his infatuation for Anne, were of course public property, and the courtiers turned to the coming constellation, whatever the common people might do. Mendoza, the Spanish ambassador, withdrew from Court in the spring after the declaration of war, and the Queen's isolation was then complete. To the Spanish Latinist in Flanders, J. Luis Vives, and to Erasmus, she wrote asking for counsel in her perplexity, but decorous epistles in stilted Latin advising resignation and Christian fortitude was all she got from either. Her nephew the Emperor had urged her, in any case, to refuse to recognise the authority of any tribunal in England to judge her case, and had done what he could to frighten the Pope against acceding to Henry's wishes. But even he was not implacable, if his political ends were served in any arrangement that might be made; and at this time he evidently hoped, as did the Pope most fervently, that as a last resource Katharine would help everybody out of the trouble by giving up the struggle and taking the veil. Her personal desire would doubtless have been to adopt this course, for the world had lost its savour, but she was a daughter of Isabel the Catholic, and tame surrender was not in her line. Her married life with Henry she knew was at an end; but her daughter was now growing into girlhood, and her legitimacy and heirship to the English crown she would only surrender with her own life. So to all smooth suggestions that she should make things pleasant all round by acquiescing in the King's view of their marriage, she was scornfully irresponsive.

Through the plague-scourged summer of 1528 Henry and Anne waited impatiently for the coming of the Legate Campeggio. He was old and gouty, hampered with a mission which he dreaded; for he could not hope to reconcile the irreconcilable, and the Pope had quietly given him the hint that he need not hurry. Clement was, indeed, in a greater fix than ever. He had been made to promise by the Emperor that the case should not be decided in England, and yet he had been forced into giving the dispensation and decretal not only allowing it to be decided there in favour of Henry, but had despatched Campeggio to pronounce judgment. He had, however, at the same time assured the Emperor that means should be found to prevent the finality of any decision in England until the Emperor had approved of it, and Campeggio was instructed accordingly. The Spaniards thought that the English Cardinal would do his best to second the efforts of the Pope without appearing to do so, and there is no doubt that they were right, for Wolsey was now (the summer of 1528) really alarmed at the engine he had set in motion and could not stop. Katharine knew that the Legate was on his way, and that the Pope had, in appearance, granted all of Henry's demands; but she did not know, or could not understand, the political forces that were operating in her favour, which made the Pope defraud the King of England, and turned her erstwhile mortal enemy Wolsey into her secret friend. Tact and ready adaptability might still have helped Katharine. The party of nobles under Norfolk, it is true, had deserted her; but Wolsey and the bureaucrats were still a power to be reckoned with, and the middle classes and the populace were all in favour of the Queen and the imperial alliance. If these elements had been cleverly combined they might have conquered, for Henry was always a coward and would have bent to the stronger force. But Katharine was a bad hand at changing sides, and Wolsey dared not openly do so.

For a few days in the summer of 1528, whilst Campeggio was still lingering on the Continent, it looked as if a mightier power than any of them might settle the question for once and all. Henry and Anne were at Greenwich when the plague broke out in London. In June one of Anne's attendants fell ill of the malady, and Henry in a panic sent his favourite to Hever, whilst he hurried from place to place in Hertfordshire. The plague followed him. Sir Francis Poyns, Sir William Compton, William Carey, and other members of his Court died in the course of the epidemic, and the dread news soon reached Henry that Anne and her father were both stricken at Hever Castle. Henry had written daily to her whilst they had been separated. "Since your last letter, mine own darling," he wrote a few days after she left, "Walter Welsh, Master Brown, Thomas Care, Grion of Brereton, and John Coke the apothecary have fallen of the sweat in this house.... By the mercy of God the rest of us be yet well, and I trust shall pass it, either not to have it, or at least as easily as the rest have done." Later he wrote: "The uneasiness my doubts about your health gave me, disturbed and alarmed me exceedingly; and I should not have had any quiet without hearing certain tidings. But now, since you have felt as yet nothing, I hope, and am assured, that it will spare you, as I hope it is doing with us. For when we were at Waltham two ushers, two valets, and your brother, master-treasurer, fell ill, but are now quite well; and since we have returned to our house at Hunsdon we have been perfectly well, and have not now one sick person, God be praised. I think if you would retire from Surrey, as we did, you would escape all danger. There is another thing may comfort you, which is, in truth, that in this distemper few or no women have been taken ill, and no person of our Court has died. For which reason I beg you, my entirely beloved, not to frighten yourself, nor be too uneasy at our absence, for wherever I am, I am yours: and yet we must sometimes submit to our misfortunes; for whoever will struggle against fate is generally but so much the further from gaining his end. Wherefore, comfort yourself and take courage, and avoid the pestilence as much as you can; for I hope shortly to make you sing *la renvoyé*. No more at present from lack of time, but that I wish you in my arms that I might a little dispel your unreasonable thoughts. Written by the hand of him who is, and always will be, yours."

When the news of Anne's illness reached him he despatched one of his physicians post haste with the following letter to his favourite: "There came to me suddenly in the night the most afflicting news that could have arrived. The first, to hear the sickness of my mistress, whom I esteem more than all the world, and whose health I desire as I do my own, so that I would gladly bear half your illness to make you well; the second, the fear that I have of being still longer harassed by my enemy— your absence— much longer ... who is, so far as I can judge, determined to spite me more, because I pray God to rid me of this troublesome tormentor; the third, because the physician in whom I have most confidence is absent at the very time when he might be of the most service to me, for I should hope by his means to obtain one of my chiefest joys on earth— that is, the care of my mistress. Yet, for want of him, I send you my second, and hope that he will soon make you well. I shall then love him more than ever. I beseech you to be guided by his advice, and I hope soon to see you again, which will be to me a greater comfort than all the precious jewels in the world." In a few days Anne was out of danger, and the hopes and fears aroused by her illness gave place to the old intrigues again.

A few weeks later Anne was with her lover at Ampthill, hoping and praying daily for the coming of the gouty Legate, who was slowly being carried through France to the coast. Wolsey had to be very humble now, for Anne had shown her ability to make Henry brave him, and the King rebuked him publicly at her bidding, but until Campeggio came and the fateful decision was given that would make Anne a

Queen, both she and Henry diplomatically alternated cajolery with the humbling process towards the Cardinal. Anne's well-known letter with Henry's postscript, so earnestly asking Wolsey for news of Campeggio, is written in most affectionate terms, Anne saying, amongst other pretty things, that she "loves him next unto the King's grace, above all creatures living." But the object of her wheedling was only to gain news of the speedy coming of the Legate. The King's postscript to this letter is characteristic of him. "The writer of this letter would not cease till she had caused me likewise to set my hand, desiring you, though it be short, to take it in good part. I assure you that there is neither of us but greatly desireth to see you, and are joyous to hear that you have escaped the plague so well; trusting the fury thereof to be passed, especially with them that keepeth good diet, as I trust you do. The not hearing of the Legate's arrival in France causeth us somewhat to muse: notwithstanding, we trust, by your diligence and vigilance, with the assistance of Almighty God, shortly to be eased out of that trouble."

Campeggio was nearly four months on his way, urged forward everywhere by English agents and letters, held back everywhere by the Pope's fears and his own ailments; but at last, one joyful day in the middle of September, Henry could write to his lady-love at Hever: "The Legate which we most desire arrived at Paris on Sunday last past, so that I trust next Monday to hear of his arrival at Calais: and then I trust within a while after to enjoy that which I have so long longed for, to God's pleasure and both our comfort. No more to you at present, mine own darling, for lack of time, but that I would you were in mine arms, or I in yours, for I think it long since I kissed you." Henry had to wait longer than in his lover-like eagerness he had expected; it was fully a fortnight before he had news of Campeggio's arrival at Dover. Great preparations had been made to entertain the Papal Legate splendidly in London, and on his way thither; but he was suffering and sorry, and begged to be saved the fatigue of a public reception. So ill was he that, rather than face the streets of London on the day he was expected, he lodged for the night at the Duke of Suffolk's house on the Surrey side of London bridge, and the next day, 8th October, was quietly carried in the Duke's barge across the river to the Bishop of Bath's palace beyond Temple Bar, where he was to lodge. There he remained ill in bed, until the King's impatience would brook no further delay; and on the 12th he was carried, sick as he was, and sorely against his will, in a crimson velvet chair for his first audience.

In the great hall of the palace of Bridewell, hard by Blackfriars, Henry sat in a chair of state, with Wolsey and Campeggio on his right hand, whilst one of the Legate's train delivered a fulsome Latin oration, setting forth the iniquitous outrages perpetrated by the imperialists upon the Vicar of Christ, and the love and gratitude of the Pontiff for his dearest son Henry for his aid and sympathy. The one thing apparently that the Pope desired was to please his benefactor, the King of England. When the public ceremony was over, Henry took Campeggio and Wolsey into a private room; and the day following the King came secretly to Campeggio's lodging, and for four long hours plied the suffering churchman with arguments and authorities which would justify the divorce. Up to this time Campeggio had fondly imagined that he might, with the Papal authority, persuade Henry to abandon his object. But this interview undeceived him. He found the King, as he says, better versed in the matter "than a great theologian or jurist"; and Campeggio opined at last that "if an angel descended from heaven he would be unable to persuade him" that the marriage was valid. When, however, Campeggio suggested that the Queen might be induced to enter a convent, Henry was delighted. If they would only prevail upon her to do that she should have everything she demanded: the title of Queen and all her dowry, revenue, and belongings; the Princess Mary should be acknowledged heiress to the crown, failing legitimate male issue to the King, and all should be done to Katharine's liking. Accordingly, the next day, 14th October, Campeggio and Wolsey took boat and went to try their luck with the Queen, after seeing the King for the third time. Beginning with a long sanctimonious rigmarole, Campeggio pressed her to take a "course which would give general satisfaction and greatly benefit herself"; and Wolsey, on his knees, and in English, seconded his colleague's advice. Katharine was cold and collected. She was, she said, a foreigner in England without skilled advice, and she declined at present to say anything. She had asked the King to assign councillors to aid her, and when she had consulted them she would see the Legates again.

As day broke across the Thames on the 25th October, Campeggio lay awake in bed at Bath House, suffering the tortures of gout, and perturbed at the difficult position in which he was placed, when Wolsey was announced, having come from York Place in his barge. When the Cardinal entered the room he told his Italian colleague that the King had appointed Archbishop Warham, Bishop Fisher, and others, to be councillors for the Queen, and that the Queen had obtained her husband's permission to come to Campeggio and confess that morning. At nine o'clock Katharine came unobserved to Bath House by water, and was closeted for long with the Italian Cardinal. What she told him was under the sacred seal of the confessional, but she prayed that the Pope might in strict secrecy be informed of certain of the particulars arising out of her statements. She reviewed the whole of her life from the day of her arrival in England, and solemnly swore on her conscience that she had only slept with young Arthur seven nights, *é che da lui restó intacta é incorrupta*; and this assertion, *as far as it goes*, we may accept as the truth, seeing the solemn circumstances under which it was made. But when Campeggio again urged Katharine to get them all out of their difficulty by retiring to a convent and letting the King have his way, she almost vehemently declared that "she would die as she had lived, a wife, as God had made her." "Let a sentence be given," she said, "and if it be against me I shall be free to do as I like, even as my husband will." "But neither the whole realm, nor, on the other hand, the greatest punishment, even being torn limb from limb, shall alter me in this, and if after death I were to return to life, I would die again, and yet again, rather than I would give way." Against such firmness as this the poor, flaccid old churchman could do nothing but hold up his hands and sigh at the idea of any one being so obstinate.

A day or two afterwards Wolsey and Campeggio saw the Queen again formally. She was on this occasion attended by her advisers, and once more heard, coldly and irresponsively, the appeals to her prudence, her worldly wisdom, her love for her daughter, and every other feeling that could lead her to cut the gordian knot that baffled them all. "She would do nothing to her soul's damnation or against God's law," she said, as she dismissed them. Whether it was at this interview, or, as it seems to me more likely, the previous one that she broke out in violent invective against Wolsey for his enmity towards the Emperor, we know not, but the storm of bitter words she poured upon him for his pride, his falsity, his ambition, and his greed; her taunts at his intrigues to get the Papacy, and her burning scorn that her marriage, unquestioned for twenty years, should be doubted now, must have finally convinced both Wolsey and Campeggio that if Henry was firm Katharine was firmer still. Campeggio was in a pitiable state of mind, imploring the Pope by every post to tell him what to do. He and Wolsey at one time conceived the horrible idea of marrying the Princess Mary to her half brother, the Duke of Richmond, as a solution of the succession difficulty, and the Pope appears to have been inclined to allow it; but it was soon admitted that the course proposed would not forward, but rather retard, the King's second marriage, and that was the main object sought.

At length Wolsey ruefully understood that conciliation was impossible; and, pressed as he was by the King, was forced to insist with Campeggio that the cause must be judicially decided without further delay. Illness, prayerful attempts to bring one side or the other to reason, and many other excuses for procrastination were tried, but at length Campeggio had to confess to his colleague that the Pope's decretal, laying down the law in the case in Henry's favour, was only a show document not to be used, or to leave his possession for a moment; and, moreover, that no final judgment could be given by him that was not submitted to the Pope's confirmation. Wolsey was aghast, and wrote in rage and indignation to the English agent with the Pope denouncing this bad faith. "I see ruin, infamy, and subversion of the whole dignity and estimation of the Apostolic See if this course be persisted in. You see in what dangerous times we are. If the Pope will consider the gravity of this cause, and how much the safety of the nation depends upon it, he will see that the course he now pursues will drive the King to adopt those remedies that are so injurious to the Pope, and are frequently instilled into the King's mind. Without the Pope's compliance I cannot bear up against the storm; and when I reflect upon the conduct of his Holiness I cannot but fear lest the common enemy of souls, seeing the King's determination, inspires the Pope with his present fears and reluctance, which will alienate all the faith and devotion from the Apostolic See.... It is useless for Campeggio to think of reviving the marriage. If he did it would lead to worse consequences. Let him therefore proceed to sentence. Prostrate at the feet of his Holiness I most urgently beg of him to set aside all delays."

This cry, wrung evidently from Wolsey's heart at the knowledge of his own danger, is the first articulate expression of the tremendous religious issue that might depend upon the conduct of the various parties in the divorce proceedings. The fire lit by Luther a few years previously had spread apace in Germany, and had reached England. All Christendom would soon have to range itself in two divisions, cutting athwart old national affinities and alliances. Charles had defied Luther at the outset; and the traditions of his Spanish house made him, the most powerful monarch in Europe, the champion of orthodoxy. But his relations with the Papacy, as we have seen, had not been uniformly cordial. To him the Pope was a little Italian prince whilst he was a great one, and he was jealous of the slightest interference of Rome with the Spanish Church. His position in Germany, moreover, as suzerain of the princes of the Empire, some of whom already leant to Lutheranism, complicated the situation: so that it was not yet absolutely certain that

Charles would finally stake everything upon the unification of the Christian Church by force, on the lines of strict Papal authority.

On the other hand, both Francis and Henry had for political reasons strongly supported the Pope in his greatest distress, and their religion was certainly no less faithful than that of the Emperor. It was inevitable that, whichever side Charles took in the coming religious struggle, would not for political reasons commend itself to Francis, and *vice versa*; and everything depended upon the weight which Henry might cast into one scale or the other. His national traditions and personal inclination would lead him to side with Charles, but at the crucial moment, when the first grain had to be dropped into the balance, he found himself bound by Wolsey's policy to Francis, and at issue with the Emperor, owing to the relationship of the latter to Katharine. Wolsey felt, in the letter quoted above, that the Pope's shilly-shally, in order not to offend the Emperor, would drive the impatient King of England to flout, and perhaps break with, the Papacy, and events proved that the Cardinal was right in his fears. We shall see later how the rift widened, but here the first fine crevice is visible.

Henry, prompted by Anne and his vanity, intended to have his way at whatever cost. Katharine could give him no son: he would marry a woman who could do so, and one that he loved far better than he ever loved his wife. In ordinary circumstances there need have been no great difficulty about the divorce, nor would there have been in this case, but for the peculiar political and religious situation of Europe at the time, and but for Katharine's unbending rigidity of character. She might have made her own terms if she had consented to the conciliatory suggestions of the churchmen. The legality of her marriage would have been declared, her daughter recognised as heiress presumptive, her own great revenues would have been left to her, and her title of Queen respected. She was not even to be asked to immure herself in a convent, or to take any conventual vow but that of chastity, if she would only consent to a divorce on the ground of her desire to devote herself to religion. As Campeggio repeated a dozen times, the only thing she would be asked to surrender was conjugal relations with the King, that had ceased for years, and in no case would be renewed. Much as we may admire her firmness, it is impossible to avoid seeing that the course recommended to her was that which would have best served, not only her own interest and happiness, but also those of her daughter, of her religion, and of the good relations between Henry and the Emperor that she had so much at heart.

Henry, on his side, was determined to allow nothing to stand in his way, whilst keeping up his appearance of impeccability. Legal and ecclesiastical authorities in England and France were besought to give their sanction to his view that no Pope had the power of dispensation for a marriage with a deceased brother's widow; and the English clergy were assured that the King only sought an impartial authoritative decision for the relief of his own conscience. The attitude of the English people gave him some uneasiness; for, like all his house, he loved popularity. "The common people, being ignorant," we are told, "and others that favoured the Queen, talked largely, and said that for his own pleasure the King would have another wife, and had sent for this Legate to be divorced from the Queen, with many foolish words; inasmuch as, whosoever spake against the marriage was of the common people abhorred and reproved." The feeling indeed in favour of Katharine was so outspoken and general that the King took the unusual course of assembling the nobles, judges, and so many of the people as could enter, in the great hall of Bridewell, on Sunday afternoon, the 8th November, to endeavour personally to justify himself in the eyes of his subjects.

As usual with him, his great aim was by sanctimonious protestations to make himself appear a pure-souled altruist, and to throw upon others the responsibility for his actions. He painted in dismal colours the dangers to his subjects of a disputed succession on his death. "And, although it hath pleased Almighty God to send us a fair daughter by a noble woman and me begotten, to our great joy and comfort, yet it hath been told us by divers great clerks that neither she is our lawful daughter, nor her mother our lawful wife, and that we live together abominably and detestably in open adultery." He swore, almost blasphemously, that for the relief of his conscience he only sought authoritatively to know the truth as to the validity of his marriage, and that Campeggio had come as an impartial judge to decide it. If Katharine was adjudged to be his wife nothing would be more pleasant or acceptable to him, and he praised her to the skies, as a noble lady against whom no words could be spoken. The measure of his sincerity is seen when we compare this hypocritical harangue with the letters now before us to and from his envoys in Rome, by which it is evident that the last thing he desired was an impartial judgment, or indeed any judgment, but one that would set him free to marry again. One of the most extraordinary means employed to influence Katharine soon after this appears to have been another visit to her of Wolsey and Campeggio. They were to say that the King had intelligence of a conspiracy against him and Wolsey by her friends and the Emperor's English partisans; and they warned her that if anything of the sort occurred she would be to blame. They were then to complain of her bearing towards the King, "who was now persuaded by her behaviour that she did not love him." "She encouraged ladies and gentlemen to dance and make merry," for instance, whereas "she had better tell them to pray for a good end of the matter at issue." "She shows no pensiveness of countenance, nor in her apparel nor behaviour. She shows herself too much to the people, rejoicing greatly in their exclamations and ill obloquy; and, by beckoning with her head and smiling, which she has not been accustomed to do in times past, rather encouraged them in doing so." For all this and many other things the King does not consider it fitting to be in her company, or to let the Princess be with her. The acme of hypocrisy was reached in the assurance the Legates were then to give the Queen, that if she would behave well and go into a convent, the King neither could, nor would, marry another wife in her lifetime; and she could come out to the world again if the sentence were in her favour. Let her go, they said, and submit to the King on her knees, and he would be good to her, but otherwise he would be more angry than ever. Scornful silence was the Queen's reply.

After this Katharine lived lonely and depressed at Greenwich, frequently closeted with Bishop Fisher and others of her councillors, whilst Henry was strengthening his case with the opinions of jurists, and by attempts to influence Campeggio. To Greenwich he went, accompanied by Anne and a brilliant Court, to show the Italian Cardinal how bounteously a Christmas could be spent in England. Campeggio's son was knighted and regaled with costly presents, and all that bribes (the Bishopric of Durham, &c.) and flattery might do was done to influence the Legate favourably; but throughout the gay doings, jousts and tourneys, banquets and maskings, "the Queen showed to them no manner of countenance, and made no great joy of nothing, her mind was so troubled." Well might it be, poor soul, for Anne was by the King's side, pert and insolent, surrounded by a growing party of Wolsey's enemies, who cared little for Pope or Emperor, and who waited impatiently for the time when Anne should rule the King alone, and they, through her, should rule England. Katharine, in good truth, was in everybody's way, for even her nephew could not afford to quarrel with England for her sake, and her death or disappearance would have made a reconciliation easy, especially if Wolsey, the friend of France, fell also.

"Anne," we are told by the French ambassador, "was lodged in a fine apartment close to that of the King, and greater court was now paid to her every day than has been paid to the Queen for a long time. I see that they mean to accustom the people by degrees to endure her, so that when the great blow comes it may not be, thought strange. But the people remain quite hardened (against her), and I think they would do more if they had more power."

Thus the months passed, the Pope being plied by alternate threats and hopes, both by English and Spanish agents, until he was nearly beside himself, Wolsey almost frantically professing his desire to forward the King's object, and Campeggio temporising and trying to find a means of conciliation which would leave the King free. Katharine herself remained immovable. She had asked for and obtained from the Emperor a copy of the Papal brief authorising her marriage with Henry, but the King's advocates questioned its authenticity, and even her own advisers urged her to obey her husband's request that she should demand of the Emperor the original document. Constrained by her sworn pledge to write nothing to the Emperor without the King's knowledge, she sent the letter dictated to her, urgently praying her nephew to send the original brief to England. The letter was carried to Spain by her young English confessor, Thomas Abel, whom she did not entirely trust, and sent with him her Spanish usher, Montoya; but they had verbal instructions from their mistress to pray the Emperor to disregard her written request, and refuse to part with the brief, and to exert all his influence to have the case decided in Rome. By this it will be seen that Katharine was fully a match in duplicity for those against whom she was pitted. She never wavered from first to last in her determination to refuse to acknowledge the sentence of any court sitting in England on her case, and to resist all attempts to induce her to withdraw voluntarily from her conjugal position and enter a nunnery. Henry, and especially Anne, in the meanwhile, were growing impatient at all this calculated delay, and began to throw the blame upon Wolsey. "The young lady used very rude words to him," wrote Du Bellay on the 25th January, and "the Duke of Norfolk and his party already began to talk big." A few days afterwards Mendoza, in a letter to the Emperor, spoke even more strongly. "The young lady that is the cause of all this disorder, finding her marriage delayed, that she thought herself so sure of, entertains great suspicion that Wolsey puts impediments in her way, from a belief that if she were Queen his power would decline. In this suspicion she is joined by her father and the Dukes of Norfolk and Suffolk, who have combined to overthrow the Cardinal."

"The King is so hot upon it (the divorce) that there is nothing he does not promise to gain his end.... Campeggio has done nothing for the Queen as yet but to press her to enter religion."

Henry at length determined that he would wait no longer. His four agents in Rome had almost driven the Pope to distraction with their importunities. Gardiner had gone to the length of threatening Clement with the secession of England from the Papacy, and Anne's cousin, Henry's boon companion Brian, deploring the Pope's obstinacy in a letter from Rome to the King, was bold enough to say: "I hope I shall not die until your Grace has been able to requite the Pope, and Popes, and not be fed with their flattering words." But in spite of it all, Clement would only palliate and temporise, and finally refused to give any fresh instructions to the Legates or help the King's cause by any new act. To Campeggio he wrote angrily, telling him, for God's sake, to procrastinate the matter in England somehow, and not throw upon his shoulders in Rome the responsibility of giving judgment; whilst Campeggio, though professing a desire to please Henry in everything— in the hope of getting the promised rich See of Durham, his enemies said— was equally determined not to go an inch beyond the Pope's written instructions, or to assume responsibility for the final decision. The churchmen indeed were shuffling and lying all round, for the position was threatening, with Lutheranism daily becoming bolder and the Emperor growing ever more peremptory, now that he had become reconciled to the Pope.

By the end of May Henry had had enough of dallying, especially as rumours came from Rome that the Pope might revoke the commission of the Legates; and the great hall of the Monastery of Blackfriars was made ready for the sittings of the Legatine Court. On a raised daïs were two chairs of state, covered with cloth of gold, and on the right side of the daïs a throne and canopy for the King, confronted by another for the Queen. The first sittings of the Legates were formal, and the King and Queen were summoned to appear before the tribunal on the 18th June 1529. Early in the morning of the day appointed the hall was full to overflowing with bishops, clerics, and councillors, and upon the crowd there fell the hush of those who consciously look upon a great drama of real life. After the Bishops of Bath and Lincoln had testified that citations to the King and Queen had been delivered, and other formal statements had been taken, an usher stood forth and cried: "Henry, King of England, appear." But Henry was at Greenwich, five miles away, and in his stead there answered the ecclesiastical lawyer, Dr. Sampson. Then "Katharine, Queen of England" rang out, and into the hall there swept the procession of the Queen, herself rustling in stiff black garments, with four bishops, amongst them Fisher of Rochester, and a great train of ladies. Standing before the throne erected for her, she made a low obeisance to the Legates; and then, in formal terms, protested against the competence of the tribunal to judge her case, consisting, as it did, of those dependent upon one of the parties, and unable to give an impartial judgment. She appealed from the Legates to the Sovereign Pontiff, who, without fear or favour of man, would decide according to divine and human law. Then with another low obeisance Katharine turned her back upon the Court, and returned to the adjoining palace of Bridewell.

On the following Monday, the 21st, the Court again sat to give judgment upon her protest, which Campeggio would have liked to accept and so to relieve him of his difficulty but for the pressure put upon him by Wolsey and the Court. To the call of his name Henry on this occasion answered in person from his throne, "Here," whilst the Queen contented herself by an inclination of the head. When the Legates had rejected her protest, the King rose, and in one of his sanctimonious speeches once more averred his admiration and affection for his wife, and swore that his fear of living sinfully was the sole cause of his having raised the question of the validity of his marriage. When his speech had ended Katharine rose. Between them the clerks and assessors sat at a large table, so that she had to make the whole circuit of the hall to approach the King. As she came to the foot of his throne she knelt before him for a last appeal to his better feelings. In broken English, and with tears coursing down her cheeks, she spoke of their long married life together, of the little daughter they both loved so well, of her obedience and devotion to him, and finally called him and God to witness that her marriage with his brother had been one in name only. Then, rising, she bowed low to the man who was still her husband, and swept from the room. When she reached the door, Henry, realising that all Christendom would cry out against him if she was judged in her absence, bade the usher summon her back, but she turned to the Welsh courtier, Griffin Richards, upon whose arm she leaned, saying: "Go on, it is no matter; this is no impartial Court to me," and thus, by an act of defiance, bade Henry do his worst. Like other things she did, it was brave, even heroic in the circumstances, but it was unwise from every point of view.

It would be profitless to follow step by step the further proceedings, which Campeggio and Wolsey, at least, must have known were hollow. The Court sat from week to week, and Henry grew more angry as each sitting ended fruitlessly, the main question at issue now being the consummation or non-consummation of the first marriage; until, at the end of July, Campeggio demanded a vacation till October, in accordance with the rule in Roman Courts. Whilst this new delay was being impatiently borne, the revocation of the powers of the Legates, so long desired by Campeggio, came from Rome, and Henry saw that the churchmen had cheated him after all. His rage knew no bounds; and the Cardinal's enemies, led by Anne and her kinsmen, cleverly served now by the new man Stephen Gardiner, fanned the flame against Wolsey. He might still, however, be of some use; and though in deadly fear he was not openly disgraced yet. One day the King sent for him to Bridewell during the recess, and was closeted with him for an hour. In his barge afterwards on his way home Wolsey sat perturbed and unhappy with the Bishop of Carlisle. "It is a very hot day," said the latter. "Yes," replied the unhappy man, "if you had been as well chafed as I have been in the last hour you would say it was hot." Wolsey in his distress went straight to bed when he arrived at York Place, but before he had lain two hours Anne's father came to his bedside to order him in the name of the King to accompany Campeggio to Bridewell, to make another attempt to move the Queen. He had to obey, and, calling at Bath House for Campeggio on his way, they sought audience of Katharine. They found her cool and serene— indeed she seems rather to have overplayed the part. She came to meet them with a skein of silk around her neck. "I am sorry to keep you waiting," she said; "I was working with my ladies." To Wolsey's request for a private audience she replied that he might speak before her people, she had no secrets with him; and when he began to speak in Latin she bade him use English. Throughout she was cool and stately, and, as may be supposed, the visit was as fruitless as others had been.

Wolsey was not quite done with even yet. He might still act as Legate alone, if the Pope's decretal deciding the law of the case in favour of Henry could be obtained from Campeggio, who had held it so tightly by the Pope's command. So when Campeggio was painfully carried into Northamptonshire in September to take leave of the King, Wolsey was ordered to accompany him. Henry thought it politic to receive them without open sign of displeasure, and sent the Italian Cardinal on his way with presents and smooth words. Wolsey escorted him a few miles on his road from Grafton, where the King was staying, to Towcester; but when next day the Cardinal returned to Grafton alone he found the King's door shut against him, and Norreys brought him an order that he was to return to London. It was a blow that struck at his heart, and he went sadly with the shadow of impending ruin upon him, never to set eyes on his master more. Before his final fall there was still one thing he might do, and he was given a few days' reprieve that he might do it. The Pope had pledged himself in writing not to withdraw the Legates' commission, and although he had done so the original commission might still be alleged as authority for Wolsey to act alone, if only the Papal decretal could be found. Campeggio's privileged character was consequently ignored, and all his baggage ransacked in the hope of finding the document before he left English soil. Alas! as an eye-witness tells us, all that the packs contained were "old hosen, old coates, and such vile stuff as no honest man would carry," for the decretal had been committed to the flames months before by the Pope's orders; and the outraged old Italian Legate, with his undignified belongings, crossed the Channel and so passes out of our history.

Anne had so far triumphed by the coalition of Wolsey's enemies. Her own hatred of him was more jealous and personal than political; for she and her paternal family were decidedly French in their sympathies, and Wolsey, at all events in the latest stages, had striven his utmost to help forward her marriage with the King. The older nobility, led by Norfolk, who had deserted Katharine their former ally, in order to use Anne for their rival's ruin, had deeper and longer-standing motives for their hate of the Cardinal. Although most of them now were heavily bribed and pensioned by France, their traditions were always towards the Imperial and Spanish alliance, and against bureaucratic ministers. There was yet another element that had joined Anne's party in order to overthrow Wolsey. It consisted of those who from patriotic sentiment resented the galling supremacy of a foreign prince over the English Church, and cast their eyes towards Germany, where the process of emancipation from the Papacy was in full swing. The party in England was not a large one, and hardly concerned itself yet with fine points of doctrine. It was more an expression of the new-born English pride and independence than the religious revolt it was to become later; and the fit mouthpiece of the feeling was bluff Charles Brandon, Duke of Suffolk, who had publicly insulted the Legates in the hall at Blackfriars.

It is obvious that a party consisting of so many factions would lose its cohesion when its main object was attained with the fall of Wolsey. The latter had bent before the storm, and at once surrendered all his plunder to the King and to Anne's relatives, which secured his personal immunity for a time, whilst he watched for the divisions amongst his opponents that might give him his chance again. Anne's uncle,

Norfolk, aristocratic and conservative, took the lead in the new government, to the annoyance of the Duke of Suffolk, who occupied a secondary place, for which his lack of political ability alone qualified him. Sir Thomas More became Chancellor, and between him and Anne there was no great love lost, whilst Anne's father, now Earl of Wiltshire, became Lord Privy Seal, and her brother, Lord Rochford, was sent as English ambassador to France. With such a government as this— of which Anne was the real head— no very distinct line of policy could be expected. The Parliament, which was summoned on Wolsey's fall, was kept busy legalising the enrichment of Anne at the expense of the Cardinal, and in clamorous complaints of the abuses committed by the clergy, but when foreign affairs had to be dealt with the voice of the government was a divided one. Anne and her paternal family were still in favour of France; but the Emperor and the Pope were close friends now, and it was felt necessary by the King and Norfolk to attempt to reconcile them to the divorce, if possible, by a new political arrangement. For this purpose Anne's father travelled to Bologna, where Charles and Clement were staying together, and urged the case of his master. The only result was a contemptuous refusal from the Emperor to consider any proposal for facilitating his aunt's repudiation; and the serving of Wiltshire, as Henry's representative, with a formal citation of the King of England to appear in person or by proxy before the Papal Court in Rome entrusted with the decision of the divorce case. This latter result drove Henry and Anne into a fury, and strengthened their discontent against the churchmen, whilst it considerably decreased the King's confidence in Wiltshire's ability. It was too late now to recall Wolsey, although the French government did what was possible to soften the King's rigour against him; but Henry longed to be able again to command the consummate ability and experience of his greatest minister, and early in the year 1530 Henry himself became a party to an intrigue for the Cardinal's partial rehabilitation. Anne, when she thought Wolsey was dying, was persuaded to send him a token and a kind message; but when, later, she learnt that an interview between the King and him was in contemplation, she took fright; and Norfolk, who at least was at one with her in her jealousy of the fallen minister, ordered the latter to go to his diocese of York, and not to approach within five miles of the King.

Anne's position in the King's household was now a most extraordinary one. She had visited the fine palace, York Place, which Wolsey had conveyed to the King at Westminster; and with the glee of a child enjoying a new toy, had inspected and appraised the splendours it contained. In future it was to be the royal residence, and she was its mistress. She sat at table in Katharine's place, and even took precedence of the Duchess of Norfolk and ladies of the highest rank. This was all very well in its way, but it did not satisfy Anne. To be Queen in name as well as in fact was the object for which she was striving, and anything less galled her. The Pope was now hand in glove with the Emperor, and could not afford to waver on Henry's side, whilst Charles was more determined than ever to prevent the close alliance between England and France that the marriage and a Boleyn predominance seemed to forebode. The natural effect of this was, of course, to drive Henry more than ever into the arms of France, and though Wolsey had owed his unpopularity largely to his French sympathies, he had never truckled so slavishly to Francis as Henry was now obliged to do, in order to obtain his support for the divorce, which he despaired of obtaining from the Pope without French pressure. The Papal Court was divided, then and always, into French and Spanish factions, and in North Italy French and Spanish agents perpetually tried to outwit each other. Throughout the Continent, wherever the influence of France extended, pressure was exerted to obtain legal opinions favourable to Henry's contention. Bribes, as lavish as they were barefaced, were offered to jurists for decisions confirming the view that marriage with a deceased brother's widow was invalid in fact, and incapable of dispensation. The French Universities were influenced until some sort of irregular dictum, afterwards formally repudiated, was obtained in favour of Henry, and in Italy French and Spanish intrigue were busy at work, the one extorting from lawyers support to the English view, the other by threats and bribes preventing its being given. This, however, was a slow process, and of doubtful efficacy after all; because, whilst the final decision on the divorce lay with the Pope, the opinions of jurists and Universities, even if they had been generally favourable to Henry, instead of the reverse, could have had ultimately no authoritative effect.

Henry began to grow restive by the end of 1530. All his life he had seemed to have his own way in everything, and here he found himself and his most ardent wishes unceremoniously set aside, as if of no account. Other kings had obtained divorces easily enough from Rome: why not he? The answer that would naturally occur to him was that his affairs were being ineptly managed by his ministers, and he again yearned for Wolsey. The Cardinal had in the meanwhile plucked up some of his old spirit at York, and was still in close communication with the French, and even with the Emperor's ambassador. Again Norfolk became alarmed, and a disclosure of the intrigue gave an excuse for Wolsey's arrest. It was the last blow, and the heart of the proud Cardinal broke on his way south to prison, leaving Henry with no strong councillor but the fair-faced woman with the tight mouth who sat in his wife's place. She was brave; "as fierce as a lioness," the Emperor's ambassador wrote, and would "rather see the Queen hanged than recognise her as her mistress"; but the party behind her was a divided one, and the greatest powers in Europe were united against her. There was only one way in which she might win, and that was by linking her cause with that of successful opposition to the Papacy. The Pope was a small Italian prince now slavishly subservient to the Emperor: Luther had defied a greater Sovereign Pontiff than he; why should Clement, a degenerate scion of the mercantile Medicis, dare to dictate to England and her King?

CHAPTER V

1530-1534

HENRY'S DEFIANCE—THE VICTORY OF ANNE

The deadlock with regard to the validity of the marriage could not continue indefinitely, for the legitimacy of the Princess Mary having been called into question, the matter now vitally touched the succession to the English crown. Katharine was immovable. She would neither retire to a convent nor accept a decision from an English tribunal, and, through her proctor in Rome, she passionately pressed for a decision there in her favour. Norfolk, at the end of his not very extensive mental resources, could only wish that both Katharine and Anne were dead and the King married to some one else. The Pope was ready to do anything that did not offend the Emperor to bring about peace; and when, under pressure from Henry and Norfolk, the English prelates and peers, including Wolsey and Warham, signed a petition to the Pope saying that Henry's marriage should be dissolved, or they must seek a remedy for themselves in the English Parliament, Clement was almost inclined to give way; for schism in England he dreaded before all things. But Charles's troops were in Rome and his agents for ever bullying the wretched Pope, and the latter was obliged to reply finally to the English peers with a rebuke. There were those both in England and abroad who urged Henry to marry Anne at once, and depend upon the recognition of the *fait accompli* by means of negotiation afterwards, but this did not satisfy either the King or the favourite. Every interview between the King and the Nuncio grew more bitter than the previous one. No English cause, swore Henry, should be tried outside his realm where he was master; and if the Pope insisted in giving judgment for the Queen, as he had promised the Emperor to do, the English Parliament should deal with the matter in spite of Rome.

The first ecclesiastical thunderclap came in October 1530, when Henry published a proclamation reminding the lieges of the old law of England that forbade the Pope from exercising direct jurisdiction in the realm by Bull or Brief. No one could understand at the time what was meant, but when the Nuncio in perturbation went and asked Norfolk and Suffolk the reason of so strange a proclamation at such a time, they replied roughly, that they "cared nothing for Popes in England ... the King was Emperor and Pope too in his own realm." Later, Henry told the Nuncio that the Pope had outraged convention by summoning him before a foreign tribunal, and should now be taught that no usurpation of power would be allowed in England. The Parliament was called, said Henry, to restrain the encroachment of the clergy generally, and unless the Pope met his wishes promptly a blow would be struck at all clerical pretensions. The reply of the Pope was another brief forbidding Henry's second marriage, and threatening Parliaments and Bishops in England if they dared to meddle in the matter. The question was thus rapidly drifting into an international one on religious lines, which involved either the submission of Henry or schism from the Church. The position of the English clergy was an especially difficult one. They naturally resented any curtailment of the privileges of their order, though they dared not speak too loudly, for they owed the enjoyment of their temporalities to the King. But they were all sons of the Church, looking to Rome for spiritual authority, and were in mortal dread of the advance of the new spirit of religious freedom aroused in Germany. The method of bridling them adopted by Henry was as clever as it was unscrupulous. The Bull giving to Wolsey independent power to judge the matrimonial cause in England as Legate, had been, as will be recollected, demanded by the King and recognised by him, as it had been, of course, by the clergy; but in January 1531, when Parliament and Convocation met, the English clergy found themselves laid under Premunire by the King for having recognised the Legatine Bull; and were told that as subjects of the crown, and not of the Pope, they had thus rendered themselves liable to the punishment for treason. The unfortunate clergy were panic-stricken at this new move, and looked in vain to Rome for support against their own King; but Rome, as usual, was trying to run with the hare and hunt with the hounds, and could only wail at the obstinacy both of Henry and Katharine.

In the previous sitting of Parliament in 1529, severe laws had been passed against the laxity and extortion of the English ecclesiastics, notwithstanding the violent indignation of Fisher of Rochester; but what was now demanded of them as a condition of their pardon for recognising the Bull was practically to repudiate the authority of the Pope over them, and to recognise the King of England as supreme head of the Church, in addition to paying the tremendous fine of a hundred thousand pounds. They were in utter consternation, and they struggled hard; but the alternative to submission was ruin, and the majority gave way. The die was cast: Henry was Pope and King in one, and could settle his own cause in his own way. When the English clergy had thus been brought to heel, Henry's opponents saw that they had driven him too far, and were aghast at his unexpected exhibition of strength, a strength, be it noted, not his own, as will be explained later; and somewhat moderated their tone. But the King of England snapped his fingers now at threats of excommunication, and cared nothing, he said, for any decision from Rome. The Emperor dared not go to war with England about Katharine, for the French were busily drawing towards the Pope, whose niece, Katharine de Medici, was to be betrothed to the son of Francis; and the imperial agents in Rome ceased to insist so pertinaciously upon a decision of the matrimonial suit.

Katharine alone clamoured unceasingly that her "hell upon earth" should be ended by a decision in her favour from the Sovereign Pontiff. Her friends in England were many, for the old party of nobles were rallying again to her side, even Norfolk was secretly in her favour, or at least against the King's marriage with his niece Anne, and Henry's new bold step against the Papacy, taken under bureaucratic influence, had aroused much fear and jealousy amongst prelates like Fisher and jurists like More, as well as amongst the aristocratic party in the country. Desperate efforts were made to prevent the need for further action in defiance of the Papacy by the decision of the matrimonial suit by the English Parliament; and early in June 1531 Henry and his Council decided to put fresh pressure upon Katharine to get her to consent to a suspension of the proceedings in Rome, and to the relegation of the case to a tribunal in some neutral territory. Katharine at Greenwich had secret knowledge of the intention, and she can hardly have been so surprised as she pretended to be when, as she was about to retire to rest, at nine o'clock at night, to learn that the Dukes of Suffolk and Norfolk, and some thirty other nobles and prelates, sought audience of her. Norfolk spoke first, and in the King's name complained bitterly of the slight put upon him by the Pope's citation. He urged the Queen, for the sake of England, for the memory of the political services of Henry to her kin, and his past kindness to her, to meet his wishes and consent to a neutral tribunal judging between them. Katharine was, as usual, cool and contemptuous. No one was more sorry than she for the King's annoyance, though she had not been the cause of it; but there was only one judge in the world competent to deal with the case. "His Holiness, who keeps the place, and has the power, of God upon earth, and is the image of eternal truth." As for recognising her husband as supreme head of the Church, that she would never do. When Dr. Lee spoke harshly, telling her that she knew that, her first marriage having been consummated, her second was never legal, she vehemently denied the fact, and told him angrily to go to Rome and argue. He would find there others than a lone woman to answer him. Dr. Sampson then took up the parable and reproached her for her determination to have the case settled so quickly; and she replied to him that if he had passed such bitter days as she had, he would be in a hurry too. Dr. Stokesley was dealt with similarly by the Queen; and she then proudly protested at being thus baited late at night by a crowd of men; she, "a poor woman without friends or counsel." Norfolk reminded her that the King had appointed the Archbishop of Canterbury, the Bishop of Durham, and the Bishop of Rochester to advise her. "Pretty councillors they are," she replied. "If I ask for Canterbury's advice he tells me he will have nothing to do with it, and for ever repeats *ira principis mors est*. The Bishop of Durham dares to say nothing because he is the King's subject, and Rochester only tells me to keep a good heart and hope for the best."

Katharine knew it not, but many of those before her were really her friends. Gardiner, now first Secretary, looked with fear upon the Lutheran innovations, Guilford the Controller, Lord Talbot, and even Norfolk wished her well, and feared the advent of Anne; and Guilford, less prudent than the rest, spoke so frankly that the favourite heard of his words. She broke out in furious invective against him before his face. "When I am Queen of England," she cried, "you will soon lose your office." "You need not wait so long," he replied, as he went straightway to deliver his seals to the King. Henry told him he ought not to mind an angry woman's talk, and was loath to accept his resignation; but the Controller insisted, and another rankling enemy was raised up to Anne. The favour she enjoyed had fairly turned her head, and her insolence, even to those who in any case had a right to her respect, had made her thoroughly detested. The Duke of Suffolk, enemy of the Papacy as he was, and the King's brother-in-law, was as anxious now as Talbot, Guilford, and Fitzwilliam to avert the marriage with Anne, who was setting all the Court by the ears. Katharine's attitude made matters worse. She still lived under the same roof as the King, though he rarely saw her except on public occasions, and her haughty replies to all his emissaries, and her constant threats of what the Emperor might do, irritated Henry beyond endurance under the taunts of Anne. The latter was bitterly jealous also of the young Princess Mary, of whom Henry was fond; and by many spiteful, petty acts of persecution, the girl's life was made unhappy. Once when Henry praised his daughter in Anne's presence, the latter broke out into violent abuse of her, and on another occasion, when Katharine begged to be allowed to visit the Princess, Henry told her roughly that she could go away as soon as she liked, and stop away. But Katharine stood her ground. She would not leave her husband, she said, even for her daughter, until she was forced to do so. Henry's patience was nearly tired out between Anne's constant importunities and Katharine's dignified immobility; and leaving his wife and daughter at Windsor, he went off on a hunting progress with Anne, in the hope that he might soon be relieved of the presence of Katharine altogether. Public feeling was indignantly in favour of the Queen; and it was no uncommon thing for people to waylay the King, whilst he was hunting, with entreaties that he would live with his wife again; and wherever Anne went the women loudly cried shame upon her.

In his distraction Henry was at a loss what to do. He always wanted to appear in the right, and he dared not imprison or openly ill-treat Katharine, for his own people favoured her, and all Europe would have joined in condemning him; yet it was clear that even Windsor Castle was not, in future, big enough for both Queen and favourite at the same time, and positive orders at length were sent to Katharine, in the autumn of 1531, to take up her residence at More in Hertfordshire, in a house formerly belonging to Wolsey. She obeyed with a heavy heart, for it meant parting— and for ever— with her daughter, who was sent to live at Richmond, and was strictly forbidden to communicate with her mother. Katharine said she would have preferred to have been sent to the Tower, to being consigned to a place so unfit for her as More, with its foul ways and ruinous surroundings, but nothing broke her spirit or humbled her pride. Her household was still regal in its extent, for we are told by an Italian visitor to her that "thirty maids of honour stood around her table when she dined, and there were fifty who performed its service: her household consisting of about two hundred persons in all." But her state was a mockery now; for Lady Anne, she knew, was with her husband, loudly boasting that within three or four months she would be a queen, and already playing the part insolently. The Privy Purse expenses of the period show how openly Anne was acknowledged as being Henry's actual consort. Not only did she accompany the King everywhere on his excursions and progresses, and partake of the receptions offered to him by local authorities and nobles, but large sums of money were paid out of the King's treasury for the gorgeous garb in which she loved to appear. Purple velvet at half a guinea a yard, costly furs and linen, bows and arrows, liveries for her servants, and all sorts of fine gear were bought for Anne. The Lord Mayor of London, in June 1530, sent her a present of cherries, and the bearer got a reward of 6s. 8d. Soon after Anne's greyhounds killed a cow, and the Privy Purse had to pay the damage, 10s. In November, 19¾ yards of crimson satin at 15s. a yard had to be paid for to make Lady Anne a robe, and £8, 8s. for budge skins was paid soon afterwards. When Christmas came and card-playing was in season, my Lady Anne must have playing money, £20 all in groats; and when she lost, as she did pretty heavily, her losings had to be paid by the treasurer, though her winnings she kept for herself. No less than a hundred pounds was given to her as a New Year's gift in 1531. A few weeks afterwards, a farm at Greenwich was bought for her for £66; and her writing-desk had to be adorned with latten and gold at a great cost. As the year 1531 advanced and Katharine's cause became more desperate, the extravagance of her rival grew; and when in the autumn of that year the Queen was finally banished from Court, Anne's bills for dressmaker's finery amounted to extravagant proportions.

The position was rendered the more bitter for Katharine when she recognised that the Pope, in a fright now at Henry's defiance, was trying to meet him half way, and was listening to the suggestion of referring the question to a tribunal at Cambray or elsewhere; whilst the Emperor himself was only anxious to get the cause settled somehow without an open affront to his house or necessary cause for quarrel with Henry. And yet, withal, the divorce did not seem to make headway in England itself. As we have seen, the common people were strongly against it: the clergy, trembling, as well they might, for their privileges between the Pope and the King, were naturally as a body in favour of the ecclesiastical view; and many of Henry and Anne's clerical instruments, such as Dr. Bennet in Rome and Dr. Sampson at Vienna, were secretly working against the cause they were supposed to be aiding: even some of the new prelates, such as Gardiner of Winchester and Stokesley of London, grew less active advocates when they understood that upon them and their order would fall ultimately the responsibility of declaring invalid a marriage which the Church and the Pope had sanctioned. Much stronger still even was the dislike to the King's marriage on the part of the older nobility, whose enmity to Wolsey had first made the marriage appear practicable. They had sided with Anne to overthrow Wolsey; but the obstinate determination of the King to rid himself of his wife and marry his favourite, had brought forward new clerical and bureaucratic ministers whose proceedings and advice alarmed the aristocracy much more than anything Wolsey had done. If Katharine had been tactful, or even an able politician, she had the materials at hand to form a combination in favour of herself and her daughter, before which Henry, coward as he was, would have quailed. But she lacked the qualities necessary for a leader: she irritated the King without frightening him, and instead of conciliating the nobles who really sympathised with her, though they were forced to do the King's bidding, she snubbed them haughtily and drove them from her.

Anne flattered and pleased the King, but it was hardly her mind that moved him to defy the powerful Papacy, or sustained him in his fight with his own clergy. From the first we have seen him leaning upon some adviser who would relieve him from responsibility whilst giving him all the honour for success. He desired the divorce above all things; but, as usual, he wanted to shelter himself behind other authority than his own. When in 1529 he had been seeking learned opinions to influence the Pope, chance had thrown the two ecclesiastics who were his instruments, Fox and Gardiner, into contact with a learned theologian and Reader in Divinity at Cambridge University. Thomas Cranmer had studied and lived much. He was a widower, and Fellow of Magdalene, Cambridge, of forty years of age; and although in orders and a Doctor of Divinity, his tastes were rather those of a learned country gentleman than of an ecclesiastic in monkish times. In conversation with Fox and Gardiner, this high authority on theology expressed the opinion that instead of enduring the delays of the ecclesiastical courts, the question of the legality of the King's marriage should be decided by divines from the words of the Scriptures themselves. The idea seemed a good one, and Henry jumped at it. In an interview soon afterwards he ordered Cranmer to put his arguments into a book, and placed him in the household of Anne's father, the Earl of Wiltshire, to facilitate the writing of it. The religious movement in Germany had found many echoes in England, and doubtless Cranmer conscientiously objected to Papal control. Certain it is that, fortified as he was by the encouragement of Anne and her father, his book was a persuasive one, and greatly pleased the King, who sent it to the Pope and others. Nor did Cranmer's activity stay there. He entered into disputation everywhere, with the object of gaining theological recruits for the King's side, and wrote a powerful refutation of Reginald Pole's book in favour of Katharine. The King thought so highly of Cranmer's controversial ability that he sent him with Lee, Stokesley, and other theologians to Rome, Paris, and elsewhere on the Continent, to forward the divorce, and from Rome he was commissioned as English Ambassador with the Emperor.

Whilst Cranmer was thus fighting the King's battle abroad, another instrument came to Henry's hand for use in England. On the disgrace of Wolsey, his secretary, Thomas Cromwell, was recommended to Henry by friends. The King disliked him, and at first refused to see him; but consented to do so when it was hinted that Cromwell was the sort of man who would serve him well in what he had at heart. The hint was a well-founded one; for Thomas Cromwell was as ambitious and unscrupulous as his master had been; strong, bold, and fortunately unhampered by ecclesiastical orders. When Henry received him in the gardens at Whitehall, Cromwell spoke as no priest, and few laymen, would have dared to do: for, apart from the divorce question, there was to be no dallying with heresy if Henry could help it, and the fires of Smithfield burning doubters were already beginning to blaze under the influence of Sir Thomas More. "Sire," said Cromwell to the King, "the Pope refuses you a divorce ... why wait for his consent? Every Englishman is master in his own house, and why should not you be so in England? Ought a foreign prelate to share your power with you? It is true the bishops make oath to your Majesty; but they make another to the Pope immediately afterwards which absolves them from it. Sire, you are but half a king, and we are but half your subjects. Your kingdom is a two-headed monster: will you bear such an anomaly any longer? Frederick and other German princes have cast off the yoke of Rome. Do likewise; become once more king, govern your kingdom in concert with your lords and commons."

With much more of such talk Cromwell flattered the King, who probably hardly knew whether to punish or reward such unheard-of boldness; but when Cromwell, prepared for the emergency, took from his pocket a copy of the prelates' oath to the Pope, Henry's indignation bore all before it, and Cromwell's fortune was made. He at once obtained a seat in Parliament (1529), and took the lead in the anti-clerical measures which culminated in the emancipation of the English clergy from the Papacy, and their submission to the King. Gardiner, ambitious and able as he was, was yet an ecclesiastic, and looked grimly upon such a religious policy as that into which Henry was being towed by his infatuation for Anne; but Cromwell was always ready with authorities and flattery to stiffen the King's resolve, and thenceforward, until his fall before a combination of nobles, his was the strong spirit to which Henry clung.

It will be seen that the influences against the King's marriage with Anne were very powerful, since it had become evident that the object could only be attained by the separation of England from the Papal communion; a step too bold and too much smacking of Lutheranism to commend itself to any but the few who might benefit by the change. The greatest danger seemed that by her isolation England might enable the two great Catholic powers to combine against her, in which case Henry's ruin was certain; and, eager as he was to divorce Katharine in England and marry Anne, the King dared not do so until he had secured at least the neutrality of France. As usual, he had to pay heavily for it. Dr. Fox, Henry's most able and zealous foreign minister, was again sent to France, and an alliance was negotiated in the spring of 1532, by which Henry bound himself to join Francis against the Emperor in case of attack, and Francis undertook to support Henry if any attempt was made by Charles to avenge his aunt. Anne was once more jubilant and hopeful; for her cause was now linked with a national alliance which had a certain party of adherents in the English Court, and an imperial attack upon England in the interests of Katharine was rendered unlikely. But, withal, the opposition in England itself had to be overcome, for Henry was ever a stickler for correctness in form, and wanted the divorce to have an appearance of defensible legality. The bishops in Parliament were sounded, but it was soon evident that they as a body would not fly in the face of the Papacy and the Catholic interests, even to please the King. Timid, tired old Warham, the Archbishop of Canterbury, was approached with a suggestion that he, as Primate, might convene a quorum of prelates favourable to Henry, who would approve of the entire repudiation of the Papal authority in England, and themselves pronounce the King's divorce. But Warham was already hastening to the grave, and flatly refused to stain his last hours by spiritual revolt. Despairing of the English churchman, Henry then turned to the lay peers and commons, and, through Norfolk, asked them to decide that the matrimonial cause was one that should be dealt with by a lay tribunal; but Norfolk's advocacy was but half-hearted, and the peers refused to make the declaration demanded.

The fact is clear that England was not yet prepared to defy spiritual authority to satisfy the King's caprice; and Anne was nearly beside herself with rage. She, indeed, was for braving everybody and getting married at once, divorce or no divorce. Why lose so much time? the French ambassador asked. If the King wanted to marry again let him do as King Louis did, and marry of his own motion. The advice pleased both Henry and his lady-love, but Norfolk and Anne's father were strongly opposed to so dangerous and irregular a step, and incurred the furious displeasure of Anne for daring to thwart her. Every one, she said, even her own kinsmen, were against her, and she was not far wrong, for with the exception of Cranmer in Germany and Cromwell, no one cared to risk the popular anger by promoting the match. Above all, Warham stood firm. The continued attacks of the King at Cromwell's suggestion against the privileges of the clergy hardened the old Archbishop's heart, and it was evident that he as Primate would never now annul the King's marriage and defy the authority of Rome. The opposition of Lord Chancellor More and of the new Bishop of Winchester, Gardiner, to Cromwell's anti-clerical proposals in Parliament angered the King, and convinced him that with his present instruments it would be as difficult for him to obtain a divorce in legal form in England as in Rome itself. More was made to feel that his position was an impossible one, and retired when Parliament was prorogued in May; and Gardiner had a convenient attack of gout, which kept him away from Court until the King found he could not conduct foreign affairs without him and brought him back.

In the meanwhile Katharine neglected the opportunities offered to her of combining all these powerful elements in her favour. Nobles, clergy, and people were almost universally on her side: Anne was cordially hated, and had no friends but the few religious reformers who hoped by her means to force the King ever further away from the Papacy; and yet the Queen continued to appeal to Rome and the Emperor, against whom English patriotic feeling might be raised by Anne's few friends. The unwisdom of thus linking Katharine's cause with threats of foreign aggression, whilst England itself was favourable to her, was seen when the Nuncio presented to Henry a half-hearted exhortation to take his lawful wife back. Henry fulminated against the foreigner who dared to interfere between him and his wife; and, very far from alarming him, the Pope's timid action only proved the impotence of Rome to harm him. But the results fell upon the misguided Katharine, who had instigated the step. She was sent from the More to Ampthill, a house belonging to one of her few episcopal enemies.

All through the summer of 1532 the coming and going of French agents to England puzzled the Queen and her foreign friends; but suddenly, late in July, the truth came out. Henry and Anne had gone with a great train on a hunting tour through the midlands in July; but only a few days after starting they suddenly returned to London. The quidnuncs whispered that the people on the way had clamoured so loudly that the Queen might be recalled to Court, and had so grossly insulted Anne, that the royal party had been driven back in disgust; and though there was no doubt some ground for the assertion, the real reason for the return was that the interview between Henry and the French king, so long secretly in negotiation, had at last been settled. To enlist Francis personally on the side of the divorce, and against the clerical influence, was good policy; for the Emperor could not afford to quarrel both with France and England for his aunt, and especially as the meeting arranged between Francis and the Pope at Nice for the betrothal of the Duke of Orleans with Katharine de Medici was already in contemplation, and threatened the Emperor with a combination of France, England, and perhaps the Papacy, which would be powerful enough to defy him. The policy was Cromwell's, who had inherited from his master, Wolsey, a leaning for the French alliance; but Norfolk and the rest of Henry's advisers were heavily bribed by France, and were on this occasion not inimical. The people at large, as usual, looked askance at the French connection. They dreaded, above all things, a war with Spain and Flanders, and recollected with apprehension the fruitless and foolish waste in splendour on the last occasion of the monarchs of France and England meeting. An attempt was made to provide that the preparations should be less costly and elaborate than those for the Field of the Cloth of Gold, but Henry could not forego the splendour that he loved, and a suite of 3000 or 4000 people were warned to accompany the King across the Channel to Boulogne and Calais.

ANNE BOLEYN
From a portrait by LUCAS CORNELISZ *in the National Portrait Gallery*

For the interview to have its full value in the eyes of Henry and his mistress, the latter must be present at the festival, and be recognised by the French royal family as being of their own caste. Francis was not scrupulous, but this was difficult to arrange. His own second wife was the Emperor's sister, and she, of course, would not consent to meet "the concubine"; nor would any other of the French princesses, if they could avoid it; but, although the French at first gave out that no ladies would be present, Anne began to get her fine clothes ready and enlist her train of ladies as soon as the interview between the kings was arranged. So confident was she now of success that she foretold to one of her friends that she would be married whilst in France. To add to her elation, in the midst of the preparations Archbishop Warham died, and the chief ecclesiastical obstacle to the divorce in England disappeared. Some obedient churchman as Primate would soon manage to enlist a sufficient number of his fellows to give to his court an appearance of authority, and the Church of England would ratify the King's release.

The effects of Warham's death (23rd August 1532) were seen immediately. There is every probability that up to that time Anne had successfully held her royal lover at arm's length; but with Cranmer, or another such as he, at Lambeth her triumph was only a matter of the few weeks necessary to carry out the formalities; and by the end of the month of August 1532 she probably became the King's mistress. This alone would explain the extraordinary proceedings when, on the 1st September, she was created Marchioness of Pembroke in her own right. It was Sunday morning before Mass at Windsor, where the new French alliance was to be ratified, that the King and his nobles and the French ambassador met in the great presence chamber and Anne knelt to receive the coronet and robe of her rank, the first peeress ever created in her own right in England: precedence being given to her before the two other English marchionesses, both ladies of the blood royal. Everything that could add prestige to the ceremony was done. Anne herself was dressed in regal crimson velvet and ermine; splendid presents were made to her by the enamoured King, fit more for a sovereign's consort than his mistress; a thousand pounds a year and lands were settled upon her, and her rank and property were to descend to the issue male of her body. But the cloven hoof is shown by the omission from the patent of the usual legitimacy clause. Even if, after all, the cup of queendom was dashed from her lips untasted, she had made not a bad bargain for herself. Her short triumph, indeed, was rapidly coming. She had fought strenuously for it for many years; and now most of the legal bars against her had fallen. But, withal, there was bitterness still in her chalice. The people scowled upon her no less now that she was a marchioness than before, and the great ladies who were ordered to attend the King's "cousin" into France did their service but sourly: whilst Francis had to be conciliated with all sorts of important concessions before he could be got to welcome "the lady" into his realm. When, at last, he consented, "because she would have gone in any case; for the King cannot be an hour without her," Francis did it gallantly, and with good grace, for, after all, Anne was just then the strongest prop in England of the French alliance.

Katharine, from afar off, watched these proceedings with scornful resentment. Henry had no chivalry, no generosity, and saved his repudiated wife no humiliation that he could deal her in reward for her obstinacy. He had piled rich gifts upon Anne, but her greed for costly gewgaws was insatiable; and when the preparations for her visit to France were afoot she coveted the Queen's jewels. Henry's sister, the Duchess of Suffolk, Queen Dowager of France, had been made to surrender her valuables to the King's favourite; but when Henry sent a message to his wife bidding her give up her jewels, the proud princess blazed out in indignant anger at the insult. "Tell the King," she said, "that I cannot send them to him; for when lately, according to the custom of this realm, I presented him with a New Year's gift, he warned me to send him no such presents for the future. Besides, it is offensive and insulting to me, and would weigh upon my conscience, if I were led to give up my jewels for such a base purpose as that of decking out a person who is a reproach to Christendom, and is bringing scandal and disgrace upon the King, through his taking her to such a meeting as this in France. But still, if the King commands me and sends specially for them himself, I will give him my jewels." Such an answer as this proves clearly the lack of practical wisdom in the poor woman. She might have resisted, or she might have surrendered with a good grace; but to irritate and annoy the weak bully, without gaining her point, was worse than useless. Anne's talk about marrying the King in France angered Katharine beyond measure; but the favourite's ambition grew as her prospect brightened, and when it was settled that Cranmer was to be recalled from Germany and made Primate, Anne said that she had changed her mind. "Even if the King wished to marry her there (in France) she would not consent to it. She will have it take place here in England, where other queens have usually been married and crowned."

Through Kent, avoiding as they might the plague-stricken towns, the King and his lady-love, with a great royal train, rode to Dover early in October 1532. At Calais, Henry's own town, Anne was received almost with regal honours; but when Henry went forth to greet Francis upon French soil near Boulogne, and to be sumptuously entertained, it was seen that, though the French armed men were threateningly numerous, there were no ladies to keep in countenance the English "concubine" and the proud dames who did her service. Blazing in gems, the two kings met with much courtly ceremony and hollow professions of affection. Banqueting, speech-making, and posturing in splendid raiment occupied five days at Boulogne, the while the "Lady Marquis" ate her heart out at Calais in petulant disappointment; though she made as brave a show as she could to the Frenchmen when they came to return Henry's visit. The chronicler excels himself in the description of the lavish magnificence of the welcome of Francis at Calais, and tells us that, after a bounteous supper on the night of Sunday 27th October, at which the two kings and their retinues sat down, "The Marchioness of Pembroke with seven other ladies in masking apparel of strange fashion, made of cloth of gold compassed with crimson tinsel satin, covered with cloth of silver, lying loose and knit with gold laces," tripped in, and each masked lady chose a partner, Anne, of course, taking the French king. In the course of the dance Henry plucked the masks from the ladies' faces, and debonair Francis, in courtly fashion, conversed with his fair partner. One of the worst storms in the memory of man delayed the English king's return from Calais till the 13th November; but when at length the *Te Deum* for his safe home-coming was sung at St. Paul's, Anne knew that the King of France had undertaken to frighten the Pope into inactivity by talk of the danger of schism in England, and that Cranmer was hurrying across Europe on his way from Italy to London, to become Primate of the Church of England.

The plot projected was a clever one, but it was still needful to handle it very delicately. Cranmer during his residence in Germany and Italy had been zealous in winning favourable opinions for Henry's contention, and his foregathering with Lutheran divines had strengthened his reforming opinions. He had, indeed, proceeded to the dangerous length of going through a form of marriage secretly with a young lady belonging to a Lutheran family. His leanings cannot have been quite unknown to the ever-watchful spies of the Pope and the Emperor, though Cranmer had done his best to hoodwink them, and to some extent had succeeded. But to ask the Pope to issue the Bulls confirming such a man in the Primacy of England was at least a risky proceeding, and Henry had to dissemble. In January, Katharine fondly thought that her husband was softening towards her, for he released her chaplain Abell, who had been imprisoned for publicly speaking in her favour. She fancied, poor soul, that "perhaps God had touched his heart, and that he was about to acknowledge his error." Chapuys attributed Henry's new gentleness to his begrudging the cost of two queenly establishments. But seen from this distance of time, it was clearly caused by a desire to disarm the suspicion of the Pope and the Emperor, who were again to meet at Bologna, until the Bulls confirming Cranmer's appointment to the Archbishopric had been issued. Henry went out of his way to be amiable to the imperial ambassador Chapuys, whilst he beguiled the Nuncio with the pretended proposal for reconciliation by means of a decision on the divorce to be given by two Cardinal Legates, appointed by the Pope, and sitting in neutral territory. In vain Chapuys warned the Emperor that Cranmer could not be trusted; but Henry's diplomatic signs of grace prevailed, and the Pope, dreading to drive England further into schism, confirmed Cranmer's election as Archbishop of Canterbury (March 1533).

It was high time; for under a suave exterior both Henry and Anne were in a fever of impatience. At the very time that Queen Katharine thought that her husband had repented, Anne conveyed to him the news that she was with child. It was necessary for their plans that the offspring should be born in wedlock, and yet no public marriage was possible, or the eyes of the Papal party would be opened before the Bulls confirming Cranmer's elevation were issued. Sometime late in January 1533, therefore, a secret marriage was performed at Greenwich, probably by the reforming Franciscan Friar, George Brown, and Anne became Henry's second wife, whilst Katharine was still undivorced. The secret was well kept for a time, and the Nuncio, Baron di Burgo, was fooled to the top of his bent by flatteries and hopes of bribes. He even sat in state on Henry's right hand, the French ambassador being on the left, at the opening of Parliament, probably with the idea of convincing the trembling English clergy that the King and the Pope were working together. In any case, the close association of the Nuncio with Henry and his ministers aroused the fears of Katharine anew, and she broke out in denunciations of the Pope's supineness in thus leaving her without aid for three and a half years, and now entertaining, as she said, a suggestion that would cause her to be declared the King's concubine, and her daughter a bastard. In vain Chapuys, the only man of his party who saw through the device, prayed that Cranmer's Bulls should not be sent from Rome, that the sentence in Katharine's favour should no longer be delayed. It was already too late. The pride of Anne and her father at the secret marriage could not much longer be kept under. In the middle of February, whilst dining in her own apartment, she said that "she was now as sure that she should be married to the King, as she was of her own death"; and the Earl of Wiltshire told the aged kinsman of Henry, the Earl of Rutland, a staunch adherent of Katharine, that "the King was determined not to be so considerate as he had been, but would marry the Marchioness of Pembroke at once, by the authority of Parliament." Anne's condition, indeed, could not continue to be concealed, and whispers of it reached the Queen at Ampthill. By March the rumour was rife at Court that the marriage had taken place— a rumour which it is plain that Anne's friends took no pains to deny, and Cranmer positively encouraged.

Cromwell, in the meanwhile, grew in power and boldness with the success of his machinations. The Chancellorship, vacant by More's resignation, was filled by Cromwell's friend Audley, and every post that fell vacant or could be vacated was occupied by known opponents of the clergy. The country and Parliament were even yet not ready to go so far as Cromwell in his policy of emancipation from Rome in spiritual affairs; and only by the most illegal pressure both in the two Houses and in Convocation was the declaration condemning the validity of the King's marriage with Katharine at last obtained. Armed with these declarations and the Bulls from Rome confirming Cranmer's appointment, Henry was ready in April to cast away the mask, and the Dukes of Norfolk and Suffolk were sent to tell Katharine at Ampthill "that she need not trouble any more about the King, for he had taken another wife, and that in future she must abandon the title of Queen, and be called Duchess; though she should be left in possession of her property." Chapuys was indignant, and urged the Emperor to make war upon England in revenge for the insult to his house. "The moment this accursed Anne gets her foot firmly in the stirrup she will do the Queen all the harm she can, and the Princess also, which is what the Queen fears most.... She (Anne) has lately boasted that she will make the Princess one of her maids, which will not give her too much to eat; or will marry her to some varlet." But the Emperor had cares and dangers that his ambassador in England knew not of, and he dared not avenge his aunt by the invasion of England.

A long and fruitless war of words was waged between Henry and Chapuys when the news of the secret marriage became known; the talk turning upon the eternal question of the consummation of Katharine's first marriage. Chapuys reminded the King that on several occasions he (Henry) had confessed that his wife had been intact by Arthur. "Ah!" replied Henry, "I only said that in fun. A man when he is frolicking and dining says a good many things that are not true. Now, I think I have satisfied you.... What else do you want to know?" A day or two after this, on Easter Eve, Anne went to Mass in truly royal state, loaded with diamonds and other precious stones, and dressed in a gorgeous suit of tissue; the train being borne by her cousin, the daughter of the Duke of Norfolk, betrothed to the King's illegitimate son, the Duke of Richmond. She was followed by a greater suite and treated with more ceremony than had formerly attended Katharine, and, to the astonishment of the people, was prayed for thenceforward in the

Church services at Court as Queen. In London the attitude of the people grew threatening, and the Lord Mayor was taken to task by the King, who ordered that proclamation should be made forbidding any unfavourable reference to the King's second marriage. But the fire of indignation glowed fiercely beneath the surface, for everywhere the cause of Katharine was bound up, as it seemed, with the old faith in which all had been born, with the security of commerce with England's best customers, and with the rights of anointed royalty, as against low-born insolence.

No humiliation was spared to Katharine. Her daughter was forbidden to hold any communication with her, her household was reduced to the meagre proportions of a private establishment, her scutcheon was taken down from Westminster Hall, and her cognisance from her barge, and, as a crowning indignity, she was summoned to appear before the Primate's court at Dunstable, a summons which, at the prompting of Chapuys, she entirely disregarded. Up to this time she had stood firm in her determination to maintain an attitude of loyalty to the King and to her adopted country; but, as she grew more bitter at her rival's triumph, and the flowing tide of religious change rose at her feet, she listened to plans for bringing a remedy for her ills by a subversion of Henry's regime. But she was a poor conspirator, and considerations of safety for her daughter, and her want of tact in uniting the English elements in her favour, always paralysed her.

In the meanwhile the preparations for the public recognition and coronation of Anne went on. The new Queen tried her best to captivate the Londoners, but without success; and only with difficulty could the contributions be obtained for the coming festivities when the new Queen passed through the city. On the 10th May Katharine was declared contumacious by the Primate's court, and on the 23rd May Cranmer pronounced the King's first marriage to have been void from the first. This was followed by a pronouncement to the effect that the second marriage, that with Anne, was legal, and nothing now stood in the way of the final fruition of so much labour and intrigue, pregnant with such tremendous results to England. On the 29th May 1533 the first scene of the pageant was enacted with the State progress by water from Greenwich to the Tower. No effort had been spared by Henry to make the occasion a brilliant one. We are told that the whole river from the point of departure to that of arrival was covered with beautifully bedizened boats; guns roared forth their salutations at Greenwich, and from the crowd of ships that lay in the stream. Flags and *feux de joie* could be bought; courtiers', guilds', and nobles' barges could be commanded, but the hearty cheers of the lieges could not be got for all King Harry's power, as the new Queen, in the old Queen's barge, was borne to the frowning fortress which so soon was to be her own place of martyrdom.

On Sunday, 31st May 1533, the procession through the crowded city sallied from the Tower betimes in the morning. Englishmen and foreigners, except Spaniards only, had been forced to pay heavily for the splendour of the day; and the trade guilds and aldermen, brave in furred gowns and gold chains, stood from one device to another in the streets, as the glittering show went by. The French element did its best to add gaiety to the occasion, and the merchants of France established in London rode at the head of the procession in purple velvet embroidered with Anne's device. Then came the nobles and courtiers and all the squires and gentlemen whom the King had brought from their granges and manor-houses to do honour to their new Queen. Anne herself was seated in an open litter of white satin covered by a golden canopy. She was dressed in a surcoat and mantle of white tissue trimmed with ermine, and wore a robe of crimson brocade stiff with gems. Her hair, which was very fine, hung over her shoulders surmounted by a coif and a coronet of diamonds, whilst around her neck was hung a necklace of great pearls, and upon her breast reposed a splendid jewel of precious stones. "And as she passed through the city she kept turning her face from one side to the other to greet the people, but, strange to see it was, that there were hardly ten persons who greeted her with 'God save your Grace,' as they used to do when the sainted Queen Katharine went by."

Lowering brows, and whispered curses of "Nan Bullen" from the citizens' wives followed the new Queen on her way; for to them she stood for war against the Emperor in the behoof of France, for harassed trade and lean larders, and, above all, for defiance of the religious principles that most of them held sacred; and they hated the long fair face with which, or with love philtres, she had bewitched the King. The very pageants ostensibly raised in her honour contrived in several cases to embody a subtle insult. At the Gracechurch corner of Fenchurch Street, where the Hanse merchants had erected a "merveilous connyng pageaunt," representing Mount Parnassus, with the fountain of Helicon spouting racked Rhenish wine all day, the Queen's litter was stayed a space to listen to the Muses playing "swete instrumentes," and to read the "epigrams" in her praise that were hung around the mount. But Anne looked aloft to where Apollo sat, and saw that the imperial eagle was blazoned in the place of honour, whilst the much-derided bogus arms of the Boleyns lurked in humble guise below; and for many a day thenceforward she was claiming vengeance against the Easterlings for the slight put upon her. As each triumphal device was passed, children dressed as angels, or muses, were made to sing or recite conceited phrases of dithyrambic flattery to the heroine of the hour. There was no grace or virtue of which she was not the true exemplar. Through Leadenhall and Cornhill and so to Chepe, between lines of liveried citizens, Anne's show progressed. At the cross on Cheapside the Mayor and corporation awaited the Queen; and the Recorder, "Master Baker," with many courtly compliments, handed her the city's gift of a thousand marks in a purse of gold, "which she thankfully received." That she did so was noted with sneering contempt by Katharine's friends. "As soon as she received the purse of money she placed it by her side in the litter: and thus she showed that she was a person of low descent. For there stood by her at the time the captain of the King's guard, with his men and twelve lacqueys; and when the sainted Queen had passed by for *her* coronation, she handed the money to the captain of the guard to be divided amongst the halberdiers and lacqueys. Anne did not do so, but kept them for herself." St. Paul's and Ludgate, Fleet Street and Temple Bar, all offered their official adulation, whilst the staring people stood by dumb. Westminster Hall, into which Anne's litter was borne for the feast, was richly hung with arras and "newly glazed." A regal throne with a canopy was set on high for Anne, and a great sideboard of gold plate testified to the King's generosity to his new wife. But after she had changed her garments and was welcomed with open arms by Henry at his new palace of Westminster, her disappointment broke out. "How like you the look of the city, sweetheart?" asked the King. "Sir," she replied, "the city itself was well enow; but I saw many caps on heads and heard but few tongues."

The next day, Sunday, Anne was crowned by Cranmer with full ceremony in Westminster Abbey, and for days thereafter banqueting, tilting, and the usual roystering went on; and the great-granddaughter of Alderman Boleyn felt that at last she was Queen indeed. Henry, too, had had his way, and again could hope that a son born in wedlock might perpetuate the name of Tudor on the throne of England. But he was in deadly fear, for the prospect was black all around him. Public indignation in England grew apace at the religious changes and at the prospect of war; but what most aroused Henry's alarm was the sudden coldness of France, and the probability of a great Catholic coalition against him. Norfolk and Lord Rochford with a stately train had gone to join in the interview between Francis and the Pope, in the hope that the joint presence of France and England might force Clement to recognise accomplished facts in order to avoid the secession of England from the Church. Although it suited Francis to promote the antagonism between Henry and the Emperor by keeping the divorce proceedings dragging on in Rome, it did not suit him for England to defy the Papacy by means of Cranmer's sentence, and so to change the balance of power in Europe by driving Henry into permanent union with German Protestants whilst Francis was forced to side with the Emperor on religious grounds. So long as Henry remained undivorced and unmarried anything might happen. He might sate of his mistress and tire of the struggle against Rome, or be driven by fear of war to take a conciliatory course, and in any of these cases he must needs pay for France's aid; but now that his divorce and remarriage were as valid as a duly authorised Archbishop could make them, the utility of Anne as an aid to French foreign policy disappeared. The actual marriage therefore deprived her of the sympathies of the French party in the English Court, which had hitherto sided with her, and the effects were immediately seen in the attitude of Francis.

Before Norfolk could reach the south of France news came to him that the Pope, coerced by the Emperor, had issued a brief declaring all of Henry's proceedings in England to be nullified and he and his abettors excommunicated, unless of his own accord he restored things to their former condition before September. It was plain, therefore, that any attempt at the coming interview to reconcile Clement with Henry's action would be fruitless. Norfolk found Francis also much cooler than before, and sent back his nephew Rochford post haste to England to beg the King's instructions. He arrived at Court in early August, at a time when Henry's perplexity was at its height. He had learnt of the determination of Francis to greet the Pope and carry through the marriage between the Duke of Orleans and Katharine de Medici, whether the King of England's demands were satisfied by Clement or not. He now knew that the dreaded sentence of excommunication pended over him and his instruments. If he had been left to his own weakness he would probably have given way, or at least have sought compromise. If Norfolk had been at his elbow, the old aristocratic English party might also have stayed the King's hand. But Cromwell, bold and astute, and Anne, with the powerful lever of her unborn child, which might be a son, knew well that they had gone too far to return, and that defiance of the Papacy was the only road open to them. Already at the end of June Henry had gone as far as to threaten an appeal from the Pope to the General Council of the Church, the meeting of which was then being discussed; but now that he knew that Francis was failing him, and the Pope had finally cast down the gage, he took the next great step which led to England's separation from Rome. Norfolk was recalled, and Gardiner accredited to Francis only with a watching brief during the Papal interview at Nice, whilst Henry's ambassadors in Rome were recalled, and English agents were sent to Germany to seek alliances with the German Protestant princes. When, therefore, Norfolk arrived in England, he found that in his two months' absence Cromwell had steered the ship of state further away than ever from the traditional policy of the English conservatives; namely, one of balance between the two great Catholic powers; and that England was isolated, but for the doubtful friendship of those vassal princes of the Empire who professed the dreaded new heresy. Thenceforward the ruin of Anne and Cromwell was one of the main objects of Norfolk and the noble party.

The treatment meted out to Katharine during the same time followed a similar impulse. Chapuys had been informed that, the King having now taken a legal wife, Katharine could no longer be called Queen, but Princess Dowager of Wales, and that her regal household could not be kept up; and on the 3rd July Katharine's principal officers were ordered to convey a similar message to her personally. The message was roughly worded. It could only be arrogance and vainglory, she was told, that made her retain or usurp the title of Queen. She was much mistaken if she imagined that her husband would ever live with her again, and by her obstinate contumacy she would cause wars and bloodshed, as well as danger to herself and her daughter, as both would be made to feel the King's displeasure. The Queen's answer, as might have been expected, was as firm as usual. She was the King's legitimate wife, and no reward or fear in the world would ever make her abandon her right to the title she bore. It was not vainglory that moved her, for to be the daughter of Ferdinand and Isabel was a greater honour than to be a Queen. Henry might punish her, she said, or even her daughter, "Yet neither for that, nor a thousand deaths, would she consent to damn her soul or that of her husband the King." The King, beside himself with rage, could do no more than warn Katharine's household that they must all treat their mistress as Princess of Wales, or suffer the penalty. As for Katharine, no punishment short of death could move her; and Cromwell himself, in admiration at her answer, said that "nature had injured her in not making her a man, for she would have surpassed in fame all the heroes of history."

When a few days after this Katharine was removed to Buckden, crowds followed her with tears and blessings along the road, even as they had followed the Princess Mary shortly before, "as if she were God Almighty," as Anne said. In defiance of Henry's threats, "God save the Queen" rang high and clear wherever she went, and the people, "wishing her joy, comfort, and all manner of prosperity, and mishap to her enemies, begged her with tears to let them serve her; for they were all ready to die for her sake." Anne's spite at such demonstrations was characteristic. Katharine possessed a very rich and gorgeous length of stuff, which she had brought from Spain to serve as a christening robe if she should have a son and heir. Anne's time was drawing near, and she would not be content until the King had demanded of his wife the Spanish material to serve as a robe for the Prince of Wales, which he was confident would be born to Anne. "God forbid," replied Katharine, "that I should ever give help or countenance in a case so horrible and abominable as this!" and the indignity of forcible searching of her chests for the stuff at least was not insisted upon then.

Anne's own position was hardly a happy one; her one hope being that the coming child would be a son, as the King was assured by astrologers that it would be. For amorous Henry was already tiring somewhat of her, and even Cromwell's tone was less confident than before. Early in August, Henry left her at Greenwich to go to Windsor alone, for the first time since they had been together. Sometime in July she had insisted upon a very sumptuous bed, which had formed part of a French royal ransom, being taken out of the treasure-room for the birth of the expected heir. It is well, sneered Chapuys, in the first days of September, that she got it betimes, "otherwise she would not have it now, for she has been for some time past very jealous of the King; and, with good cause, spoke about it in words that he did not like. He told her that she must wink at such things, and put up with them, as her betters had done before her. He could at any time cast her down as easily as he had raised her." Frequent bickerings of this sort went on during the last weeks of Anne's pregnancy; but on Sunday, 7th September, the day that was to heal all differences came. Henry had defied the greatest power in the world, had acted basely and brutally to his legal wife, and had incurred the reprobation of his own people for the sake of having a son, and on the fateful day mentioned a fair girl baby was born to Anne at Greenwich.

The official rejoicings were held, but beneath the surface every one knew that a tragedy lurked, for unless a son was born to Anne her doom was sealed. Henry had asserted his mastership in his own realm and had defied Christendom. He had found that his subjects, however sulkily, had accepted his action without open revolt; and that Charles, notwithstanding the insult to his house, was still speaking softly through his ambassadors. If a great princess like Katharine could thus be repudiated without disaster to his realm, it would indeed be easy for him to cast away "that noughty pake, Nan Bullen," if she failed to satisfy his desire for a son. But in the meanwhile it was necessary for him to secure, so far as he could, the succession of his new daughter, since Cranmer's decision had rendered Mary, Princess of Wales, of whom her father had been so proud, illegitimate. Accordingly, immediately after the child Elizabeth was christened, heralds proclaimed in the King's name that Princess Mary was thenceforward to lose her title and pre-eminence, the badge upon her servants' coats being replaced by the arms of the King, and the baby Lady Elizabeth was to be recognised as the King's only legitimate heir and Princess of Wales. In vain the imperial ambassador protested and talked to Cromwell of possible war, in which England might be ruined, which Cromwell admitted but reminded him that the Emperor would not benefit thereby; in vain Katharine from her retirement at Buckden urged Chapuys and the Emperor to patronise Reginald Pole as a possible threat to Henry; in vain Princess Mary herself, in diplomatic language, told her father that he might give her what title he liked, but that she herself would never admit her illegitimacy or her mother's repudiation; in vain Bishop Fisher and Chapuys counselled the invasion of England and the overturn of Henry: Cromwell knew that there was no drawing back for him, and that the struggle must go on now to the bitter end.

Anne with the birth of her daughter became more insolent and exacting than ever. Nothing would satisfy her but the open degradation of Katharine and her daughter, and Henry in this respect seems to have had no spark of generous or gentlemanly feeling. Irritated by what he considered the disobedience of his wife and child, and doubtless also by their constant recourse for support and advice to the Emperor's ambassador against him, he dismissed Mary's household and ordered her to go to Hatfield and serve as maid the Princess Elizabeth. Mary was ready with her written protest, which Chapuys had drafted for her, but, having made it, decided to submit; and was borne to Hatfield in scornful dudgeon, to serve "the bastard" of three months old. When she arrived the Duke of Suffolk asked her if she would go and pay her respects to "the Princess." "I know of no other princess but myself," replied Mary. "The daughter of Lady Pembroke has no right to such a title. But," added she, "as the King acknowledges her I may call her sister, as I call the Duke of Richmond brother." Mary was the true daughter of her proud mother, and bluff Charles Brandon got many a tart answer from her before he gave her up in despair to perform a similar mission to her mother at Buckden.

Katharine had never changed her tone. Knowing Henry's weakness, she had always pressed for the final Papal decision in her favour, which she insisted would bring her husband to his knees, as it doubtless would have done if he had stood alone. For a time the Pope and the King of France endeavoured to find a *via media* which should save appearances, for Charles would not bind himself to carry out by force the Papal deposition of Henry, which Clement wanted. But Katharine would have no compromise, nor did it suit Cromwell or Anne, though the former was apparently anxious to avoid offending the Emperor. Parliament, moreover, was summoned for the 15th January 1534, to give the sanction of the nation to Henry's final defiance of Rome; and persistence in the path to which the King's desire for a son and his love for Anne had dragged England, was now the only course open to him. Suffolk and a deputation of councillors were consequently sent once more with an ultimatum to Katharine. Accompanied by a large armed force to intimidate the Queen and the people who surrounded her, the deputation saw her on the 18th December; and Suffolk demanded that she should recognise Cranmer's decision and abandon her appeal to Rome; whilst her household and herself were to take the oath of allegiance to the King in the new form provided. The alternative was that she should be deprived of her servants and be removed to Fotheringay or Somersame, seated in the midst of pestilential marshes. Suffolk was rough in his manner, and made short work of the English household, nearly all of whom were dismissed and replaced by others; but he found Katharine the same hard woman as ever. Considering all the King had done for her and hers, he said, it was disgraceful that she should worry him as she had done for years, putting him to vast expense in embassies to Rome and elsewhere, and keeping him in turmoil with his neighbours. Surely she had grown tired of her obstinacy by this time, and would abandon her appeal to Rome. If she did so the King would do anything for her; but if not he would clip her wings and effectually punish her. As a beginning, he said, they were going to remove her to Fotheringay. Katharine had heard such talk many times before, though less rudely worded; and she replied in the usual tone. She looked to the Pope alone, and cared nothing for the Archbishop of Canterbury. As for going to Fotheringay, that she would not do. The King might work his will; but unless she was dragged thither by main force she would not go, or she would be guilty of suicide, so unhealthy was the place.

Some of the members of the household were recalcitrant, and the two priests, Abell and Barker, were sent to the Tower. The aged Spanish Bishop of Llandaff, Jorge de Ateca, the Queen's confessor, was also warned that he must go, and De la Sá, her apothecary, and a physician, both Spaniards; but at her earnest prayers they were allowed to remain pending an appeal. The Queen's women attendants were also told they must depart, but upon Katharine saying that she would not undress or go to bed unless she had proper help, two of them were allowed to stay. For a whole week the struggle went on, every device and threat being employed to break down the Queen's resistance. She was as hard as adamant. All the servants who remained but the Spaniards, who spoke no English, had to swear not to treat her as Queen, and she said she would treat them as gaolers. On the sixth day of Suffolk's stay at Buckden, pack animals were got ready, and preparations made for removing the establishment to Fotheringay. But they still had to reckon with Katharine. Locking herself in her chamber, she carried on a colloquy with her oppressors through a chink in the wall. "If you wish to take me," she declared, "you must break down my door;" but, though the country gentlemen around had been summoned to the aid of the King's commissioners, and the latter were well armed, such was the ferment and indignation in the neighbourhood— and indeed throughout the country— that violence was felt to be unwise, and Katharine was left in such peace as she might enjoy. Well might Suffolk write, as he did, to Norfolk: "We find here the most obstinate woman that may be; inasmuch as we think surely there is no other remedy than to convey her by force to Somersame. Concerning this we have nothing in our instructions; we pray your good lordship that we may have knowledge of the King's pleasure." All this petty persecution was, of course, laid at the door of Anne by Katharine's friends and the Catholic majority; for Cromwell was clever in avoiding his share of the responsibility. "The lady," they said, "would never be satisfied until both the Queen and her daughter had been done to death, either by poison or otherwise; and Katharine was warned to take care to fasten securely the door of her chamber at night, and to have the room searched before she retired.

In the meantime England and France were drifting further apart. If Henry finally decided to brave the Papal excommunication, Francis dared not make common cause with him. The Bishop of Paris (Du Bellay) once more came over, and endeavoured to find a way out of the maze. Anne, whom he had befriended before, received him effusively, kissing him on the cheek and exerting all her witchery upon him;

but it was soon found that he brought an ultimatum from his King; and when Henry began to bully him and abuse Francis for deserting him, the bishop cowed him with a threat of immediate war. The compromise finally arrived at was that if the Pope before the following Easter (1534) would withdraw his sentence against Henry, England would remain within the pale of the Church. Otherwise the measure drafted for presentation to Parliament entirely throwing off the Papal supremacy would be proceeded with. This was the parting of the ways, and the decision was left to Clement VII.

Parliament opened on the 15th January, perhaps the most fateful assembly that ever met at Westminster. The country, as we have seen, was indignant at the treatment of Katharine and her daughter, but the instinct of loyalty to the King was strong, and there was no powerful centre around which revolt might crystallise. The clergy especially— even those who, like Stokesley, Fox, and Gardiner, were Henry's instruments— dreaded the great changes that portended; and an attempt to influence Parliament by a declaration of the clergy in Convocation against the King's first marriage, failed, notwithstanding the flagrant violence with which signatures were sought. With difficulty, even though the nobles known to favour Katharine were not summoned, a bill granting a dowry to the Queen as Dowager Princess of Wales was passed; but the House of Commons, trembling for the English property in the imperial dominions, threw it out. The prospect for a time looked black for the great ecclesiastical changes that were contemplated, and the hopes of Katharine's friends rose again.

The Bishop of Paris in the meanwhile had contrived to frighten Clement and his Cardinals, by his threatening talk of English schism and the universal spread of dissent, into an insincere and half-hearted acquiescence in a compromise that would submit the question of a divorce to a tribunal of two Cardinals sitting at Cambray to save appearances, and deciding in favour of Henry. When the French ambassador Castillon came to Henry with this news (early in March 1534) the King had experienced the difficulty of bringing Parliament and Convocation to his views; and, again, if left to himself, he would probably have yielded. But Anne and Cromwell, and indeed Cranmer, were now in the same boat; and any wavering on the part of the King would have meant ruin to them all. They did their best to stiffen Henry, but he was nearly inclined to give way behind their backs; and after the French ambassador had left the Council unsuccessful, Henry had a long secret talk with him in the garden, in which he assured him that he would not have anything done hastily against the Holy See.

But whilst the rash and turbulent Bishop of Paris was hectoring Clement at Rome and sending unjustifiably encouraging messages to England, circumstances on both sides were working against the compromise which the French desired so much. Cromwell and Anne were panic-stricken at the idea of reopening the question of the marriage before any Papal tribunal, and kept up Henry's resentment against the Pope. Henry's pride also was wounded by a suggestion of the French that, as a return for Clement's pliability, Alexander de Medici, Duke of Florence, might marry the Princess Mary. Cromwell's diplomatic management of the Parliamentary opposition and the consequent passage of the bill abolishing the remittance of Peter's pence to Rome, also encouraged Henry to think that he might have his own way after all; and the chances of his making further concessions to the Pope again diminished. A similar process was going on in Rome. Whilst Clement was smilingly listening to talk of reconciliation for the sake of keeping England under his authority, he well knew that Henry could only be moved by fear; and all the thunderbolts of the Church were being secretly forged to launch upon the King of England.

On the 23rd March 1534 the consistory of Cardinals sat, the French Cardinals being absent; and the final judgment on the validity of Henry's marriage with Katharine was given by the head of the Church. The cause which had stirred Europe for five years was settled beyond appeal so far as the Roman Church could settle it. Katharine was Henry's lawful wife, and Anne Boleyn was proclaimed by the Church to be his concubine. Almost on the very day that the gage was thus thrown down by the Pope, Henry had taken similar action on his own account. In the previous sitting of Parliament the King had been practically acknowledged as head of the Church in his own dominions; and now all appeals and payments to the Pope were forbidden, and the bishops of England were entirely exempt from his spiritual jurisdiction and control. To complete the emancipation of the country from the Papacy, on the 23rd March 1534 a bill (the Act of Succession) was read for the third time, confirming the legality of the marriage of Henry and Anne, and settling the succession to the crown upon their issue to the exclusion of the Princess Mary. Cranmer's divorce decision was thus ratified by statute; and any person questioning in word or print the legitimacy of Elizabeth's birth was adjudged guilty of high treason. Every subject of the King, moreover, was to take oath to maintain this statute on pain of death. The consummation was reached: for good or for evil England was free from Rome, and the fair woman for whose sake the momentous change had been wrought, sat planning schemes of vengeance against the two proud princesses, mother and daughter, who still refused to bow the neck to her whom they proclaimed the usurper of their rights.

CHAPTER VI

1534~1536

A FLEETING TRIUMPH—POLITICAL INTRIGUE AND THE BETRAYAL OF ANNE

In the previous pages we have witnessed the process by which a vain, arrogant man, naturally lustful and held by no moral or material restraint, had been drawn into a position which, when he took the first step that led to it, he could not have contemplated. In ordinary circumstances there would have been no insuperable difficulty in his obtaining a divorce, and he probably expected little. The divorce, however, in this case involved the question of a change in the national alliance and a shifting of the weight of England to the side of France; and the Emperor by his power over the Pope had been able to frustrate the design, not entirely on account of his family connection with Katharine, but rather as a question of international policy. The dependent position of the Pope had effectually stood in the way of the compromise always sought by France, and the resistance to his will had made Henry the more determined to assert himself, with the natural result that the dispute had developed into religious schism. There is a school of historians which credits Henry personally with the far-reaching design of shaking off the ecclesiastical control of Rome in order to augment the national greatness; but there seems to me little evidence to support the view. When once the King had bearded the Papacy, rather than retrace the steps he had taken and confess himself wrong, it was natural that many of his subjects who conscientiously leant towards greater freedom in religion than Rome would allow, were prepared to carry the lesson further, as the German Lutherans had done, but I can find no reason to believe that Henry desired to initiate any change of system in the direction of freedom: his aim being, as he himself said, simply to make himself Pope as well as King within his own realm. Even that position, as we have seen in the aforegoing chapters, was only reached gradually under the incentive of opposition, and by the aid of stouter hearts and clearer brains than his own: and if Henry could have had his way about the marriage, as he conceivably might have done on many occasions during the struggle by a very slight change in the circumstances, there would have been, so far as he personally was concerned, no Reformation in England at the time.

One of the most curious phases in the process here described is the deterioration notable in Henry's character as the ecclesiastical and moral restraints that influenced him were gradually cast aside. We have seen him as a kind and courteous husband, not more immoral than other men of his age and station; a father whose love for his children was intense; and a cultured gentleman of a headstrong but not unlovable character. Resistance to his will had touched his pride and hardened his heart, until at the period which we have now reached (1534) we see him capable of brutal and insulting treatment of his wife and elder daughter, of which any gentleman would be ashamed. On the other hand, the attitude of Katharine and Mary was exactly that best calculated to drive to fury a conceited, overbearing man, loving his supreme power as Henry did. It was, of course, heroic and noble of the two ladies to stand upon their undoubted rights as they did; but if Katharine by adopting a religious life had consented to a divorce, the decree of nullity would not have been pronounced; her own position would have been recognised, her daughter's legitimacy saved, and the separation from Rome at least deferred, if not prevented. There was no such deterioration in Anne's character as in that of Henry; for it was bad from the first, and consistently remained so. Her ambition was the noblest trait in her nature; and she served it with a petty personal malignity against those who seemed to stand in her way that goes far to deprive her of the pity that otherwise would go out to her in her own martyrdom at the hands of the fleshly tyrant whose evil nature she had been so greatly instrumental in developing.

It was undoubtedly to Anne's prompting that the ungenerous treatment of the Princess Mary was due, a treatment that aroused the indignation even of those to whom its execution was entrusted. Henry was deeply attached to his daughter, but it touched his pride for her to refuse to submit without protest to his behest. When Norfolk told him of the attitude of the Princess on her being taken to Hatfield to attend upon Elizabeth, he decided to bring his parental authority to bear upon her personally, and decided to see her. But Anne, "considering the easiness or rather levity of the King, and that the great beauty and goodness of the Princess might overcome his displeasure with her, and, moved by her virtues and his fatherly pity for her, be induced to treat her better and restore her title to her, sent Cromwell and other messengers posting after the King to prevent him, at any cost, from seeing or speaking to the Princess." When Henry arrived at Hatfield and saw his baby daughter Elizabeth, the elder Princess begged to be allowed to salute him. The request was not granted; but when the King mounted his horse in the courtyard Mary stood upon a terrace above to see him. The King was informed of her presence, or saw her by chance; and, as she caught his eye, she threw herself upon her knees in an attitude of prayer, whereupon the father touched his bonnet, and bowed low and kindly to the daughter he was wronging so bitterly. He explained afterwards that he avoided speaking to her as she was so obstinate with him, "thanks to her Spanish blood." When the French ambassador mentioned her kindly, during the conversation, he noted that Henry's eyes filled with tears, and that he could not refrain from praising her. But for Anne's jealousy for her own offspring, it is probable that Mary's legitimacy would have been established by Act of Parliament; as Cromwell at this time was certainly in favour of it: but Anne was ever on the watch, especially to arouse Henry's anger by hinting that Mary was looking to foreigners for counsel, as indeed she was. It was this latter element in which danger principally lurked. Katharine naturally appealed to her kin for support; and all through her trouble it was this fact, joined with her firm refusal to acknowledge Henry's supreme power, that steeled her husband's heart. But for the King's own daughter and undoubted born subject to act in the same way made her, what her mother never had been, a dangerous centre around which the disaffected elements might gather. The old nobility, as we have seen, were against Anne: and Henry quite understood the peril of having in his own family a person who commanded the sympathies of the strongest foreign powers in Europe, as well as the most influential elements in England. He angrily told the Marquis of Exeter that it was only confidence in the Emperor that made Mary so obstinate; but that he was not afraid of the Emperor, and would bring the girl to her senses: and he then went on to threaten Exeter himself if he dared to communicate with her. The same course was soon afterwards taken with Norfolk, who as well as his wife was forbidden to see the Princess, although he certainly had shown no desire to extend much leniency to her.

The treatment of Katharine was even more atrocious, though in her case it was probably more the King's irritated pride than his fears that was the incentive. When the wretched Elizabeth Barton, the Nun of Kent, was prosecuted for her crazy prophecies against the King every possible effort was made to connect the unfortunate Queen with her, though unsuccessfully, and the attempt to force Katharine to take the oath prescribed by the new Act of Succession against herself and her daughter was obviously a piece of persecution and insult. The Commission sent to Buckden to extort the new oath of allegiance to Henry, and to Anne as Queen, consisted of Dr. Lee, the Archbishop of York, Dr. Tunstall, Bishop of Durham; and the Bishop of Chester; and the scene as described by one of the Spanish servants is most curious. When the demand was made that she should take the oath of allegiance to Anne as Queen, Katharine with fine scorn replied, "Hold thy peace, bishop: speak to me no more. These are the wiles of the devil. I am Queen, and Queen will I die: by right the King can have no other wife, and let this be your answer." Assembling her household, she addressed them, and told them they could not without sin swear allegiance to the King and Anne in a form that would deny the supreme spiritual authority of the Pope: and taking counsel with her Spanish chamberlain, Francisco Felipe, they settled between them that the Spaniards should answer interrogatories in Spanish in such a way that by a slight mispronunciation their answer could be interpreted, "I acknowledge that the King has made himself head of the Church" (*se ha hecho cabeza de la iglesia*), whereas the Commissioners would take it as meaning "that the King be created head of the Church" (*sea hecho cabeza de la iglesia*); and on the following morning the wily chamberlain and his countrymen saved appearances and their consciences at the same time by a pun. But when the formal oath of allegiance to Anne was demanded, Felipe, speaking for the rest, replied, "I have taken one oath of allegiance to my lady Queen Katharine. She still lives, and during her life I know no other Queen in this realm." Lee then threatened them with punishment for refusal, and a bold Burgundian lackey, Bastian, burst out with, "Let the King banish us, but let him not order us to be perjurers." The bishop in a rage told him to begone at once; and, nothing loath, Bastian knelt at his mistress's feet and bade her farewell; taking horse at once to ride to the coast. Katharine in tears remonstrated with Lee for dismissing her servant without reference to her; and the bishop, now that his anger was calmed, sent messengers to fetch Bastian back; which they did not do until he had reached London.

This fresh indignity aroused Katharine's friends both in England and abroad. The Emperor had already remonstrated with the English ambassador on the reported cruel treatment of the Queen and her daughter, and Henry now endeavoured to justify himself in a long letter (June 1534). As for the Queen, he said, she was being treated "in everything to the best that can be devised, whom we do order and entertain as we think most expedient, and as to us seemeth prudent. And the like also of our daughter the Lady Mary: for we think it not meet that any person should prescribe unto us how we should order our own daughter, we being her natural father." He expressed himself greatly hurt that the Emperor should think him capable of acting unkindly, notwithstanding that the Lady Katharine "hath very disobediently behaved herself towards us, as well in contemning and setting at naught our laws and statutes, as in many other ways." Just lately, he continues, he had sent three bishops to exhort her, "in most loving fashion," to obey the law; and "she hath in most ungodly, obstinate, and inobedient wise, wilfully resisted, set at naught and contemned our laws and ordinances: so if we would administer to her any rigour or extremity she were undoubtedly within the extreme danger of our laws."

The blast of persecution swept over the land. The oaths demanded by the new statutes were stubbornly resisted by many. Fisher and More, as learned and noble as any men in the land, were sent to the Tower (April 1534) to be entrapped and done to death a year later. Throughout the country the Commissioners with plenary powers were sent to administer the new oaths, and those citizens who cavilled at taking them were treated as traitors to the King. But all this did not satisfy Anne whilst Katharine and Mary remained recalcitrant and unpunished for the same offence. Henry was in dire fear, however, of some action of the Emperor in enforcement of the Papal excommunication against him and his kingdom, which according to the Catholic law he had forfeited by the Pope's ban. Francis, willing as he was to oppose the Emperor, dared not expose his own kingdom to excommunication by siding with Henry, and the latter was statesman enough to see, as indeed was Cromwell, that extreme measures against Mary would turn all Christendom against him, and probably prove the last unbearable infliction that would drive his own people to aid a foreign invasion. So, although Anne sneered at the King's weakness, as she called it, and eagerly anticipated his projected visit to Francis, during which she would remain Regent in England, and be able to wreak her wicked will on the young Princess, the King, held by political fear, and probably, too, by some fatherly regard, refused to be nagged by his wife into the murder of his daughter, and even relinquished the meeting with Francis rather than leave England with Anne in power.

In the meanwhile Katharine's health grew worse. Henry told the French ambassador in January, soon after Suffolk's attempt to administer the first oath to her, that "she was dropsical and could not live long": and his enemies were ready with the suggestion— which was probably unfounded— that she was being poisoned. She shut herself up in her own chamber, and refused to eat the food prepared by the new servants; what little food she took being cooked in her own room by her one maid. Early in the summer (May) she was removed from Buckden to Kimbolton Castle, within the miasmic influence of the fens, and there was no attempt to conceal the desire on the part of the King and those who had brought him to this pass that Katharine should die, for by that means alone, it seemed, could foreign intervention and civil war be averted. Katharine herself was, as we have seen, full of suspicion. In March Chapuys reported that she had sent a man to London to procure some old wine for her, as she refused to drink the wine provided for her use. "They were trying," he said, "to give her artificial dropsy." Two months later, just after the stormy scene when Lee and Tunstall had endeavoured to extort from the Queen the oath to the new Act of Succession, Chapuys in hot indignation suddenly appeared at Richmond, where the King was, to protest against such treatment. Henry was intensely annoyed and offended, and refused to see the ambassador. He was master, he said, in his own realm; and it was no good coming to him with such remonstrances. No wonder that Chapuys concluded, "Everybody fears some ill turn will be done to the Queen, seeing the rudeness to which she is daily subjected, both in deeds and words; especially as the concubine has said that she will not cease till she has got rid of her; and as the prophecies say that one Queen of England is to be burnt, she hopes it will be Katharine."

Early in June Katharine urged strongly that Chapuys should travel to Kimbolton to see her, alleging the bad condition of her health as a reason. The King and Cromwell believed that her true object in desiring an interview was to devise plans with her nephew's ambassador for obtaining the enforcement of the papal censure, which would have meant the subversion of Henry's power; and for weeks Chapuys begged for permission to see her in vain. "Ladies were not to be trusted," Cromwell told him; whilst fresh Commissioners were sent, one after the other, to extort, by force if necessary, the oath of Katharine's lady attendants to the Act of Succession, much to the Queen's distress. At length, tired of waiting, the ambassador told Cromwell that he was determined to start at once; which he did two days later, on the 16th July. With a train of sixty horsemen, his own household and Spaniards resident in England, he rode through London towards the eastern counties, ostensibly on a religious pilgrimage to Our Lady of Walsingham. Riding through the leafy lanes of Hertfordshire in the full summer tide, solaced by music, minstrelsy, and the quaint antics of Chapuys' fool, the party were surprised on the second day of their journey to see gallop past them on the road Stephen Vaughan, one of the King's officers who spoke Spanish; and later, when they had arrived within a few miles of Kimbolton, they were met by the same man, accompanied this time by a humble servitor of Katharine, bringing to the pilgrims wine and provisions in abundance, but also the ill news that the King had ordered that Chapuys was to be forbidden access to the Queen. The ambassador was exceedingly indignant. He did not wish to offend the King, he said, but, having come so far and being now in the immediate neighbourhood, he would not return unsuccessful without an effort to obtain a more authoritative decision. Early the next morning one of Katharine's old officers came to Chapuys and repeated the prohibition, begging him not even to pass through the village, lest the King should take it ill. Other messages passed, but all to the same effect. Poor Katharine herself sent secret word that she was as thankful for Chapuys' journey as if it had been successful, and hinted that it would be a consolation to her if some of her countrymen could at least approach the castle. Needless to say that the Spaniards gathered beneath the walls of the castle and chatted gallantly across the moat to the ladies upon the terraces, and some indeed, including the jester, are asserted to have found their way inside the castle, where they were regaled heartily, and the fool played some of the usual tricks of his motley. Chapuys, in high dudgeon, returned by another road to London without attempting to complete his pilgrimage to Walsingham, secretly spied upon as he was, the whole way, by the King's envoy, Vaughan. "Tell Cromwell," he said to the latter, as he discovered himself on the outskirts of London, "that I should have judged it more honourable if the King and he had informed me of his intention before I left London, so that all the world should not have been acquainted with a proceeding which I refrain from characterising. But the Queen," he continued, "nevertheless had cause to thank him (Cromwell) since the rudeness shown to her would now be so patent that it could not well be denied."

Henry and Cromwell had good reason to fear foreign machinations to their detriment. The Emperor and Francis were in ominous negotiations; for the King of France could not afford to break with the Papacy, the rising of Kildare in Ireland was known to have the sympathy, if not the aid, of Spain, and it was felt throughout Christendom that the Emperor must, sooner or later, give force to the Papal sentence against England to avoid the utter loss of prestige which would follow if the ban of Rome was after all seen to be utterly innocuous. A sympathetic English lord told Chapuys secretly that Cromwell had ridiculed the idea of the Emperor's attacking England; for his subjects would not put up with the consequent loss of trade. But if he did, continued Cromwell, "the death of Katharine and Mary would put an end to all the trouble." Chapuys told his informant, for Cromwell's behoof, that if any harm was done to either of the ladies the Emperor would have the greater cause for quarrel.

In the autumn Mary fell seriously ill. She had been obliged to follow "the bastard," Elizabeth, against her will, for ever intriguing cleverly to avoid humiliation to herself. But the long struggle against such odds broke down her health, and Henry, who, in his heart of hearts, could hardly condemn his daughter's stubbornness, so like his own, softened to the extent of his sending his favourite physician, Dr. Butts, to visit her. A greater concession was to allow Katharine's two medical men to attend the Princess; and permission was given to Katharine herself to see her, but under conditions which rendered the concession nugatory. The Queen wrote a pathetic letter in Spanish to Cromwell, praying that Mary might be permitted to come and stay with her. "It will half cure her," she urged. As a small boon, Henry had consented that the sick girl should be sent to a house at no great distance from Kimbolton. "Alas!" urged Katharine, "if it be only a mile away, I cannot visit her. I beseech that she be allowed to come to where I am. I will answer for her security with my life." But Cromwell or his master was full of suspicion of imperial plots for the escape of Mary to foreign soil, and Katharine's maternal prayer remained unheard.

The unhappy mother tried again soon afterwards to obtain access to her sick daughter by means of Chapuys. She besought for charity's sake that the King would allow her to tend Mary with her own hands. "You shall also tell his Highness that there is no need for any other person but myself to nurse her: I will put her in my own bed where I sleep, and will watch her when needful." When Chapuys saw the King with this pathetic message Henry was less arrogant than usual. "He wished to do his best for his daughter's health; but he must be careful of his own honour and interests, which would be jeopardised if Mary were conveyed abroad, or if she escaped, as she easily might do if she were with her mother; for he had some suspicion that the Emperor had a design to get her away." Henry threw all the blame for Mary's obstinacy upon Katharine, who he knew was in close and constant touch with his opponents: and the fear he expressed that the Emperor and his friends in England would try to spirit Mary across the sea to Flanders, where, indeed, she might have been made a thorn in her father's side, were perfectly well founded, and these plans were at the time the gravest peril that threatened Henry and England.

Cruel, therefore, as his action towards his daughter may seem, it was really prompted by pressing considerations of his own safety. Apart from this desire to keep Mary away from foreign influence working against him through her mother, Henry exhibited frequent signs of tenderness towards his elder daughter, much to Anne's dismay. In May 1534, for instance, he sent her a gentle message to the effect that he hoped she would obey him, and that in such case her position would be preserved. But the girl was proud and, not unnaturally, resentful, and sent back a haughty answer to what she thought was an attempt to entrap her. To her foreign friends she said that she believed her father meant to poison her, but that she cared little. She was sure of going to heaven, and was only sorry for her mother.

In the meanwhile Anne's influence over the King was weakening. She saw the gathering clouds from all parts of Christendom ready to launch their lightning upon her head, and ruin upon England for her sake; and her temper, never good, became intolerable. Henry, having had his way, was now face to face with the threatening consequences, and could ill brook snappish petulance from the woman for whom he had brought himself to brave the world. As usual with weak men, he pitied himself sincerely, and looked around for comfort, finding none from Anne. Francis, eldest son of the Church and most Christian King, was far from being the genial ally he once had been, now that Henry was excommunicate; the German Protestant princes even stood apart and rejected Henry's approaches for an alliance to the detriment of their own suzerain; and, worst of all, the English lords of the North, Hussey, Dacre, and the rest of them, were in close conspiracy with the imperialists for an armed rising aided from abroad; which, if successful, would make short work of Henry and his anti-Papal policy. In return for all this danger, the King could only look at the cross, discontented woman by his side, who apparently was as incapable of bearing him a son as Katharine had been. For some months in the spring of 1534 Anne had endeavoured to retain her hold upon him by saying that she was again with child, and during the royal progress in the midland counties in the summer Henry was more attentive than he had been to the woman he still hoped might bear him a son, although her shrewish temper sorely tried him and all around her. At length, however, the truth had to be told, and Henry's hopes fled, and his eyes again turned elsewhere for solace.

Anne knew that her position was unstable, and her husband's open flirtation with a lady of the Court drove her to fury. Presuming upon her former influence, she imperiously attempted to have her new rival removed from the proximity of the King. Henry flared up at this, and let Anne know, as brutally as language could put it, that the days of his complaisance with her were over, and that he regretted having done so much for her sake. Who the King's new lady-love was is not certain. Chapuys calls her "a very beautiful and adroit young lady, for whom his love is daily increasing, whilst the credit and insolence of the concubine (*i.e.* Anne) decreases." That the new favourite was supported by the aristocratic party that opposed Anne and the religious changes is evident from Chapuys' remark that "there is some good hope that if this love of the King's continues the affairs of the Queen (Katharine) and the Princess will prosper, for the young lady is greatly attached to them." Anne and her family struggled to keep their footing, but when Henry had once plucked up courage to shake off the trammels, he had all a weak man's violence and obstinacy in following his new course. One of Princess Mary's household came to tell Chapuys in October that "the King had turned Lady Rochford (Anne's sister-in-law) out of the Court because she had conspired with the concubine by hook or by crook to get rid of the young lady." The rise of the new favourite immediately changed the attitude of the courtiers towards Mary. "On Wednesday before leaving the More she (Mary) was visited by all the ladies and gentlemen, regardless of the annoyance of Anne. The day before yesterday (October 22nd) the Princess was at Richmond with the brat (*garse, i.e.* Elizabeth), and the lady (Anne) came to see her daughter accompanied by the Dukes of Norfolk and Suffolk and others, all of whom went and saluted the Princess (Mary) with some of the ladies; which was quite a new thing."

The death of Pope Clement and the advent of Cardinal Farnese as Paul III., known to be not too well affected towards the Emperor, seemed at this time to offer a chance of the reconciliation of England with the Papacy: and the aristocratic party in Henry's counsels hoped, now that the King had grown tired of his second wife, that they might influence him by a fresh appeal to his sensuality. France also took a hand in the game in its new aspect, the aim being to obtain the hand of Mary for the Dauphin, to whom, it will be recollected, she had been betrothed as a child, with the legitimisation of the Princess and the return of Henry to the fold of the Church with a French alliance. This would, of course, have involved the repudiation of Anne, with the probable final result of a French domination of England after the

King's death. The Admiral of France, Chabot de Brion, came to England late in the autumn to forward some such arrangement as that described, and incidentally to keep alive Henry's distrust of the Emperor, whilst threatening him that the Dauphin would marry a Spanish princess if the King of England held aloof. But, though Anne's influence over her husband was gone, Cromwell, the strong spirit, was still by his side; and reconciliation with the Papacy in any form would have meant ruin to him and the growing interests that he represented.

Even if Henry had now been inclined to yield to the Papacy, of which there is no evidence, Cromwell had gone too far to recede; and when Parliament met in November the Act of Supremacy was passed, giving the force of statute law to the independence of the Church of England. Chabot de Brion's mission was therefore doomed to failure from the first, and the envoy took no pains to conceal his resentment towards Anne, the origin of all the trouble that dislocated the European balance of power. There was much hollow feasting and insincere professions of friendship between the two kings, but it was clear now to the Frenchmen that, with Anne or without her, Henry would bow his neck no more to the Papacy; and it was to the Princess Mary that the Catholic elements looked for a future restoration of the old state of things. A grand ball was given at Court in Chabot's honour the day before he left London, and the dignified French envoy sat in a seat of state by the side of Anne, looking at the dancing. Suddenly, without apparent reason, she burst into a violent fit of laughter. The Admiral of France, already in no very amiable mood, frowned angrily, and, turning to her, said, "Are you laughing at me, madam, or what?" After she had laughed to her heart's content, she excused herself to him by saying that she was laughing because the King had told her that he was going to fetch the Admiral's secretary to be introduced to her, and on the way the King had met a lady who had made him forget everything else.

Though Henry would not submit to the Papacy at the charming of Francis, he was loath to forego the French alliance, and proposed a marriage between the younger French prince, the Duke of Angoulême, and Elizabeth; and this was under discussion during the early months of 1535. But it is clear that, although the daughter of the second marriage was to be held legitimate, Anne was to gain no accession of strength by the new alliance, for the French flouted her almost openly, and Henry was already contemplating a divorce from her. We are told by Chapuys that he only desisted from the idea when a councillor told him that "if he separated from 'the concubine' he would have to recognise the validity of his first marriage, and, worst of all, submit to the

Pope." Who the councillor was that gave this advice is not stated; but we may fairly assume that it was Cromwell, who soon found a shorter, and, for him, a safer way of ridding his master of a wife who had tired him and could bear him no son. A French alliance, with a possible reconciliation with Rome in some form, would not have suited Cromwell; for it would have meant a triumph for the aristocratic party at Henry's Court, and the overthrow of the men who had led Henry to defy the Papacy.

If the aristocratic party could influence Henry by means of the nameless "new young lady," the Boleyns and reformers could fight with the same weapons, and early in February 1535 we find Chapuys writing, "The young lady formerly in this King's good graces is so no longer, and has been succeeded by a cousin-german of the concubine, the daughter of the present governess of the Princess." This new mistress, whilst her little reign lasted, worked well for Anne and Cromwell, but in the meantime the conspiracy amongst the nobles grew and strengthened. Throughout the upper classes in the country a feeling of deep resentment was felt at the treatment of Mary, and there was hardly a nobleman, except Anne's father and brother, who was not pledged to take up arms in her cause and against the religious changes. Cromwell's answer to the disaffection, of which he was quite cognisant, was the closer keeping than ever of the royal ladies, with threats of their death if they were the cause of a revolt, and the stern enforcement of the oath prescribed by the Act of Supremacy. The martyrdom of the London Carthusians for refusing to take the oath of supremacy, and shortly afterwards the sacrifice of the venerable Bishop Fisher, Sir Thomas More and Katharine's priest Abel, and the renewed severity towards her favourite confessor, Friar Forest, soon also to be martyred with atrocious cruelty, shocked and horrified England, and aroused the strongest reprobation in France and Rome, as well as in the dominions of the Emperor; destroying for a time all hope of a French alliance, and any lingering chance of a reconciliation with Rome during Henry's life. All Catholic aspirations both at home and abroad centred for the next year or so in the Princess Mary, and her father's friendship was shunned even by Francis, except upon impossible conditions. Henry's throne, indeed, was tottering. His country was riddled with disaffection and dislike of his proceedings. The new Pope had forged the final thunderbolt of Rome, enjoining all Christian potentates to execute the sentence of the Church, though as yet the fiat was held back at the instance of the Emperor. The dread of war and the general unrest arising from this state of things had well-nigh destroyed the English oversea trade; the harvest was a bad one, and food was dear. Ecclesiastics throughout the country were whispering to their flocks curses of Nan Bullen, for whose sake the Church of Christ was being split in twain and its ministers persecuted. Anne, it is true, was now quite a secondary personage as a political factor, but upon her unpopular head was heaped the blame for everything. The wretched woman, fully conscious that she was the general scapegoat, could only pray for a son, whose advent might save her at the eleventh hour; for failing him she knew that she was doomed.

In the meanwhile the struggle was breaking Katharine's heart. For seven years she had fought as hard against her fate as an outraged woman could. She had seen that her rights, her happiness, were only a small stake in the great game of European politics. To her it seemed but righteous that her nephew the Emperor should, at any cost, rise in indignant wrath and avenge the insult put upon his proud line, and upon the Papacy whose earthly champion he was, by crushing the forces that had wrought the wrong. But Charles was held back by all sorts of considerations arising from his political position. Francis was for ever on the look-out for a weak spot in the imperial armour; the German Protestant princes, although quite out of sympathy with Henry's matrimonial vagaries, would look askance at a crusade to enforce the Pope's executorial decree against England, the French and moderate influence in the College of Cardinals was strong, and Charles could not afford by too aggressive an action against Henry to drive Francis and the cardinals into closer union against imperial aims, especially in the Mediterranean and Italy, where, owing to the vacancy in the duchy of Milan, they now mainly centred. So Katharine clamoured in vain to those whose sacred duty she thought it was to vindicate her honour and the faith. Both she, and her daughter at her instigation, wrote burning letters to the Pope and the imperial agents, urging, beseeching, exhorting the Catholic powers to activity against their oppressor. Henry and Cromwell knew all this, and recognising the dire danger that sooner or later Katharine's prayer to a united Christendom might launch upon England an avalanche of ruin, strove as best they might to avert such a catastrophe. Every courier who went to the Emperor from England carried alarmist rumours that Katharine and Mary were to be put out of the way; and the ladies, in a true spirit of martyrdom, awaited without flinching the hour of their sacrifice. Cromwell himself darkly hinted that the only way out of the maze of difficulty and peril was the death of Katharine; and in this he was apparently right. But at this distance of time it seems evident that much of the threatening talk, both of the King's friends and those of the Catholic Church in

England, was intended, on the one hand to drive Katharine and her daughter into submission, and prevent them from continuing their appeals for foreign aid, and on the other to move the Emperor to action against Henry. So, in the welter of political interests, Katharine wept and raged fruitlessly. The Papal decree directing the execution of the deprivation of Henry, though signed by the Pope, was still held back; for Charles could not afford to invade England himself, and was determined to give no excuse for Francis to do so.

Though there is no known ground for the then prevailing belief that Henry was aiding nature in hastening the death of his first wife, the long unequal combat against invincible circumstances was doing its work upon a constitution never robust; and by the late autumn of 1535 the stout-hearted daughter of Isabel the Catholic was known to be sick beyond surgery. In December 1535 Chapuys had business with Cromwell, and during the course of their conversation the latter told him that he had just sent a messenger to inform the King of Katharine's serious illness. This was the first that Chapuys had heard of it, and he at once requested leave to go and see her, to which Cromwell replied that he might send a servant to inquire as to her condition, but that the King must be consulted before he (Chapuys) himself could be allowed to see her. As Chapuys was leaving Whitehall a letter was brought to him from Katharine's physician, saying that the Queen's illness was not serious, and would pass off; so that unless later unfavourable news was sent Chapuys need not press for leave to see her. Two days afterwards a letter reached him from Katharine herself, enclosing one to the Emperor. She wrote in the deepest depression, praying again, and for the hundredth time, in words that, as Chapuys says, "would move a stone to compassion," that prompt action should be taken on behalf of herself and her daughter before the Parliament could do them to death and consummate the apostasy of England. It was her last heart-broken cry for help, and like all those that had preceded it during the seven bitter years of Katharine's penance, it was unheard amidst the din of great national interests that was ringing through Europe.

It was during the feast of Christmas 1535, which Henry passed at Eltham, that news came to Chapuys from Dr. De la Sá that Katharine had relapsed and was in grave peril. The ambassador was to see the King on other business in a day or two, in any case, but this news caused him to beg Cromwell to obtain for him instant leave to go to the Queen. There would be no difficulty about it, the secretary replied, but Chapuys must see the King first at Greenwich, whither he would go to meet him. The ambassador found Henry in the tiltyard all amiability. With a good deal of overdone cordiality, the King walked up and down the lists arm in arm with Chapuys, the while he reverted to the proposal of a new friendship and alliance with the Emperor. The French, he said, were up to their old pranks, especially since the Duke of Milan had died, but he should at last be forced into an intimate alliance with them, unless the Emperor would let bygones be bygones, and make friends with him. Chapuys was cool and non-committal. He feared, he said, that it was only a device to make the French jealous, and after much word-bandying between them, the ambassador flatly asked Henry what he wanted the Emperor to do. "I want him," replied the King, "not only to cease to support Madam Katharine and my daughter, but also to get the Papal sentence in Madam's favour revoked." To this Chapuys replied that he saw no good reason for doing either, and had no authority to discuss the point raised; and, as a parting shot, Henry told him that Katharine could not live long, and when she died the Emperor would have no need to follow the matter up. When Chapuys had taken his leave, the Duke of Suffolk came after him and brought him back to the King, who told him that news had just reached him that Katharine was dying— Chapuys might go and see her, but he would hardly find her alive; her death, moreover, would do away with all cause for dissension between the Emperor and himself. A request that the Princess Mary might be allowed to see her dying mother was at first met with a flat refusal, and after Chapuys' remonstrance by a temporising evasion which was as bad, so that Mary saw her mother no more in life.

Chapuys instantly took horse and sped to London, and then northward to Kimbolton, anxious to reach the Queen before she breathed her last, for he was told that for days the patient had eaten and drank nothing, and slept hardly at all. It took Chapuys two days of hard travel over the miry roads before he reached Kimbolton on the morning of the 2nd January 1536. He found that the Queen's dearest friend, Lady Willoughby (Doña Maria de Sarmiento), had preceded him by a day and was with her mistress. She had prayed in vain for license to come before, and even now Katharine's stern guardian, Bedingfield, asked in vain to see Lady Willoughby's permit, which she probably had not got. She had come in great agitation and fear, for, according to her own account, she had fallen from her horse, and had suffered other adventures on her way, but she braved everything to receive the last sigh of the Queen, whose girlhood's friend she had been. Bedingfield looked askance at the arrival of "these folks"; and at Chapuys' first interview with Katharine he, the chamberlain, and Vaughan who understood

Spanish, were present, and listened to all that was said. It was a consolation, said the Queen, that if she could not recover she might die in
the presence of her nephew's ambassador and not unprepared. He tried
to cheer her with encouraging promises that the King would let her be
removed to another house, and would accede to other requests made
in her favour; but Katharine only smiled sadly, and bade him rest after
his long journey. She saw the ambassador again alone later in the day,
and spoke at length with him, as she did on each day of the four that
he stayed, her principal discourse being of the misfortune that had
overtaken England by reason of the long delay of the Emperor in en-
forcing justice to her.

After four days' stay of Chapuys, Katharine seemed better, and the
apothecary, De la Sá, gave it as his opinion that she was out of immediate danger. She even laughed a little at the antics of Chapuys' fool,
who was called in to amuse her; and, reassured by the apparent im-
provement, the ambassador started on his leisurely return to London. On the second day after his departure, soon after midnight, the
Queen asked if it was near day, and repeated the question several times
at short intervals afterwards. When at length the watchers asked her the
reason for her impatience for the dawn, she replied that it was because
she wished to hear Mass and receive the Holy Sacrament. The aged
Dominican Bishop of Llandaff (Jorge de Ateca) volunteered to cele-
brate at four o'clock in the morning, but Katharine refused, and quoted
the Latin authorities to prove that it should not be done before dawn.
With the first struggling of the grey light of morning the offices of the
Church for the dying were solemnly performed, whilst Katharine
prayed fervently for herself, for England, and for the man who had so
cruelly wronged her. When all was done but the administration of extreme unction, she bade her physician write a short memorandum of a
few gifts she craved for her faithful servants; for she knew, and said,
that by the law of England a married woman could make no valid will.
The testament is in the form of a supplication to Henry, and is remarkable as the dictation of a woman within a few hours of her death. Each
of her servants is remembered: a hundred pounds to her principal
Spanish lady, Blanche de Vargas, "twenty pounds to Mistress Darrel
for her marriage"; his wages and forty pounds were to be paid to Francisco Felipe, the Groom of the Chambers, twenty pounds to each of
the three lackeys, including the Burgundian Bastian, and like bequests,
one by one, to each of the little household. Not even the sum she owed
for a gown was forgotten. For her daughter she craved her furs and the
gold chain and cross she had brought from Spain, all that was left of

her treasures after Anne's greed had been satisfied; and for the Convent of Observant Franciscans, where she begged for sepulture, "my gowns which he (the King) holdeth." It is a sad little document, compliance with which was for the most part meanly evaded by Henry; even Francisco Felipe "getting nothing and returning poor to his own country."

Thus, dignified and saintly, at the second hour after midday on the 8th January 1536, Katharine of Aragon died unconquered as she had lived; a great lady to the last, sacrificed in death, as she had been in life, to the opportunism of high politics. "*In manus tuas Domine commendo spiritum meum*," she murmured with her last breath. From man she had received no mercy, and she turned to a gentler Judge with confidence and hope. As usual in such cases as hers, the people about her whispered of poison; and when the body was hastily cered and lapped in lead, "by the candlemaker of the house, a servant and one companion," not even the Queen's physician was allowed to be present. But the despised "candlemaker," who really seems to have been a skilled embalmer, secretly told the Bishop of Llandaff, who waited at the door, that all the body was sound "except the heart, which was black and hideous," with a black excrescence "which clung closely to the outside"; on which report Dr. De la Sá unhesitatingly opined that his mistress had died of poison.

The news, the joyous news, sped quickly to Greenwich; and within four-and-twenty hours, on Saturday, 9th January, Henry heard with exultation that the incubus was raised from his shoulders. "God be praised," was his first exclamation, "we are free from all suspicion of war." Now, he continued, he would be able to manage the French better. They would be obliged to dance to his tune, for fear he should join the Emperor, which would be easy now that the cause for disagreement had gone. Thus, heartlessly, and haggling meanly over his wife's little bequests, even that to her daughter, Henry greeted the death of the woman he once had seemed to love. He snivelled a little when he read the affecting letter to him that she had dictated in her last hour; but the word went forth that on the next day, Sunday, the Court should be at its gayest; and Henry and Anne, in gala garb of yellow finery, went to Mass with their child in full state to the sound of trumpets. After dinner the King could not restrain his joy even within the bounds of decency. Entering the hall in which the ladies were dancing, he pirouetted about in the exuberance of his heart, and then, calling for his fair little daughter Elizabeth, he proudly carried her in his arms from one courtier to another to be petted and praised. There was only one drop of gall in the cup for the Boleyns, and they made no secret of it, namely, that the Princess Mary had not gone to accompany her mother. If Anne had only known it, her last chance of keeping at the King's side as his wife was the survival of Katharine; and lamentation instead of rejoicing should have been her greeting of the news of her rival's death. Henry, in fact, was tired of Anne already, and the cabal of nobles against her and the religious system she represented was stronger than ever; but the repudiation of his second wife on any excuse during the life of the first would have necessitated the return of Katharine as the King's lawful spouse, with all the consequences that such a change would entail, and this Henry's pride, as well as his inclinations, would never permit. Now that Katharine was dead, Anne was doomed to speedy ruin by one instrumentality or another, and before many weeks the cruel truth came home to her.

Katharine was buried not in such a convent as she had wished, for Henry said there was not one in England, but in Peterborough Cathedral, within fifteen miles of Kimbolton. The honours paid to her corpse were those of a Dowager Princess of Wales, but the country folk who bordered the miry tracks through which the procession ploughed paid to the dead Katharine in her funeral litter the honours they had paid her in her life. Parliament, far away in London, might order them to swear allegiance to Nan Bullen as Queen, and to her daughter as heiress of England; King Harry on his throne might threaten them, as he did, with stake and gibbet if they dared to disobey; but, though they bowed the head and mumbled such oaths as were dictated to them, Katharine to them had always been Queen Consort of England, and Mary her daughter was no bastard, but true Princess of Wales, whatever King and Parliament might say.

All people and all interests were, as if instinctively, shrinking away from Anne. Her uncle Norfolk had quarrelled with her and retired from Court; the French were now almost as inimical as the imperialists; and even the time-serving courtiers turned from the waning favourite. She was no longer young, and her ill temper and many anxieties had marred her good looks. Her gaiety and lightness of manner had to a great extent fled; and sedate occupations, reading, needlework, charity, and devotion occupied most of her time. "Oh for a son!" was all the unhappy woman could sigh in her misery; for that, she knew, was the only thing that could save her, now that Katharine was dead and Anne might be repudiated by her husband without the need for taking back his first discarded wife. Hope existed again that the prayed-for son might come into the world, and at the first prospect of it Anne made an attempt to utilise the influence it gave her by cajoling or crushing Mary into submission to the King's will. The girl was desolate at her mother's death; but she had her mother's proud spirit, and her answers to Anne's approaches were as cold and haughty as before. "The concubine (writes Chapuys, 21st January 1536) has thrown out the first bait to the Princess, telling her by her aunt (Lady Shelton) that if she will discontinue her obstinacy, and obey her father like a good girl, she (Anne) will be the best friend in the world to her, and like another mother will try to obtain for her all she wants. If she will come to Court she shall be exempt from carrying her (Anne's) train and shall always walk by her side." But obedience meant that Mary should recognise Cranmer's sentence against her mother, the repudiation of the Papal authority and her own illegitimacy, and she refused the olive branch held out to her. Then Anne changed her tone, and wrote to her aunt a letter to be put into Mary's way, threatening the Princess. In her former approaches, she said, she had only desired to save Mary out of charity. It was no affair of hers: she did not care; but when she had the son she expected the King would show no mercy to his rebellious daughter. But Mary remained unmoved. She knew that all Catholic Europe looked upon her now as the sole heiress of England, and that the Emperor was busy planning her escape, in order that she might, from the safe refuge of his dominions, be used as the main instrument for the submission of England to the Papacy and the destruction of Henry's rule. For things had turned out somewhat differently in this respect from what the King had expected. The death of Katharine, very far from making the armed intervention of Charles in England more improbable, had brought it sensibly nearer, for the great war-storm that had long been looming between the French and Spaniards in Italy was now about to burst. Francis could no longer afford to alienate the Papacy by even pretending to a friendship with the excommunicated Henry, whilst England might be paralysed, and all chance of a diversion against imperial arms in favour of France averted, by the slight aid and subsidy by the Emperor of a Catholic rising in England against Henry and Anne.

On the 29th January 1536 Anne's last hope was crushed. In the fourth month of her pregnancy she had a miscarriage, which she attributed passionately to her love for the King and her pain at seeing him flirting with another woman. Henry showed his rage and disappointment brutally, as was now his wont. He had hardly spoken to Anne for weeks before; and when he visited her at her bedside he said that it was quite evident that God meant to deny him heirs male by her.

"When you get up," he growled in answer to the poor woman's complaints, as he left her, "I will talk to you." The lady of whom Anne was jealous was probably the same that had attracted the King at the ball given to the Admiral of France two months previously, and had made him, as Anne hysterically complained, "forget everything else." This lady was Mistress Jane Seymour, a daughter of Sir John Seymour of Wolf Hall, Wilts. She was at the time just over twenty-five years of age, and had been at Court for some time as a maid of honour to Katharine, and afterwards to Anne. During the King's progress in the autumn of 1535, he had visited Wolf Hall, where the daughter of the house had attracted his admiring attention, apparently for the first time. Jane is described as possessing no great beauty, being somewhat colourless as to complexion; but her demeanour was sweet and gracious; and the King's admiration for her at once marked her out as a fit instrument for the conservative party of nobles at Court to use against Anne and the political and religious policy which she represented. Apparently Jane had no ability, and none was needed in the circumstances. Chapuys, moreover, suggests with unnecessary spite that in morals she was no better than she should have been, on the unconvincing grounds that "being an Englishwoman, and having been so long at Court, whether she would not hold it a sin to be still a maid." Her supposed unchastity, indeed, is represented as being an attraction to Henry: "for he may marry her on condition that she is a maid, and when he wants a divorce there will be plenty of witnesses ready to testify that she was not." This, however, is mere detraction by a man who firmly believed that the cruelly wronged Katharine whose cause he served had just been murdered by Henry's orders. That Jane had no strength of character is plain, and throughout her short reign she was merely an instrument by which politicians sought to turn the King's passion for her to their own ends.

The Seymours were a family of good descent, allied with some of the great historic houses, and Jane's two brothers, Edward and Thomas, were already handsome and notable figures at Henry's Court: the elder, Sir Edward Seymour, especially, having accompanied the showy visits of the Duke of Suffolk, Cardinal Wolsey, and the King himself to France. So far as can be ascertained, however, the brothers, prompt as they were to profit by their sister's elevation, were no parties to the political intrigue of which Jane was probably the unconscious tool. She was carefully indoctrinated by Anne's enemies, especially Sir Nicholas Carew, how she was to behave. She must, above all, profess great devotion and friendship to the Princess Mary, to assume a mien of rigid virtue and high principles which would be likely to pique a sensual man like Henry without gratifying his passion except by marriage. Many of the enemies of the French connection, which included the great majority of the nation, looked with hope towards the King's new infatuation as a means of luring back England to the comity of Catholic nations and friendship with the Emperor; though there was still a section, especially in the north of England, which believed that their best interests would be served by an open rebellion in the interests of Mary, supported from Flanders by her cousin the Emperor. All this was, of course, well known to Cromwell. He had been one of the first to counsel defiance of the Pope, but throughout he had been anxious to avoid an open quarrel with the Emperor, or to pledge England too closely to French interests; and now that even the French had turned against Anne, Cromwell saw that, unless he himself was to be dragged down when she fell, he must put the break hard down upon the religious policy that he had initiated, and make common cause with Anne's enemies.

In a secret conference that he held with Chapuys at the Austin Friars, which in future was to be his own mansion, Cromwell proposed a new alliance between England and the Emperor, which would necessarily have to be accompanied by some compromise with the Pope and the recognition of Mary's legitimacy. He assured the imperial ambassador that Norfolk, Suffolk, and the rest of the nobles formerly attached to France were of the same opinion as himself, and tried earnestly to convince his interlocutor that he had no sympathy with Anne, whom he was ready to throw overboard to save himself. When Charles received this news from his ambassador, he took a somewhat tortuous but characteristic course. He was willing to a great extent to let bygones be bygones, and to forget the sufferings, and perhaps the murder, of his aunt Katharine, if Henry would come to terms with the Papacy and legitimise the Princess Mary; but, curiously enough, he preferred that Anne should remain at Henry's side, instead of being repudiated. Her marriage, he reasoned, was obviously invalid, and any children she might have by Henry would consequently be unable to interfere with Mary's rights to the succession: whereas if Henry were to divorce Anne and contract a legal marriage, any son born to him would disinherit Mary. To this extent was Charles ready to descend if he could obtain English help and money in the coming war; and Cromwell, at all events, was anxious to go quite as far to meet him. He now showed ostentatious respect to the Princess Mary, restoring to her the little gold cross that had been her mother's, and of which she had been cruelly deprived, condemned openly the continued execution of his own policy of spoliation of the monasteries, and quarrelled both with Anne and the only man now in the same boat with her, Archbishop Cranmer, who trembled in his shoes at the ruin he saw impending upon his patroness, ready at any moment to turn his coat, but ignorant of how to do it; for Cranmer, however able a casuist he might be, possessed little statesmanship and less courage.

Lady Exeter was the go-between who brought the imperial ambassador into the conspiracy to oust Anne. The time was seen to be ripening. Henry was already talking in secret about "his having been seduced into the marriage with Anne by sorcery, and consequently that he considered it to be null, which was clearly seen by God's denying a son. He thought he should be quite justified in taking another wife," and Jane Seymour's company seemed daily more necessary to his comfort.

Sir Edward Seymour was made a Gentleman of the Privy Chamber early in March; and a fortnight later the Marchioness of Exeter reported to her friend Chapuys that the King, who was at Whitehall, had sent a loving letter, and a purse of gold, to his new lady-love. The latter had been carefully schooled as to the wise course to pursue, and played prudery to perfection. She kissed the royal letter fervently without opening it; and then, throwing herself upon her knees, besought the messenger to pray the King in her name to consider that she was a gentlewoman of fair and honourable lineage and without reproach. "She had nothing in the world but her honour, which for a thousand deaths she would not wound. If the King deigned to make her a present of money she prayed that it might be when she made an honourable marriage." According to Lady Exeter's report, this answer inflamed even more the King's love for Jane. "She had behaved herself in the matter very modestly," he said; "and in order to let it be seen that his intentions and affection were honourable, he intended in future only to speak to her in the presence of some of her relatives." Cromwell, moreover, was turned out of a convenient apartment to which secret access could be obtained from the King's quarters, in order that Sir Edward Seymour, now Viscount Beauchamp, and his wife should be lodged there, and facility thus given for the King's virtuous billing and cooing with Jane, whilst saving the proprieties.

When it was too late, even Anne attempted to desert her own political party and to rally to the side of the Emperor, whether because she understood the indulgent way in which the latter now regarded her union with Henry, or whether from mere desperation at the ruin impending, it is not easy to say. But the conspiracy for her destruction had already gone too far when the Emperor's diplomatic instructions came to his ambassador. It was understood now at Court that the King intended somehow to get rid of his doubtful wife and marry another woman, and Cromwell, with a hypocritical smile behind his hand, whispered to Chapuys that though the King might divorce Anne he would live more virtuously in future. When the imperial ambassador with his master's friendly replies to Henry's advances saw the King at Greenwich on the 18th April 1536 the Court was all smiles for him, and Anne desperately clutched at the chance of making friends with him. Chapuys was cool, and declined to go and salute her, as he was invited to do. He was ready, as he said, to hold a candle to the devil, or a hundred of them, if his master's interests would thereby be served; but he knew that Anne was doomed, and notwithstanding his master's permission he made no attempt to conciliate her. All the courtiers were watching to see how he would treat her on this the first occasion that they had met since Katharine's death. As Anne passed into the chapel to high Mass she looked eagerly around to greet her enemy. Where was he? In the chapel, she knew, and to sit close by her side; but he was nowhere to be seen. He was, in fact, standing behind the open door by which she entered; but, determined not to be balked, she turned completely round and made him a profound courtesy, which, as he was bound to do, he returned. In Anne's rooms afterwards, where the King and the other ambassadors dined, Chapuys was not present, much to the "concubine's" chagrin; but the Princess Mary and her friends in the conspiracy were suspicious and jealous even of the bow that had been exchanged under such adverse circumstances in the chapel. Anne at dinner coarsely abused the King of France, and strove her utmost to lead people to think that she, too, was hand in glove with the imperialists, as her enemies were, whilst Henry was graciousness itself to Chapuys, until he came to close quarters and heard that the Emperor was determined to drive a hard bargain, and force his English uncle to eat a large piece of humble pie before he could be taken to his bosom again. Then Henry hectored and vaunted like the bully that he was, and upon Cromwell fell his ill humour, for having, as Henry thought, been too pliant with the imperialists; and for the next week Cromwell was ill and in disgrace.

Submission to the Pope to the extent that Charles demanded was almost impossible now, both in consequence of Henry's own vanity, and because the vast revenues and estates of the monasteries had in many cases replenished the King's exchequer, or had endowed his nobles and favourites, Catholics though many of them were. A surrender of these estates and revenues would have been resisted, even if such had been possible, to the death, by those who had profited by the spoliation; and unless the Pope and the Emperor were willing to forget much, the hope of reconciling England with the Church was an impossible dream. The great nobles who had battened upon the spoils, especially Norfolk, themselves took fright at the Emperor's uncompromising demands, and tried to play off France against Charles, during Cromwell's short disgrace. The Secretary saw that if the friends of France once more obtained the control over Henry's fickle mind, the revolutionary section of the Catholic party in favour of Mary and the imperial connection would carry all before them, and that in the flood of change Cromwell and all his works would certainly be swept away. If Anne could be got rid of, and the King married to Mistress Seymour, jointly with the adoption of a moderate policy of compromise with Rome and the Emperor, all might be well, and Cromwell might retain the helm, but either an uncompromising persistence in the open Protestant defiance with probably a French alliance against the Emperor, or, on the other hand, an armed Catholic revolution in England, subsidised from Flanders, would have been inevitable ruin to Cromwell.

Anne, then, must be destroyed at any cost, and the King be won to the side of the man who would devise a means of doing it. But how? A repudiation or formal divorce on the ground of invalidity would, of course, have been easy; but it would have been too scandalous. It would also have convicted the King of levity, and above all have bastardised his second daughter, leaving him with no child that the law of the realm regarded as legitimate. Henry himself, as we have seen, talked about his having been drawn into the marriage by sorcery, and ardently desired to get rid of his wife. His intercourse with Jane Seymour, who was being cleverly coached by Anne's enemies and Mary's friends, plainly indicated that marriage was intended; but it was the intriguing brain of Cromwell that devised the only satisfactory way in which the King's caprice and his own interests could be served in the treatment of Anne. Appearances must, at any cost, be saved for Henry. He must not appear to blame, whatever happened. Cromwell must be able, for his own safety, to drag down Anne's family and friends at the same time that she was ruined, and the affair must be so managed that some sort of reconciliation could be patched up with the Emperor, whilst Norfolk and the French adherents were thrust into the background. Cromwell pondered well on the problem as he lay in bed, sick with annoyance at

Henry's rough answer to the Emperor's terms, and thus he hit upon the scheme that alone would serve the aims he had in view.

The idea gave him health and boldness again, and just as Henry under Norfolk's influence was smiling upon the French ambassador, Cromwell appeared once more before his master after his five days' absence. What passed at their interview can only be guessed by the light of the events that followed. It is quite possible that Cromwell did not tell the King of his designs against Anne, but only that he had discovered a practice of treason against him. But whether the actual words were pronounced or not, Henry must have understood, before he signed and gave to Cromwell the secret instrument demanded of him, that evil was intended to the woman of whom he had grown tired. It was a patent dated the 24th April, appointing the Lord Chancellor Audley and a number of nobles, including the Duke of Norfolk and Anne's father, the Earl of Wiltshire, together with the judges, a Commission to inquire into any intended treasonable action, no matter by whom committed, and to hold a special Court to try the persons accused. With this instrument in his pocket, Cromwell held at will the lives of those whom he sought to destroy. Anne, as we have seen, had loved and courted the admiration of men, even as her daughter Elizabeth afterwards did to an extent that bordered upon mania. Her manners were free and somewhat hysterical, and her reputation before marriage had been more than doubtful, but the stern Act of Succession, which in 1534 made it treason to question the legitimacy of Anne's daughter, barred all accusation against her except in respect to actions after Elizabeth's birth.

Cromwell was well served by spies, even in Anne's chamber; for her star was visibly paling, and people feared her vengeance little; and not many days passed before the Secretary had in his hand testimony enough to strike his first blow. It was little enough according to our present notions of evidence, and at another time would have passed unnoticed. A young fellow of humble origin, named Mark Smeaton, had by Anne's influence been appointed one of Henry's grooms of the chamber in consequence of his skill as a lute player. Anne herself, who was a fine musician and composer, delighted in listening to Mark's performances; and doubtless, as was her wont, she challenged his admiration because he was a man. A contemporary who repeated the tattle of the Court says that she had fallen in love with the lute player, and had told him so; and that she had aroused the jealousy of her rival admirers, Norreys, Brereton, and others, by her lavish gifts and open favour to Mark Smeaton. According to this story, she endeavoured to appease the former by renewed flirting with them, and to silence Mark's discontent by large gifts of money. Others of her courtiers, especially Sir Thomas Percy, indignant that an upstart like Mark should be treated better than themselves, insulted and picked quarrels with the musician; and it is evident that Anne, at the very time that Cromwell was spreading his nets for her, was hard put to it to keep the peace between a number of idle, jealous young men whose admiration she had sought for pastime.

On the 29th April, Mark Smeaton was standing sulkily in the deep embrasure of a window in Anne's chamber in the palace of Greenwich. The Queen asked him why he was so out of humour. He replied that it was nothing that mattered. She evidently knew the real reason for his gloom, for she reminded him that he could not expect her to speak to him as if he were a nobleman. "No, no!" said Mark, "a look sufficeth for me, and so fare you well." Sir Thomas Percy seems to have heard this little speech, and have conveyed it, with many hints of Mark's sudden prosperity, to Cromwell. "It is hardly three months since Mark came to Court, and though he has only a hundred pounds a year from the King, and has received no more than a third, he has just bought three horses that have cost him 500 ducats, as well as very rich arms and fine liveries for his servants for the May-day ridings, such as no gentleman at Court has been able to buy, and many are wondering where he gets the money." Mark Smeaton was a safe quarry, for he had no influential friends, and it suited Cromwell's turn to begin with him to build up his case against Anne.

There was to be a May-day jousting in the tilt-yard at Greenwich, at which Anne's brother, Lord Rochford, was the challenger, and Sir Henry Norreys was the principal defender. Early in the morning of the day, Cromwell, who of course took no part in such shows, went to London, and asked Smeaton to accompany him and dine, returning in the afternoon to Greenwich in time for the ridings. Mark accepted the invitation, and was taken ostensibly for dinner to a house at Stepney, that probably being a convenient half-way place between Greenwich and Westminster by water. No sooner had the unsuspecting youth entered the chamber than he saw the trap into which he had fallen. Six armed men closed around him, and Cromwell's face grew grave, as the Secretary warned the terrified lad to confess where he obtained so much money. Smeaton prevaricated, and "then two stout young fellows were called, and the Secretary asked for a rope and a cudgel. The rope, which was filled with knots, was put around Mark's head and twisted with the cudgel until Mark cried, 'Sir Secretary, no more! I will tell the truth. The Queen gave me the money.'" Then, bit by bit, by threats of torture, some sort of confession incriminating Anne was wrung out of the poor wretch: though exactly what he confessed is not on record. Later, when the affair was made public, the quidnuncs of London could tell the most private details of his adultery with the Queen; for Cromwell took care that such gossip should be well circulated.

Whatever confession was extorted from Smeaton, it implicated not only himself but the various gentlemen who shared with him the Queen's smiles, and was quite sufficient for Cromwell's purpose. Hurrying the unfortunate musician to the Tower in the strictest secrecy, Cromwell sent his nephew Richard post haste to Greenwich with a letter divulging Smeaton's story to the King. Richard Cromwell arrived at the tiltyard as the tournament was in progress, the King and Anne witnessing the bouts from a glazed gallery. Several versions of what then happened are given; but the most probable is that as soon as Henry had glanced at the contents of the letter and knew that Cromwell had succeeded, he abruptly rose and left the sports; starting almost immediately afterwards for London without the knowledge of Anne. With him went a great favourite of his, Sir Henry Norreys, Keeper of the Privy Purse, who was engaged to be married to Madge Shelton, Anne's cousin, who had at one time been put forward by the Boleyn interest as the King's mistress. Norreys had, no doubt, flirted platonically with the Queen, who had openly bidden for his admiration, but there is not an atom of evidence that their connection was a guilty one. On the way to London the King taxed him with undue familiarity with Anne. Horror-stricken, Norreys could only protest his innocence, and resist all the temptations held out to him to make a clean breast of the Queen's immorality. One of the party of Anne's enemies, Sir William Fitzwilliam, was also in attendance on the King; and to him was given the order to convey Norreys to the Tower. After the King's departure from Greenwich, Anne learnt that he had gone without a word of farewell, and that Smeaton was absent from the joust, detained in London.

The poor woman's heart must have sunk with fear, for the portents of her doom were all around her. She could not cry for mercy to the flabby coward her husband, who, as usual, slunk from bearing the responsibility of his own acts, and ran away from the danger of personal appeal from those whom he wronged. Late at night the dread news was whispered to her that Smeaton and Norreys were both in the Tower; and early in the morning she herself was summoned to appear before a quorum of the Royal Commissioners, presided over by her uncle and enemy, the Duke of Norfolk. She was rudely told that she was accused of committing adultery with Smeaton and Norreys, both of whom had confessed. She cried and protested in vain that it was untrue. She was told to hold her peace, and was placed under arrest until her barge was ready and the tide served to bear her up stream to the Tower. With her went a large guard of halberdiers and the Duke of Norfolk. Thinking that she was being carried to her husband at Westminster, she was composed and tranquil on the way; but when she found that the Traitors' Gate of the Tower was her destination, her presence of mind deserted her. Sir William Kingston, one of the chief conspirators in Mary's favour, and governor of the fortress, stood upon the steps under the gloomy archway to receive her, and in sign of custody took her by the arm as she ascended. "I was received with greater ceremony the last time I entered here," she cried indignantly; and as the heavy gates clanged behind her and the portcullis dropped, she fell upon her knees and burst into a storm of hysterical tears. Kingston and his wife did their best to tranquillise her; but her passionate protestations of innocence made no impression upon them.

Her brother, Lord Rochford, had, unknown to her, been a few hours before lodged in the same fortress on the hideous and utterly unsupported charge of incest with his sister; and Cromwell's drag-net was cast awide to bring in all those whose names were connected, however loosely, with that of the Queen by her servants, all of whom were tumbling over each other in their haste to denounce their fallen mistress. Sir Thomas Weston and William Brereton, with both of whom Anne had been fond of bandying questionable compliments, were arrested on the 4th May; and on the 5th Sir Thomas Wyatt, the poet, and a great friend of the King, was put under guard on similar accusations. With regard to Wyatt there seems to have been no doubt, as has been shown in an earlier chapter, that some love passages had passed between him and Anne before her marriage; and there is contemporary assertion to support the belief that their connection had not been an innocent one; but the case against him was finally dropped and he was again taken into Henry's favour; a proof that there was no evidence of any guilt on his part since Anne was Queen. He is asserted to have begged Henry not to contract the marriage, and subsequently to have reminded him that he had done so, confessing after her arrest that Anne had been his mistress before she married the King.

The wretched woman babbled hysterically without cessation in her chamber in the Tower; all her distraught ravings being carefully noted and repeated by the ladies, mostly her personal enemies, who watched her night and day; artful leading questions being put to her to tempt her to talk the more. She was imprudent in her speech at the best of times, but now, in a condition of acute hysteria, she served the interests of her enemies to the full, dragging into her discourse the names of the gentlemen who were accused and repeating their risky conversations with her, which were now twisted to their worst meaning. At one time she would only desire death; then she would make merry with a good dinner or supper, chatting and jesting, only to break down into hysterical laughter and tears in the midst of her merriment. Anon she would affect to believe that her husband was but trying her constancy, and pleaded with all her heart to be allowed to see him again. But he, once having broken the shackles, was gaily amusing himself in gallant guise with Mistress Seymour, who was lodged, for appearance' sake, in the house of her mentor, Sir Nicholas Carew, a few miles from London, but within easy reach of a horseman. Anne in her sober moments must have known that she was doomed. She hoped much from Cranmer, almost the only friend of hers not now in prison; but Cranmer, however strong in counsel, was a weak reed in combat; and hastened to save himself at the cost of the woman upon whose shoulders he had climbed to greatness. The day after Anne's arrest, Cranmer wrote to the King "a letter of consolation; yet wisely making no apology for her, but acknowledging how divers of the lords had told him of certain of her faults, which, he said, he was sorry to hear, and concluded desiring that the King would continue his love to the gospel, lest it should be thought that it was for her sake only that he had favoured it." Before he had time to despatch the letter, the timorous archbishop was summoned across the river to Westminster to answer certain disquieting questions of the Commissioners, who informed him of the evidence against the Queen; and in growing alarm for himself and his cause, he hurried back to Lambeth without uttering a word in favour of the accused, whose guilt he accepted without question.

Thenceforward Anne's enemies worked their way unchecked, even her father being silenced by fear for himself. For Cromwell's safety it was necessary that none of the accused should escape who later might do him injury; and now that he and his imperialistic policy had been buttressed by the "discovery" of Anne's infidelity, not even the nobles of the French faction dared to oppose it by seeming to side with the unhappy woman. The Secretary did his work thoroughly. The indictments were laid before the grand juries of Middlesex and Kent, as the offences were asserted to have been committed over a long period both at Greenwich and Whitehall or Hampton Court. To the charges against

Anne of adultery with Smeaton, who it was asserted had confessed, Norreys, Weston, Brereton, and Lord Rochford, was added that of having conspired with them to kill the King. There was not an atom of evidence worth the name to support any of the charges except the doubtful confession of Smeaton, wrung from him by torture; and it is certain that at the period in question the death of Henry would have been fatal to the interests of Anne. But a State prosecution in the then condition of the law almost invariably meant a condemnation of the accused; and when Smeaton, Weston, Norreys, and Brereton were arraigned in Westminster Hall on the 12th May, their doom was practically sealed before the trial. Smeaton simply pleaded guilty of adultery only, and prayed for mercy: the rest of the accused strenuously denied their guilt on the whole of the charges; but all were condemned to the terrible death awarded to traitors, though on what detailed evidence, if any, does not now appear. Every effort was made to tempt Norreys to confess, but he replied that he would rather die a thousand deaths than confess a lie, for he verily believed the Queen innocent.

In the meanwhile Anne in the Tower continued her strange behaviour, at times arrogantly claiming all her royal prerogatives, at times reduced to hysterical self-abasement and despair. On the 15th May she and her brother were brought to the great hall of the Tower before a large panel of peers under the presidency of the Duke of Norfolk. All that could add ignominy to the accused was done. The lieges were crowded into the space behind barriers at the end of the hall, the city fathers under the Lord Mayor were bidden to attend, and with bated breath the subjects saw the woman they had always scorned publicly branded as an incestuous adulteress. The charges, as usual at the time, were made in a way and upon grounds that now would not be permitted in any court of justice. Scraps of overheard conversation with Norreys and others were twisted into sinister significance, allegations unsupported, and not included in the indictment, were dragged in to prejudice the accused; and loose statements incapable of proof or disproof were liberally introduced for the same purpose. The charge of incest with Rochford depended entirely upon the assertion that he once remained in his sister's room a long time; and in his case also loose gossip was alleged as a proof of crime: that Anne had said that the King was impotent, that Rochford had thrown doubts upon the King being the father of Anne's child, and similar hearsay ribaldry. Both Anne and her brother defended themselves, unaided, with ability and dignity. They pointed out the absence of evidence against them, and the inherent improbability of the charges. But it was of no avail, for her death had already been settled between Henry and Cromwell: and the Duke of Norfolk, with his sinister squint, condemned his niece, Anne Queen of England, to be burnt or beheaded at the King's pleasure; and Viscount Rochford to a similar death. Both denied their guilt after sentence, but acknowledged, as was the custom of the time, that they deserved death, this being the only way in which mercy might be gained, so far as forfeiture of property was concerned.

Anne had been cordially hated by the people. Her rise had meant the destruction of the ancient religious foundations, the shaking of the ecclesiastical bases of English society; but the sense of justice was not dead, and the procedure at the trial shocked the public conscience. Already men and women murmured that the King's goings on with Mistress Seymour whilst his wife was under trial for adultery were a scandal, and Anne in her death had more friends than in her life. On all sides in London now, from the Lord Mayor downwards, it was said that Anne had been condemned, not because she was guilty, but because the King was tired of her: at all events, wrote Chapuys to Granvelle, there was surely never a man who wore the horns so gaily as he. On the 17th May the five condemned men were led to their death upon Tower Hill, all of them, including Smeaton, being beheaded. As usual in such cases, they acknowledged general guilt, but not one (except perhaps Smeaton) admitted the particular crimes for which they died, for their kin might have suffered in property, if not in person, if the King's justice had been too strongly impugned.

Anne, in alternate hope and despair, still remained in the Tower, but mostly longing for the rapid death she felt in her heart must come. Little knew she, however, why her sacrifice was deferred yet from day to day. In one of her excited, nervous outbursts she had cried that, no matter what they did, no one could prevent her from dying Queen of England. She had reckoned without Henry's meanness, Cromwell's cunning, and Cranmer's suppleness. Her death warrant had been signed by the King on the 16th May, and Cranmer was sent to receive her last confession. The coming of the archbishop— *her* archbishop, as she called him— gave her fresh hope. She was not to be killed after all, but to be banished, and Cranmer was to bring her the good news. Alas! poor soul, she little knew her Cranmer even yet. He had been primed by Cromwell for a very different purpose, that of worming out of Anne some admission that would give him a pretext for pronouncing her marriage with the King invalid from the first. The task was a repulsive one for the Primate, whose act alone had made the marriage possible; but Cranmer was— Cranmer. The position was a complicated one.

Henry, as he invariably did, wished to save his face and seem in the right before the world, consequently he could not confess that he had been mistaken in the divorce from Katharine, and get rid of Anne's marriage in that way, nor did he wish to restore Mary to the position of heiress to the crown. What he needed Cranmer's help for was to render Elizabeth also illegitimate, but still his daughter, in order that any child he might have by Jane Seymour, or failing that, his natural son, the Duke of Richmond, might be acknowledged his successor.

At intervals during Anne's career her alleged betrothal to the Earl of Northumberland before her marriage (see p. 126) had been brought up to her detriment; and the poor hare-brained earl had foresworn himself more than once on the subject. He was dying now, but he was again pressed to say that a regular betrothal had taken place with Anne. But he was past earthly fear, and finally asserted that no contract had been made. Foiled in this attempt, Henry— or rather Cromwell— sent Cranmer to the Tower on the 16th May on his shameful errand: to lure the poor woman by hopes of pardon to confess the existence of an impediment to her marriage with the King. What the impediment was was never made public, but Anne's latest biographer, Mr. Friedmann, adduces excellent reasons for arriving at the conclusions that I have drawn, namely, that Mary Boleyn having been Henry's mistress, he and Anne were within the prohibited degrees of affinity for husband and wife; the fact that no marriage had taken place between Henry and Mary Boleyn being regarded as canonically immaterial. In any case, the admission of a known impediment having been made by Anne, no time was lost. The next day, the 17th May, Cranmer sat, with Cromwell and other members of the Council, in his Primate's court at Lambeth to condemn the marriage that he himself had made. Anne was formally represented, but nothing was said on her behalf; and sentence was hurriedly pronounced that the King's marriage with Anne Boleyn had never been a marriage at all. At the same time order was sent to Sir William Kingston that the "concubine" was to suffer the last penalty on the following morning. When the sleepless night for Anne had passed, mostly in prayer, she took the sacrament with the utmost devotion, and in that most solemn moment swore before the Host, on her hopes of eternal life, that she had never misused her body to the King's dishonour.

In the meanwhile her execution had been deferred until the next day, and Anne again lost her nerve. It was cruel, she said, to keep her so long in suspense: pray, she petitioned, put her out of her misery now that she was prepared. The operation would not be painful, Kingston assured her. "My neck is small enough," she said, spanning it with her fingers, and again burst into hysterics. Soon she became calm once more; and thenceforward only yearned for despatch. "No one ever had a better will for death than she," wrote Chapuys to his master: and Kingston, hardened as he was to the sight of the condemned in their last hours, expressed surprise to Cromwell that instead of sorrow "this lady has much joy and pleasure in death." Remorse for her ungenerous treatment of the Princess Mary principally troubled her. She herself, she said, was not going to execution by the divine judgment for what she had been accused of, but for having planned the death of the Princess. And so, in alternate prayer and light chatter, passed Anne's last night on earth, and at nine o'clock on the spring morning of the 19th May she was led forth to the courtyard within the Tower, where a group of gentlemen, including Cromwell and the Dukes of Richmond and Suffolk, stood on or close to a low scaffold or staging reached by four steps from the ground. Anne was dressed in grey damask trimmed with fur, over a crimson petticoat, and cut low at the neck, so as to offer no impediment to the executioner's steel; and for the same reason the brown hair was dressed high in a net under the pearl-bordered coif. Kept back by guards to some little distance from the platform stood a large crowd of spectators, who had flocked in at the heels of the Lord Mayor and Sheriffs; though foreigners had been rigidly excluded.

When Anne had ascended the steps she received permission to say a few words; and followed the tradition of not complaining against the King's justice which had condemned her. She had not come thither to preach, she said, but to die, though she was not guilty of the particular crimes for which she had been condemned. When, however, she began to speak of Jane Seymour being the cause of her fall, those on the scaffold stopped her, and she said no more. A headsman of St. Omer had been brought over from Calais, in order that the broadsword instead of the axe might be used; and this man, who was undistinguishable by his garb from the other bystanders, now came forward, and, kneeling, asked the doomed woman's pardon, which granted, Anne herself knelt in a distraught way, as if to pray, but really gazed around her in mute appeal from one pitiless face to another. The headsman, taking compassion upon her, assured her that he would not strike until she gave the signal. "You will have to take this coif off," said the poor woman, and one of the ladies who attended her did so, and partially bound her eyes with a handkerchief; but Anne still imagined that her headdress was in the way, and kept her hand upon her hair, straining her eyes and ears towards the steps where from the headsman's words she expected the sword to be handed to him. Whilst she was thus kneeling erect in suspense, the sword which was hidden in the straw behind her was deftly seized by the French executioner, who, swinging the heavy blade around, in an instant cut through the erect, slender neck; and the head of Anne Boleyn jerked from the shoulders and rolled upon the cloth that covered the platform.

Katharine in her neglected tomb at Peterborough was avenged, but the fissure that had been opened up between England and the Papacy for the sake of this woman had widened now past bridging. Politicians might, and did, make up their differences now that the "concubine" was dead, and form alliances regardless of religious affinities; but submission to the Papacy in future might mean that the most powerful people in England would be deprived of the fat spoils of the Church with which Cromwell had bought them, and that the vainest king on earth must humbly confess himself in the wrong. Anne herself was a mere straw upon a whirlpool, though her abilities, as Cromwell confessed, were not to be despised. She did not plan or make the Reformation, though she was forced by her circumstances to patronise it. The real author of the great schism of England was not Anne or Cranmer, but Luther's enemy, Charles V., the champion of Catholicism. But for the pressure he put upon the Pope to refuse Henry's divorce, in order to prevent a coalition of England and France, Cranmer's defiance of the Papacy would not have been needed, and Henry might have come back to Rome again easily. But with Cranmer to provide him with plausible pretexts for the repeated indulgence of his self-will, and Cromwell to feed his pride and cupidity by the plunder of the Church, Henry had already been drawn too far to go back. Greed and vanity of the ruling powers thus conspired to make permanent in England the influence of evanescent Anne Boleyn.

JANE SEYMOUR
From a painting by HOLBEIN in the Imperial Collection at Vienna

CHAPTER VII

1536~1540

PLOT AND COUNTERPLOT—JANE SEYMOUR AND ANNE OF CLEVES

From the moment that Henry abruptly left the lists at May-day on the receipt of Cromwell's letter detailing the admissions of Smeaton, he saw Anne no more. No pang of remorse, no wave of compassion passed over him. He easily believed what he wished to believe, and Anne was left to the tender mercies of Cromwell, to be done to death. Again Henry was a prey to profound self-pity for ever having fallen under the enchantment of such a wicked woman. He, of course, was not to blame for anything. He never was. He was always the clement, just man whose unsuspecting goodness of heart had been abused by others, and who tried to find distraction and to forget the evil done him. On the very night of the day that Anne was arrested the Duke of Richmond, Henry's son, now a grown youth, went, as was his custom, into his father's room at Whitehall to bid him good night and ask his blessing. The King, we are told, fell a-weeping as he blessed his son, "saying that he and his sister (Mary) might well be grateful to God for saving them from the hands of that accursed and venomous harlot who had intended to poison them." That Anne may have planned the assassination of Mary is quite probable, even if she had no hand in the shortening of Katharine's days, and this may have been the real hidden pretext of her death acting upon Henry's fears for himself. But if such were the case, Henry, at least, was deserving of no pity, for when it was only Katharine's life that was in danger he was, as we have seen, brutally callous, and only awoke to the enormity of the "venomous harlot" when Cromwell made him believe that his own safety was jeopardised. Then no fate was too cruel for the woman he once had loved.

On the day preceding Anne's trial, Jane Seymour was brought from Sir Nicholas Carew's house to another residence on the river bank, only a mile from Whitehall Stairs, to be ready for her intended elevation as soon as the Queen was disposed of. Here Jane was served for the few days she stayed "very splendidly by the cooks and certain officers of the King, and very richly adorned." So certain was Henry that nothing would now stand in the way of his new marriage that Jane was informed beforehand that on the 15th, by three in the afternoon, she would hear of her predecessor's condemnation; and Anne's cousin and enemy, Sir Francis Brian, eagerly brought the news to the expectant lady at the hour anticipated. The next day, when the sword of the French heads-man had made Henry indeed a widower, the King only awaited receipt of the intelligence to enter his barge and seek the consolation of Jane Seymour. At six o'clock in the morning of the 20th May, when the headless body of Anne, barely cold, still awaited sepulture huddled in an old arrow-box in the Church of St. Peter within the Tower, Jane was secretly carried by water from her residence to Hampton Court; and before nine o'clock she had been privately married to the King, by vir-tue of a dispensation issued the day previously by the accommodating Cranmer. It would seem probable that the day after the private espous-als Jane travelled to her home in Wiltshire, where she stayed for several days whilst preparations were being made in the King's abodes for her reception as Queen: for all the A's had to be changed to J's in the royal ciphers, and traces of Anne's former presence abolished wherever pos-sible. Whether Henry accompanied his new wife to Wiltshire on this occasion is not quite certain, though from Sir John Russell's account it is probable that he did. In any case the King and his new wife visited Mercer's Hall, in Cheapside, on the 29th May, St. Peter's Eve, to wit-ness from the windows the civic ceremony of the annual setting of the watch; and on the following day, 30th May, the pair were formally mar-ried in the Queen's closet at Whitehall.

The people at large looked somewhat askance at this furious haste to marry the new wife before the shed blood of the previous one was dry; but the Court, and those who still recollected the wronged Princess Mary and her dead mother, were enthusiastic in their welcome to Jane. The Emperor's friends, too, were in joyous mood; and Princess Mary at Hunsdon was full of hope, and eager to be allowed to greet her father and his wife now that "that woman" was dead. Chapuys, we may be sure, did not stand behind the door now when he went to Court. On the contrary, when he first visited Whitehall a few days after the wedding, Henry led him by the hand to Jane's apartments, and allowed the diplomatist to kiss the Queen— "congratulating her upon her mar-riage and wishing her prosperity. I told her that, although the device of the lady who had preceded her on the throne was 'The happiest of women,' I had no doubt that she herself would realise that motto. I was sure that the Emperor would be equally rejoiced as the King himself had been at meeting such a virtuous and amiable Queen, the more so that her brother (*i.e.* Sir E. Seymour, afterwards the Duke of Somerset) had been in the Emperor's service. I added that it was almost impossible to believe the joy and pleasure which Englishmen generally had felt at the marriage; especially as it was said that she was continually trying to persuade the King to restore the Princess to his favour, as formerly." Most of Chapuys' courtly talk with Jane, indeed, was directed to this point of the restoration of Mary; but the new Queen, though inexperienced, had been well coached, and did not unduly commit herself; only promising to favour the Princess, and to endeavour to deserve the title that Chapuys had given her of "peacemaker." Henry strolled up to the pair at this point, and excused his new wife for any want of expertness: "as I was the first ambassador she had received, and she was not used yet to such receptions. He (Henry) felt sure, however, that she would do her utmost to obtain the title of 'peacemaker,' with which I (Chapuys) had greeted her, as, besides being naturally of a kind and amiable disposition and much inclined to peace, she would strive to prevent his (Henry's) taking part in a foreign war, if only out of the fear of being separated from him."

But all these fine hopes were rapidly banished. Jane never possessed or attempted to exercise any political influence on her husband. She smiled sweetly and in a non-committal way upon the Princess Mary, and upon the imperialist and moderate Catholic party that had hoped to make the new Queen their instrument; but Cromwell's was still the strong mind that swayed the King. He had obtained renewed control over his master by ridding him of Anne; and had, at all events, prevented England from being drawn into a coalition with France against the Emperor; but he had no intention, even if it had been possible, of going to the other extreme and binding his country to go to war against France to please the Emperor. Henry's self-will and vanity, as well as his greed, also stood in the way of a complete submission to the Papacy, and those who had brought Jane Seymour in, hoping that her advent would mean a return to the same position as that previous to Anne's rise, now found that they had been over sanguine. Charles and Francis were left to fight out their great duel alone in Italy and Provence, to the general discomfiture of the imperial cause; and, instead of hastening to humble himself at the feet of Paul III., as the pontiff had fondly expected, Henry summoned Parliament, and gave stronger statutory sanction than ever to his ecclesiastical independence of Rome. Anne's condemnation and Elizabeth's bastardy were obediently confirmed by the Legislature, and the entire freedom of the English Church from Rome reasserted.

But the question of the succession was that which aroused the strongest feeling, and its settlement the keenest disappointment. Now that Anne's offspring was disinherited, Princess Mary and her friends naturally expected that she, with the help of the new Queen, would once more enter into the enjoyment of her birthright. Eagerly Mary wrote to Cromwell bespeaking his aid, which she had been led to expect that he would give; and by his intercession she was allowed to send her humble petition to her father, praying for leave to see him. Her letters are all couched in terms of cringing humility, praying forgiveness for past offences, and promising to be a truly dutiful daughter in future. But this did not satisfy Henry. Cromwell, desirous, in pursuance of his policy of keeping friendly with the Emperor without going to war with France, or kneeling to Rome, hoped to bring about peace between Mary and her father. But the strongest passions of Henry's nature were now at stake, and he would only accept his daughter's submission on terms that made her a self-confessed bastard, and against this the girl, as obstinate as her father and as righteously proud as her mother, still rebelled. Henry's son, the Duke of Richmond, was now a straight stripling of eighteen, already married to Norfolk's daughter, and, failing issue by Jane, here was an heir to the Crown that might carry the Tudor line onward in the male blood, if Parliament could be chicaned or threatened into acknowledging him. So Mary was plied with letters from Cromwell, each more pressing and cruel than the previous one, driving the girl to distraction by the King's insistence upon his terms. Threats, cajolery, and artful casuistry were all tried. Again Mary turned to her foreign advisers and the King's rebellious subjects for support, and again her father's heart hardened when he knew it. Norfolk, who with others was sent to persuade her, was so incensed with her firmness that he said if she had been his daughter he would have knocked her head against the wall until it was as soft as a codlin. But Norfolk's daughter was the Duchess of Richmond, and might be Queen Consort after Henry's death if Mary were disinherited, so that there was some excuse for his violence. Those who were in favour of Mary were dismissed from the Council— even Cromwell was in fear— and Jane Seymour was rudely snubbed by the King for daring to intercede for the Princess. At length, with death threatening her, Mary could stand out no longer. Without even reading it, she signed with a mental reservation, and confident of obtaining the Papal absolution for which she secretly asked, the shameful declaration forced upon her, repudiating the Papal authority, and specifically acknowledging herself a bastard.

Then Henry was all amiability with his wronged daughter. He and Jane went to visit her at Richmond, whither she had been brought, giving her handsome presents of money and jewels; liberty was given to her to come to Court, and stately service surrounded her. But it was all embittered by the knowledge that Parliament had been induced to acknowledge that all the King's children were illegitimate, and to grant to Henry himself the right of appointing his own successor by letters patent or by will. Alas! the youth in whose immediate interest the injustice was done was fast sinking to his grave; and on the 22nd July 1536 the Duke of Richmond breathed his last, to Henry's bitter grief, Mary's prospects again became brighter, and all those who resented the religious policy and Henry's recalcitrancy now looked to the girl as their only hope of a return to the old order of things. Chapuys, too, was ceaseless in his intrigues to bring England once more into a condition of obedience to the Pope, that should make her a fit instrument for the imperial policy, and soon the disappointment that followed on the elevation of Jane Seymour found vent in the outbreak of rebellion in Lincolnshire and Yorkshire.

The priests and the great mass of the people had bent the neck patiently to the King's violent innovations in the observances that they had been taught to hold sacred. They had seen the religious houses, to which they looked for help and succour in distress, destroyed and alienated. The abuses of the clergy had doubtless been great, and the first measures against them had been welcomed; but the complete confiscation of vast properties, in the main administered for the benefit of the lowly, the continued enclosure of common lands by the gentry newly enriched by ecclesiastical plunder, and the rankling sense of the scandalous injustice that had been suffered by Katharine and Mary, for the sake, as the people said, of the King's lustful caprice, at last provided the extreme militant Catholic party with the impetus needed for revolt against the Crown. Imperious Henry was beside himself with rage; and for a time it looked as if he and his system might be swept away in favour of his daughter, or one of the Poles, who were being put forward by the Pope. The Bull of excommunication against Henry and England, so long held back, was now launched, making rebellion righteous; and the imperial interest in England, which was still strong, did its best to aid the rising of Henry's lieges against him. But the rebels were weakly led: the greater nobles had for the most part been bought by grants of ecclesiastical lands; and Norfolk, for all his moral baseness, was an experienced and able soldier. So the Pilgrimage of Grace, threatening as it looked for a time, flickered out; and the yoke was riveted tighter than ever upon the neck of rural England. To the party that had hoped to make use of her, Jane Seymour was thus, to some extent, a disappointment; but her placid submissiveness, which made her a bad political instrument, exactly suited a husband so imperious as Henry; and from a domestic point of view the union was successful. During the summer Jane shared in her husband's progresses and recreations, but as the months rolled on and no hope came of offspring, ominous rumours ran that Jane's coronation would be deferred until it was proved that she might bear children to the King; and some said that if she proved barren a pretext would be found for displacing her in favour of another. Indeed, only a few days after the public marriage, Henry noticed two very beautiful girls at Court, and showed his annoyance that he had not seen them before taking Jane.

After six months of marriage without sign of issue, Henry began to take fright. The Duke of Richmond was dead, and both the King's daughters were acknowledged by the law of England to be illegitimate. He was already forty-six years of age, and had lately grown very obese; and his death without further issue or a resettlement of the succession would inevitably lead to a dynastic dispute, with the probable result of the return of the House of York to the throne in the person of one of the Poles under the ægis of Rome. Whenever possible, Jane had said a good word for the Princess Mary, and Henry began to listen more kindly than before to his wife's well-meant attempts to soften him in favour of his daughter. The Catholic party was all alert with new hopes that the King, convinced that he could father no more sons, would cause his elder daughter to be acknowledged his heir; but the reformers, who had grown up numerously, especially in and about London, during Henry's defiance of Rome, looked askance at a policy which in time they feared might bring back the old order of things. The mainstay of this party at Court, apart from the professed Lutherans and the new bishops, were those who, having received grants of ecclesiastical property, despaired of any return to the Roman communion and the imperial alliance without the restoration of the Church property. Amongst these courtiers was Jane's brother, Edward Seymour, Viscount Beauchamp, who had received large grants of ecclesiastical lands at intervals since 1528. He was a personal friend of the King, and had taken no active part in the intrigue that accompanied his sister's elevation, though after the marriage he naturally rose higher than before in the favour of the King. He was a clever and superficially brilliant, but ostentatious and greedy man, of no great strength of purpose, whose new relationship to the King marked him out as a dominating influence in the future. The Dukes of Norfolk and Suffolk, upon whom Henry had depended as generals, were now very old and ailing, and there was no other peer but Cromwell of any ability in the Councils.

Even thus early it was clear that Seymour's weight would, notwithstanding the circumstances of his sister's rise, be thrown on to the anti-Papal side when the crucial struggle came. He was, moreover, a new man; and as such not welcomed by the older nobility, who, though desirous of retaining their Church plunder, were yet bound by their traditions against bureaucrats such as Cromwell, and the policy of defiance of the Papacy that he and his like had suggested and carried out. Cromwell's own position at this time (1536-37) was a paradoxical one. It was he who had led Henry on, step by step, to entire schism and the plunder of the Church; it was he who not only had shown how to get rid of Katharine, but how to destroy her successor; and it was he whom the Catholic party hated with a whole-hearted detestation, for the King's acts as well as his own. On the other hand, he was hardly less distrusted by the reforming party; for his efforts were known to be directed to a reconciliation with the Emperor, which could only be effected conjointly with some sort of arrangement with the Papacy. His efforts to please the imperialists by siding with the Princess Mary during her dispute with her father led him to the very verge of destruction. Whilst the young Princess was being badgered into making her shameful and insincere renunciation of her faith and birthright, Cromwell, the very man who was the instrument for extorting her submission, sat, as he says, for a week in the Council considering himself "a dead man," because the King believed that he was encouraging Mary to resist. Cromwell, therefore, like most men who endeavour to hold a middle course, was distrusted and hated by every one; and it must have been obvious to him that if he could ensure the adhesion of the rising Seymour interest his chance of weathering the storm would be infinitely improved. His son had recently married Jane Seymour's sister, and this brought him into close relationship with the family, and, as will be seen, led in the next year to a compact political union between the Seymour brothers, Cromwell, and the reforming party, as against the nobles and traditional conservatives.

For the time, however, Cromwell held on his way, endeavouring to keep in with the imperialists and Mary; and it was doubtless to his prompting that Jane used her influence, when at its highest point, to reconcile the Princess personally to her father. To the great joy of the

King, in March 1537, Jane was declared to be with child. The Emperor had already opened a negotiation for the marriage of Mary with his brother-in-law, the Infante Luiz of Portugal, and Henry was playing a waiting game till he saw if Jane would bear him a child. If so, Mary might go; although he still refused to legitimise her; but if no more issue was to be born to him, he could hardly allow his elder daughter to leave England and fall into the hands of the Emperor. Charles, on the other hand, was extremely anxious to obtain possession of so valuable a pledge for the future as Mary; and was willing to go to almost any lengths to get her, either by fair means or foul, fearing, as he did, that the girl might be married discreditably in England— he thought even to Cromwell himself— in order to destroy her international value to Henry's rivals.

As soon, however, as Jane's pregnancy was announced Mary's position changed. If a child was born in wedlock to the King, especially if it were a son, there would be no need to degrade Mary by joining her to a lowly husband; she might, on the contrary, become a good international marriage asset in the hands of her father, who might bargain with Charles or Francis for her. The fresh move of Jane Seymour, therefore, in her favour, in the spring of 1537, when the Queen's pregnancy had given her greater power over her husband, was probably welcome both to the King and Cromwell, as enhancing Mary's importance at a time when she might be used as an international political pawn without danger. Jane was sad one day in the early period of her pregnancy. "Why, darling," said the King, "how happeneth it you are not merrier?" "It hath pleased your Grace," replied the Queen, "to make me your wife, and there are none but my inferiors with whom to make merry, withal, your Grace excepted; unless it would please you that we might enjoy the company of the Lady Mary at Court. I could be merry with her." "We will have her here, darling, if that will make thee merry," said the King. And before many days had gone, Mary, with a full train of ladies, was brought from Hunsdon, magnificently dressed, to Whitehall, where, in the great presence chamber, Henry and his wife stood before the fire. The poor girl was almost overcome at the tenderness of her reception, and fell upon her knees before her father and his wife. Henry, as usual anxious to throw upon others the responsibility of his ill-treatment of his daughter, turned to his Councillors, who stood around, and said, "Some of you were desirous that I should put this jewel to death." "That were a pity," quoth the Queen, "to have lost your chiefest jewel of England." The hint was too much for Mary, who changed colour and fell into a swoon, greatly to her father's concern.

At length the day long yearned and prayed for by Henry came. Jane had for some months lived in the strictest quietude, and prayers and masses for her safe delivery were offered in the churches for weeks before. In September she had travelled slowly to Hampton Court, and on the 12th October 1537 a healthy son was born to her and Henry. The joy of the King was great beyond words. The gross sensualist, old beyond his years, had in vain hoped through all his sturdy youth for a boy, who, beyond reproach, might bear his regal name. He had flouted Christendom and defied the greatest powers on earth in order to marry a woman who might bear him a man child. When she failed to do so, he had coldly stood aside whilst his instruments defamed her and did her to death; and now, at last, in his declining years, his prayer was answered, and the House of Tudor was secure upon the future throne of England. Bonfires blazed and joy bells rang throughout the land; feasts of unexampled bounteousness coarsely brought home to the lieges the blessing that had come to save the country from the calamity of a disputed succession. The Seymour brothers at once became, next the King and his son, the most important personages in England, the elder, Edward, being created Earl of Hertford, and both receiving great additional grants of monastic lands. In the general jubilation at the birth, the interests of the mother were forgotten. No attempt appears to have been made to save her from the excitement that surrounded her; and on the very day of her delivery she signed an official letter "Jane the Quene" to Cromwell, directing him to communicate to the Privy Council the joyful news.

The most sumptuous royal christening ever seen was in bustling preparation in and about her sick-chamber; and that no circumstance of state should be lacking, the mother herself, only four days after the birth, was forced to take part in the exhausting ceremony. In the chapel at Hampton Court, newly decorated like the splendid banqueting-hall adjoining, where the initials of Jane carved in stone with those of the King, and her arms and device on glowing glass and gilded scutcheon still perpetuate her fleeting presence, the christening ceremony was held by torchlight late in the chill autumn evening. Through the long draughty corridors, preceded by braying trumpets and followed by rustling crowds of elated courtiers, the sick woman was carried on her stately pallet covered with heavy robes of crimson velvet and ermine. Under a golden canopy, supported by the four greatest nobles in the land, next to Norfolk, who was one of the godfathers, the Marchioness of Exeter bore the infant in her arms to the scene of the ceremony; and the Princess Mary, fiercely avid of love as she ever was, held the prince at the font. Suffolk, Arundel, and doomed Exeter, with a host of other magnates, stood around; whilst one towering handsome figure, with a long brown beard, carried aloft in his arms the tiny fair girl-child of Anne, the Lady Elizabeth, holding in her dainty hands the holy chrisom. It was Edward Seymour, Earl of Hertford, looked at askance by the rest as a new man, but already overlapping them all as the uncle of the infant prince. During the *Te Deum* and the long, pompous ceremony of the baptism the mother lay flushed and excited upon her couch; whilst the proud father, his broad face beaming with pride, sat by her side, holding her hand.

It was hard upon midnight when the Queen gave her blessing to her child and was carried back to her chamber, with more trumpet blasts and noisy gratulation. The next day, as was to be expected, she was in a high fever, so ill that she was confessed and received extreme unction. But she rallied, and seemed somewhat amended for the next few days, though ominous rumours were rife in London that her life had purposely been jeopardised in order to save that of the child at birth. They were not true, but they give the measure of the public estimate of Henry's character, and have been made the most of by Sanders, Rivadeneyra, and the other Jesuit historians. On the 23rd October the Queen fell gravely ill again, and in the night was thought to be dying. Henry had intended to ride to Esher that day, but "could not find it in his heart" to go; and the next night, the 24th October, Jane Seymour died, a sacrifice to improper treatment and heartlessly exacted ceremonial. Henry had not been married long enough to her to have become tired of her, and her somewhat lethargic placidity had suited him. She had, moreover, borne him the long-looked-for son; and his grief for her loss was profound, and no doubt sincere. Much as he hated signs of mortality, he wore black mourning for her for three months, and shut himself up at Windsor away from the world, and above all away from the corpse of his dead wife, for a fortnight. Jane's body, embalmed, lay in the presence chamber at Hampton Court for a week. Blazing tapers surrounded the great hearse, and masses went on from dawn to midday in the chamber. All night long the Queen's ladies, with Princess Mary, watched before the bier, until the end of the month, when the catafalque had been erected in the chapel for the formal lying in state. On the 12th November, with the greatest possible pomp, the funeral procession bore the dead Queen to Windsor for burial in a grave in St. George's Chapel, destined to receive the remains of Henry as well as that of his third wife, the mother of his son. The writers of the time, following the lead of Henry and his courtiers, never mentioned their grief for the Queen without promptly suggesting that it was more than counterbalanced by their joy at the birth of her son, who from his first appearance in the world was hailed as a paragon of beauty and perfection. Thanksgivings for the boon of a male heir to the King blended their sounds of jubilation with the droning of the masses for the mother's soul, and the flare of the bonfires died down into the flickering tapers that dimly lit the funerals. Even Henry himself, in writing to give the news of his son's birth, confessed that his joy at the event had far exceeded his grief for Jane's death.

So far as the Catholic party that had promoted it was concerned, the marriage with Jane had been a failure. The Pilgrimage of Grace had been drowned in the blood of ruthless slaughter: and partly because of Mary's scruples and fears, partly because they themselves had been gorged with the plunder of the Church, nearly all the great nobles stood aside and raised no voice whilst Cromwell and his master still worked havoc on the religious houses, regardless of Jane's timid intercession. Boxley, Walsingham, and even the sacred shrine of Canterbury, yielded their relics and images, venerated for centuries, to be scorned and destroyed; whilst the vast accumulated treasures of gold and gems that enriched them went to fill the coffers of the King, and their lands to bribe his favourites. Throughout England the work of confiscation was carried on now with a zeal which only greed for the resultant profit can explain. The attacks upon superstition in the Church by those in authority naturally aroused a feeling of greater freedom of thought amongst the mass of the people. The establishment of an open Bible in English in every church for the perusal of the parishioners, due, as indeed most of the doctrinal changes were, to Cranmer, encouraged men to think to some extent for themselves. But though, for purposes to which reference will be made presently, Henry willingly concurred in Cranmer's reforming tendencies and Cromwell's anti-ecclesiastical plans for providing him with abundant money, he would allow no departure from orthodoxy as he understood it. His love for theological controversy, and his undoubted ability and learning in that direction, enabled him to enforce his views with apparently unanswerable arguments, especially as he was able, and quite ready, to close the dispute with an obstinate antagonist by prescribing the stake and the gibbet either to those who repudiated his spiritual supremacy or to those who, like the Anabaptists, questioned the efficacy of a sacrament which he had adopted. For Henry it was to a great extent a matter of pride and self-esteem now to show to his own subjects and the world that he was absolutely supreme and infallible, and this feeling unquestionably had greatly influenced the progress effected by the reformation and emancipation from Rome made after the disappointing marriage with Jane Seymour.

But there was also policy in Henry's present action. Throughout the years 1536 and 1537 Francis and the Emperor had continued at war; but by the close of the latter year it was evident that both combatants were exhausted, and would shortly make up their differences. The Papal excommunication of Henry and his realm was now in full force, making rebellion against the King a laudable act for all good Catholics; and any agreement between the two great Continental sovereigns in union with Rome boded ill for England and for its King. There were others, too, to whom such a combination boded ill. The alliance between France and the infidel Turk to attack the Christian Emperor had aroused intense indignation amongst Catholics throughout the world against Francis; and the Pope, utilising this feeling, strove hard to persuade both Christian sovereigns to cease their fratricidal struggle and to recognise that the real enemy to be feared and destroyed was Lutheranism or heresy in their midst. During the Emperor's absence, and the war, Protestantism in Germany had advanced with giant strides. The Princes had boldly refused to recognise any conciliatory Council of the Church under the control of the Pope; and the pressure used by the Emperor to compel them to do so aroused the suspicion that the day was fast approaching when Lutheranism would have to fight for its life against the imperial suzerain of Germany.

Already the forces were gathering. George of Saxony, the enemy of Luther, was hurrying to the grave, and Henry his brother and heir was a strong Protestant. Philip of Hesse had two years before thrown down the gage, and had taken by force from the Emperor the territory of Würtemburg, and had restored the Protestant Duke Ulrich. Charles' brother Ferdinand, who ruled the empire, clamoured as loudly as did Mary of Hungary in Flanders and Eleanor of Austria in France, for a peace between the two champions of Christendom, the repudiation by France of the Turkish alliance, and a concentration of the Catholic forces in the world before it was too late to crush the hydra of heresy which threatened them all. It was natural in the circumstances that the enemies of the Papacy should be drawn together. A fellow-feeling makes us wondrous kind, and a common danger drew Henry of England and Philip of Hesse together. Henry was no Lutheran, and did not pretend to be. He had been drawn into the Reformation by the process that we have followed, in which interested advisers had worked upon his passions and self-esteem; but he had gone too far in defiance of Rome now to turn back, and was forced to look to his own safety by such policy as was possible to him. For several months after Jane Seymour's death the envoys of the German Protestants were in England in close negotiation with Henry and Cromwell. In order that a close league should be made, it was necessary that some common doctrinal standpoint should be agreed upon, and infinite theological discussions took place to bring this about. Henry would not give way on any principal point, and the Protestant ambassadors went home again without a formal understanding. But though Henry remained, as he intended to do, thus unpledged, it was good policy for him to impress upon the Germans by his ruthless suppression of the monasteries, and his prohibition of the ancient superstitions, that he was the enemy of their enemy; and that if he was attacked for heresy, it would be incumbent upon the Lutherans to be on his side even against their own suzerain.

This was not, however, the only move made by Henry against the threatening danger of a joint attack of the Catholic powers. He had hardly thrown off his mourning for Jane before he turned his hand to the old game of dividing his rivals. His bluff was as audacious and brilliant as usual. To the imperial and French ambassadors in turn he boasted that either of their masters would prefer his friendship and alliance to that of the other; and, rightly convinced that he would really be more likely to gain latitudinarian Francis than Charles, he proposed in the spring of 1538 that he should marry a French princess. As the two great Catholic sovereigns drew closer together, though still nominally at war in Italy, Henry became, indeed, quite an eager wooer. His friend, Sir Francis Brian, was sent to Paris, secretly to forward his suit, and obtained a portrait of the Duke of Guise's second daughter, the sister of the King of Scotland's bride, Mary of Lorraine; with which Henry confessed himself quite smitten. He had, before this, only three months after Jane's death, made a desperate attempt to prevail upon Francis to let him have Mary of Lorraine herself; though she was already betrothed to the King of Scots, his nephew; but this had been positively and even indignantly refused. Even the younger daughter of Guise, beautiful as she was, did not quite satisfy his vanity. Both he and his agent Brian, who was a fit representative for him, disgusted Francis by suggesting that three other French princesses should be taken to Calais by the Queen of Navarre— Francis' sister— in order that they might be paraded before the King of England for his selection, "like hackneys," as was said at the time. He thought that the angry repudiation of such an insulting proposal was most unreasonable. "How can I choose a wife by deputy?" he asked. "I must depend upon my own eyes"; besides, he added, he must hear them sing, and see how they comported themselves. Perhaps, suggested the French ambassador sarcastically, he would like to go further and test the ladies in other ways, as the knights of King Arthur used to do. Henry coloured at this; but vauntingly replied that he could, if he pleased, marry into the imperial house; but he would not marry at all unless he was quite sure that his new relation would prefer his alliance to all others. When, at length, in June, the truce of Nice was signed, and soon afterwards the fraternal meeting and close community between Francis and Charles was effected at Aigues Mortes, Henry began to get seriously alarmed. His matrimonial offers, to his surprise, were treated very coolly; all his attempts to breed dissension between the imperial and French ambassadors, who were now hand and glove, were laughed at; and the intimate confidence and friendship between his two Catholic rivals seemed at last to bring disaster to Henry's very doors; for it was not concealed that the first blow to be struck by the Catholic confederacy was to be upon the schismatic heretic who ruled England.

With Francis there was no more to be done; for Henry and Brian, by their want of delicacy, had between them deeply wounded all the possible French brides and their families. But, at least, Henry hoped that sufficient show of friendship with Charles might be simulated to arouse Francis' jealousy of his new ally. Henry therefore began to sneer at the patched-up friendship, as he called it. "And how about Milan?" he asked the French ambassador, knowing that that was the still rankling sore; and soon he began to boast more openly that he himself might have Milan by the cession of it as a dower to Dom Luiz of Portugal, on his marriage with the Princess Mary; whilst Henry himself married the young widowed Duchess of Milan, Charles' niece, Christina of Denmark, that clever, quick-witted woman, whose humorous face lives for ever on the canvas of Holbein in the English National Gallery. There had been a Spanish ambassador, Diego Hurtado de Mendoza, in England since the spring of 1537, to negotiate the Portuguese marriage of the Princess Mary; but the eternal questions of dowry, security, and the legitimacy of the Princess had made all negotiations so far abortive. Now they were taken up more strongly, by means of Wyatt at Madrid, and by special envoys to Mary of Hungary in Flanders. But it was all "buckler play," as the imperial agents and Charles himself soon found out. Henry and Cromwell knew perfectly well that no stable alliance with the Emperor was possible then unless their religious policy was changed; and they had gone too far to change it without humiliation, if not destruction, to Henry; the real object of the negotiations being simply to obtain some sort of promise about the cession of Milan, by which Francis might be detached from the imperial alliance. But it was unsuccessful; and, for once, the two great antagonists held together for a time against all Lutheranism and heresy.

Then Henry and Cromwell had to look anxiously for support and alliances elsewhere. To the King it was a repugnant and humiliating necessity. He had puffed himself into the belief that he was the most potent and infallible of sovereigns, and he found himself, for the first time, scorned by all those he had reason to fear. He, the embodiment of the idea of regal omnipotence, would be forced to make common cause with those who, like the German Protestants, stood for resistance to supreme authority; with usurpers like Christian III. of Denmark, and trading democracies like Lübeck. With much hesitation and dislike, therefore, he listened, whilst Cromwell urged the inevitable policy upon him, which led him farther and farther away from the inner circle of potentates to which he and his father had gained entrance in the course of the events related in the first chapters of this book.

Cromwell's arguments would probably have been unavailing but for the opportune "discovery," in the usual fortuitous Cromwell fashion, of a dangerous aristocratic conspiracy against Henry himself. Cardinal Pole had been entrusted with the Papal excommunication, and everywhere impressed upon English Catholics the duty of obeying their spiritual father by deposing the King. Whether anything in the form of a regular conspiracy to do this existed in England is extremely doubtful; but the Cardinal had naturally written to his relatives in England, especially to his brother Geoffrey, and perhaps to his mother, the Countess of Salisbury, a princess of the blood royal of York. First Geoffrey was seized and carried to the Tower, and some sort of incriminating admission drawn from him by threats of torture, though, so far as can be gathered, nothing but the repetition of disaffected conversations. It was enough, however, for Cromwell's purpose when he needed it; and the fatal net was cast over Pole's elder brother, Lord Montague, the Marquis of Exeter, allied to the royal house, the Master of the Horse, Sir Nicholas Carew, Sir Edward Neville, and half a score of other high gentlemen, known to be faithful to the old cause— all to be unjustly sacrificed on the scaffold to the fears of Henry and the political exigencies of Cromwell. Even the women and children of the supposed sympathisers with the Papacy were not spared; and the aged Countess of

Salisbury, with her grandson, and the Marchioness of Exeter, with her son, were imprisoned with many humbler ones.

The defences of the kingdom on the coast and towards Scotland were rapidly made ready to resist attack from abroad, which indeed looked imminent; and when the noble and conservative party had been sufficiently cowed by the sight of the blood of the highest of its members, when the reign of terror over the land had made all men so dumb and fearsome that none dared say him nay, Cromwell felt himself strong enough to endeavour to draw England into the league of Protestant princes and defy the Catholic world. The position for Henry personally was an extraordinary one. He had gradually drifted into a position of independence from Rome; but he still professed to be a strict Catholic in other respects. His primate, Cranmer, and several other of his bishops whose ecclesiastical status was unrecognised by the Pope, were unquestionably, and not unnaturally, Protestant in their sympathies; whilst Cromwell was simply a politician who cared nothing for creeds and faiths, except as ancillary to State policy. Francis, and even on occasion Charles himself, made little of taking Church property for lay purposes when he needed it: he had more than once been the ally of the infidel against Catholic princes, and his religious belief was notoriously lax; and yet he remained "the eldest son of the Church." Charles had struggled successfully against the Papal pretensions to control the temporalities of the Spanish Church, his troops had sacked Rome and imprisoned the Pope, and his ministers for years had bullied pontiffs and scolded them as if they were erring schoolboys. Excommunication had fallen upon him and his, and as hard things had been said of him in Rome as of Henry; and yet he was the champion of Catholic Christendom. The conclusion is obvious that Henry's sin towards the Papacy was not primarily the spoliation of the Church, the repudiation of Katharine, or even the assumption of control over the temporalities, but that he had arrogated to himself the spiritual headship in his realm. In most other respects he was as good a Catholic as Charles, and a much better one than Francis; and yet under stress of circumstances he was forced into common cause with the growing party of reform in Europe, whose separation from the Church was profoundly doctrinal, and arose from entirely different motives from those of Henry.

The danger that threatened England at the time (early in 1539) was not really quite so serious as it seemed; for, close as the alliance between Charles and Francis was, old jealousies were not dead, and a joint war against England would have revived them; whilst the Papal plan of treating England commercially as outside the pale of civilisation would have ruined Charles' subject and was impracticable. But, in any case, the peril was real to Henry and Cromwell; and under the stress of it they were driven into the attempted policy of a Protestant confederacy. At the end of January 1539, Christopher Mont was sent to Germany with the first overtures. He carried letters of credence to Philip of Hesse, and Hans Frederick of Saxony, with the ostensible object of asking whether they had come to any conclusion respecting the theological disputations held in the previous year between their envoys and the English bishops to establish a common doctrinal basis. This, of course, was a mere pretext, the real object of the mission being to discover to what extent Henry could depend upon the German Protestant princes if he were attacked by their suzerain the Emperor. A private instruction was given to Mont by Cromwell, to remind one of the Saxon ministers who had come to England of a former conversation about a possible marriage between the young Duke of Cleves and the Princess Mary; and he was to take the opportunity of finding out all he could about the "beauty and qualities, shape, stature, and complexion" of the elder of the two unmarried daughters of the old Duke of Cleves, whose eldest daughter, Sybilla, had married Hans Frederick of Saxony himself, and was as bold a Protestant as he was. At the same time approaches were made to Christian III. of Denmark, who had joined the Evangelical league; and gradually the forces against the Papacy were to be knitted together. An excuse also was found to send English envoys to Cleves itself to offer an alliance in the matter of the Duchy of Gueldres, which the Duke of Cleves had just seized without the Emperor's connivance or consent. Carne and Wotton, the envoys, were also to offer the hand of the Princess Mary to the young Duke, and cautiously to hint at a marriage between his sister Anne and Henry, if conditions were favourable; and, like Mont in Saxony, were to close the ranks of Protestantism around the threatened Henry, from whose Court both the imperial and French ambassadors had now been withdrawn.

Whilst these intrigues for Protestant support on the Continent were being carried on, and the defences of England on all sides were being strengthened, Henry, apparently for the purpose of disarming the Catholic elements, and proving that, apart from the Papal submission, he was as good a Catholic as any, forced through Parliament (May 1539) the extraordinary statute called the Six Articles, or the Bloody Statute, which threw all English Protestants into a panic. The Act was drafted on Henry's instructions by Bishop Gardiner, and was called an "Act to abolish diversity of opinions." The articles of faith dictated by the King to his subjects under ferocious penalties included the main Catholic doctrine; the real presence in the Sacrament in its fullest sense; the celibacy of the clergy; that the administration of the Sacrament in two kinds is not necessary; that auricular confession is compulsory, that private masses may be said, and that vows of chastity must be kept for ever. Cranmer, who was married and had children, dared to argue against the Bill when the Duke of Norfolk introduced it in the House of Lords, and others of the new bishops timidly did likewise; but they were overborne by the old bishops and the great majority of the lay peers, influenced by their traditions and by the peremptory arguments of the King himself. Even more important was an Act passed in the same servile Parliament giving to the King's proclamations the force of law; and an Act of attainder against every one, living or dead, in England or abroad, who had opposed the King, completed the terror under which thenceforward the country lay. Henry was now, indeed, master of the bodies and souls of his subjects, and had reduced them all, Protestants and Catholics alike, to a condition of abject subjection to his mere will. The passage of these Acts, especially the Six Articles, marks a temporarily successful attempt of the conservative party, represented by the old bishops and the nobles under Norfolk, to overcome the influence of Cromwell, who was forwarding the Protestant league; but to Henry the policy must in any case have seemed a good one, as it tended to increase his personal power and prestige, and to keep both parties dependent upon him.

Before the summer of 1539 had passed it was evident to Henry that the new combination against him would not stand the strain of a joint attack upon England. Charles was full of cares of his own. The Lutherans were increasingly threatening; even his own city of Ghent had revolted, and it was plain from his reception of Pole at Toledo that he could not proceed to extremes against Henry. It certainly was not the intention of Francis to do so; and the panic in England— never fully justified— passed away. The French ambassador came back, and once more Henry's intrigues to sow dissension between the Catholic powers went ceaselessly on. In the circumstances it was natural that, after the passage of the Six Articles and the resumption of diplomatic relations with France, the negotiations with the German Protestants slackened. But the proposed marriage of Henry with the Princess of Cleves offered too good an opportunity, as Cromwell pointed out to him, of troubling the Emperor when he liked, to be dropped, even though no general political league was effected with the German Lutherans. Her brother-in-law, Hans Frederick of Saxony, was cool about it. He said that some sort of engagement had been made by her father and the Duke of Lorraine to marry her to the heir of the latter, but finally in August Wotton reported from Duren that Hans Frederick would send envoys to Cleves to propose the match, and they would then proceed to England to close the matter. Wotton had been somewhat distrustful about the previous engagement of Anne with the Duke of Lorraine's son, but was assured by the Council of Cleves that it was not binding upon the Princess, "who was free to marry as she pleased." "She has been brought up," he writes, "with the Lady Duchess, her mother ... and in a manner never from her elbow; the Lady Duchess being a wise lady, and one that very straitly looketh to her children. All report her (Anne) to be of very lowly and gentle conditions, by the which she hath so much won her mother's favour that she is loth to suffer her to depart from her. She occupieth her time mostly with her needle, wherewithal ... she can read and write (Dutch); but as to French, Latin, or any other language, she hath none. Nor yet she cannot sing nor play any instrument, for they take it here in Germany for a rebuke, and an occasion of lightness that great ladies should be learned or have any knowledge of music. Her wit is good, and she will no doubt learn English soon when she puts her mind to it. I could never hear that she is inclined to the good cheer of this country; and marvel it were if she should, seeing that her brother ... doth so well abstain from it. Your Grace's servant Hans Holbein hath taken the effigies of my Lady Anne and the Lady Amelia, and hath expressed their images very lively."

Holbein was not usually a flattering painter to his sitters, and the portrait he sent of Anne was that of a somewhat masculine and large-featured, but handsome and intellectual young woman, with fine, soft, contemplative brown eyes, thick lashes, and strong eyebrows. The general appearance is dignified, though handicapped by the very unbecoming Dutch dress of the period; and though there is nothing of the *petite* sprightliness and soft rotundity that would be likely to attract a man of Henry's characteristics, the Princess cannot have been ill-favoured. Cromwell some months earlier had reported to Henry that Mont informed him that "everybody praises the lady's beauty, both of face and body. One said she excelled the Duchess (of Milan ?) as the golden sun did the silver moon." If the latter statement be near the truth, Anne, in her own way, must have been quite good-looking. There was no delay or difficulty in carrying through the arrangements for the marriage. The envoys from Cleves and Saxony arrived in London in September, and saw Henry at Windsor. They could offer no great dowry, for Cleves was poor; but they would not be exacting about the appanage to be settled upon the Queen by her husband, to whom they left the decision of the sum; and the other covenants as to the eventual succession to her brother's duchy, in case of his death without heirs, were to be the same as those under which her elder sister married Hans Frederick.

This was the sort of spirit that pleased Henry in negotiators, and with such he was always disposed to be liberal. He practically waived the dowry, and only urged that the lady should come at once, before the winter was too far advanced. When he suggested that she should come from her home down the Rhine through Holland, and thence by sea to England, the envoys prayed that she might go through Germany and Flanders by land to Calais, and so across. For, said they, by sea there will be great peril of capture and insult by some too zealous subjects of the Emperor. "Besides, they fear lest, the time of year being now cold and tempestuous, she might there, though she never were so well ordered, take such cold or other disease, considering she never was before upon the seas, as should be to her great peril.... She is, moreover, young and beautiful; and if she should be transported by sea they fear much how it might alter her complexion." No sooner was the marriage treaty signed than splendid preparations were made for the reception of the King's coming bride. The Lord Admiral (Fitzwilliam) was ordered to prepare a fleet of ten vessels to escort her from Calais; repairs and redecorations of the royal residences went on apace; and especially in the Queen's apartments, where again the initials of poor Jane had to be altered to those of her successor, and the "principal lords have bought much cloth of gold and silk, a thing unusual for them except for some great solemnity."

The conclusion of the treaty was a triumph for Cromwell and the Protestant party in Henry's Council; and the Commissioners who signed it reflect the fact. Cranmer, Cromwell, the Duke of Suffolk, Lord Chancellor Audley, and Lord Admiral Fitzwilliam, were all of them inclined to the reforming side, whilst Bishop Tunstal, though on the Catholic side, was a personal friend of the King; and the new man, Hertford, Jane Seymour's brother, though not one of the Commissioners, gave emphatic approval of the match. "I am as glad," he wrote to Cromwell, "of the good resolution (of the marriage) as ever I was of a thing since the birth of the Prince; for I think the King's Highness could not in Christendom marry in any place meet for his Grace's honour that should be less prejudicial to his Majesty's succession." Henry himself was in his usual vaunting mood about the alliance. He had long desired, he said, to cement a union with the German confederation, and could now disregard both France and the Emperor; besides, his influence would suffice to prevent the Lutherans from going too far in their religious innovations. As for the lady, he had only one male child, and he was convinced that his desire for more issue could not be better fulfilled "than with the said lady, who is of convenient age, healthy temperament, elegant stature, and endowed with other graces."

The news of the engagement was ill received by Francis and Charles. They became more ostentatiously friendly than ever; and their ambassadors in London were inseparable. When Marillac and the Emperor's temporary envoy went together to tell Cromwell that the Emperor was so confident of the friendship of Francis that he was riding through France from Spain to Flanders, the English minister quite lost his composure. He was informed, he told the ambassadors, that this meeting of the monarchs was "merely with the view to making war on this poor King (Henry), who aimed at nothing but peace and friendship." Ominous mutterings came, too, from Flanders at the scant courtesy Henry had shown in throwing over the match with the Duchess of Milan in the midst of the negotiation. Cromwell was therefore full of anxiety, whilst the elaborate preparations were being made in Calais and in England for the new Queen's reception. Not only was a fresh household to be appointed, the nobility and gentry and their retinues summoned, fine clothes galore ordered or enjoined for others, the towns on the way from Dover to be warned of the welcome expected from them, and the hundred details dependent upon the arrival and installation of the King's fourth wife, but Henry himself had to be carefully handled, to prevent the fears engendered by the attitude of his rivals causing him to turn to the party opposed to Cromwell before the Protestant marriage was effected.

In the meanwhile, Anne with a great train of guards and courtiers, three hundred horsemen strong, rode from Dusseldorf towards Calais through Cleves, Antwerp, Bruges, and Dunkirk. It was ordered that Lord Lisle, Lord Deputy of Calais, should meet the Queen on the English frontier, near Gravelines, and that at St. Pierre, Lord Admiral Fitzwilliam, who had a fleet of fifty sail in the harbour, should greet her in the name of his King, gorgeously dressed in blue velvet, smothered with gold embroidery, and faced with crimson satin, royal blue and crimson, the King's colours, in velvet, damask, and silk, being the universal wear, even of the sailors and men-at-arms. The aged Duke of Suffolk and the Lord Warden were to receive her on her landing at Dover; and at Canterbury she was to be welcomed and entertained by Archbishop Cranmer. Norfolk and a great company of armed nobles were to greet the new Queen on the downs beyond Rochester; whilst the Queen's household, with Lady Margaret Douglas, the King's niece, and the Duchess of Richmond, his daughter-in-law, were to join her at Deptford, and the whole vast and glittering multitude were to convey her thence to where the King's pavilions were erected for her reception at Blackheath.

In the midwinter twilight of early morning, on the 11th December 1539, Anne's cavalcade entered the English town of Calais, and during the long time she remained weather-bound there she was entertained as sumptuously as the nobles and townsmen could entertain her. The day she had passed through Dunkirk in the Emperor's dominions, just before coming to Calais, a sermon was preached against her and all Lutherans; but with that exception no molestation was offered to her. The ship that was to carry her over, dressed fore and aft with silken flags, streamers, and banners, was exhibited to her admiration by Fitzwilliam, royal salutes thundered welcome to her, bands of martial music clashed in her honour, and banquets and jousts were held to delight her. Good sense and modesty were shown by her in many ways at this somewhat trying time. Her principal mentor, Chancellor Olsiliger, begged Fitzwilliam to advise her as to her behaviour; and she herself asked him to teach her some game of cards that the King of England usually played. He taught her a game which he calls "Sent, which she did learn with good grace and countenance"; and she then begged him to come to sup with her, and bring some noble folk with him to sit with her in the German way. He told her that this was not the fashion in England, but he accepted her invitation.

Thus Anne began betimes to prepare for what she hoped— greatly daring— would be a happy married life in England; whilst the wind and the waves thundering outside the harbour forbade all attempt to convey the bride to her now expectant bridegroom. Henry had intended to keep Christmas with unusual state at Greenwich in the company of his new wife; but week after week slipped by, with the wind still contrary, and it was the 27th December before a happy change of weather enabled Anne to set sail for her new home. She had a stout heart, for the passage was a rough though rapid one. When she landed at Deal, and thence, after a short rest, was conducted in state to Dover Castle, the wind blew blusterously, and the hail and winter sleet drove "continually in her Grace's face"; but she would hear of no delay in her journey forward, "so desirous was her Grace of reaching the King's presence." At Canterbury the citizens received her with a great torchlight procession and peals of guns. "In her chamber were forty or fifty gentlewomen waiting to receive her in velvet bonnets; all of which she took very joyously, and was so glad to see the King's subjects resorting to her so lovingly, that she forgot all the foul weather and was very merry at supper."

And so, with an evident determination to make the best of everything, Anne rode onward, accompanied by an ever-growing cavalcade of sumptuously bedizened folk, through Sittingbourne, and so to Rochester, where she was lodged at the bishop's palace, and passed New Year's Day 1540. News daily reached the King of his bride's approach, whilst he remained consumed with impatience at Greenwich. At each successive stage of her journey forward supple courtiers had written to Henry glowing accounts of the beauty and elegance of the bride. Fitzwilliam from Calais had been especially emphatic, and the King's curiosity was piqued to see the paragon he was to marry. At length, when he knew that Anne was on the way from Sittingbourne to Rochester, and would arrive there on New Year's Eve, he told Cromwell that he himself, with an escort of eight gentlemen clad in grey, would ride to Rochester incognito to get early sight of his bride, "whom he sorely desired to see." He went, he said, "to nourish love"; and full of hopeful anticipation, Henry on a great courser ambled over Gad's Hill from Gravesend to Rochester soon after dawn on New Year's Day 1540, with Sir Anthony Browne, his Master of the Horse, on one side, and Sir John Russell on the other. It was in accordance with the chivalrous tradition that this should be done, and that the lady should pretend to be extremely surprised when she was informed who her visitor was; so that Anne must have made a fair guess as to what was coming when Sir Anthony Browne, riding a few hundred yards ahead of his master, entered her presence, and, kneeling, told her that he had brought a New Year's gift for her. When the courtier raised his eyes and looked critically upon the lady before him, experienced as he was in Henry's tastes, "he was never more dismayed in his life to see her so far unlike that which was reported."

Anne was about twenty-four years of age, but looked older, and her frame was large, bony, and masculine, which in the facial portraits that had been sent to Henry was not indicated, and her large, low-German features, deeply pitted with the ravages of smallpox, were, as Browne knew, the very opposite of the type of beauty which would be likely to stimulate a gross, unwholesome voluptuary of nearly fifty. So, with a sinking heart, he went back to his master, not daring to prepare him for what was before him by any hint of disparagement of the bride. As soon as Henry entered with Russell and Browne and saw for himself, his countenance fell, and he made a wry face, which those who knew him understood too well; and they trembled in their shoes at what was to come of it. He nevertheless greeted the lady politely, raising her from the kneeling position she had assumed, and kissed her upon the cheek, passing a few minutes in conversation with her about her long journey. He had brought with him some rich presents of sables and other furs; but he was "so marvellously astonished and abashed" that he had not the heart to give them to her, but sent them the next morning with a cold message by Sir Anthony Browne.

In the night the royal barge had been brought round from Gravesend to Rochester, and the King returned to Greenwich in the morning by water. He had hardly passed another word with Anne since the first meeting, though they had supped together, and it was with a sulky, frowning face that he took his place in the shelter of his galley. Turning to Russell, he asked, "Do you think this woman so fair or of such beauty as report has made her?" Russell, courtier-like, fenced with the question by feigning to misunderstand it. "I should hardly take her to be fair," he replied, "but of brown complexion." "Alas!" continued the King, "whom should men trust? I promise you I see no such thing in her as hath been showed unto me of her, and am ashamed that men have so praised her as they have done. I like her not." To Browne he was quite as outspoken. "I see nothing in this woman as men report of her," he said angrily, "and I am surprised that wise men should make such reports as they have done." Whereat Browne, who knew that his brother-in-law, Fitzwilliam, was one of the "wise men" referred to, scented danger and was silent. The English ladies, too, who had accompanied Anne on the road began to whisper in confidence to their spouses that Anne's manners were coarse, and that she would never suit the King's fastidious taste.

But he who had most to lose and most to fear was Cromwell. It was he who had drawn and driven his master into the Protestant friendship against the Emperor and the Pope, of which the marriage was to be the pledge, and he had repeated eagerly for months the inflated praises of Anne's beauty sent by his agents and friends in order to pique Henry to the union. He knew that vigilant enemies of himself and his policy were around him, watching for their opportunity, Norfolk and the older nobles, the Pope's bishops, and, above all, able, ambitious Stephen Gardiner, now sulking at Winchester, determined to supplant him if he could. When, on Friday the 2nd January, Henry entered his working closet at Greenwich after his water journey from Rochester, Cromwell asked him "how he liked the Lady Anne." The King answered gloomily, "Nothing so well as she was spoken of," adding that if he had known before as much as he knew then, she should never have come within his realm. In the grievous self-pity usual with him in his perplexity, he turned to Cromwell, the man hitherto so fertile in expedients, and wailed, "What is the remedy?" Cromwell, for once at a loss, could only express his grief, and say he knew of none. In very truth it was too late now to stop the state reception; for preparations had been ordered for such a pageant as had rarely been seen in England. Cromwell had intended it for his own triumph, and as marking the completeness of his victory over his opponents. Once more ambition o'erleaped itself, and the day that was to establish Cromwell's supremacy sealed his doom.

What Anne thought of the situation is not on record. She had seen little of the world, outside the coarse boorishness of a petty low-German court; she was neither educated nor naturally refined, and she probably looked upon the lumpishness of her lover as an ordinary thing. In any case, she bated none of her state and apparent contentment, as she rode gorgeously bedight with her great train towards Greenwich. At the foot of Shooter's Hill there had been erected an imposing pavilion of cloth of gold, and divers other tents warmed with fires of perfumed wood; and here a company of ladies awaited the coming of the Queen on Saturday, 3rd January 1540. A broad way was cleared from the pavilion, across Woolwich Common and Blackheath, for over two miles, to the gates of Greenwich Park; and the merchants and Corporation of London joined with the King's retinue in lining each side of this long lane. Cromwell had recently gained the goodwill of foreigners settled in London by granting them exemption from special taxation for a term of years, and he had claimed, as some return, that they should make the most of this day of triumph. Accordingly, the German merchants of the Steelyard, the Venetians, the Spaniards, the French, and the rest of them, donned new velvet coats and jaunty crimson caps with white feathers, each master with a smartly clad servant behind him, and so stood each side of the way to do honour to the bride at the Greenwich end of the route. Then came the English merchants, the Corporation of London, the knights and gentlemen who had been bidden from the country to do honour to their new Queen, the gentlemen pensioners, the halberdiers, and, around the tent, the nobler courtiers and Queen's household, all brave in velvet and gold chains. Behind the ranks of gentlemen and servitors there was ample room and verge enough upon the wide heath for the multitudes who came to gape and cheer King Harry's new wife; more than a little perplexed in many cases as to the minimum amount of enthusiasm which would be accepted as seemly. Cromwell himself marshalled the ranks on either side, "running up and down with a staff in his hand, for all the world as if he had been a running postman," as an eye-witness tells us.

It was midday before the Queen's procession rode down Shooter's Hill to the tents, where she was met by her official household and greeted with a long Latin oration which she did not understand, whilst she sat in her chariot. Then heartily kissing the great ladies sent to welcome her, she alighted and entered the tent to rest and warm herself over the perfumed fires, and to don even more magnificent raiment than that she wore. When she was ready for her bridegroom's coming she must have been a blaze of magnificence. She wore a wide skirt of cloth of gold with a raised pattern in bullion and no train, and her head was covered first with a close cap and then a round cap covered with pearls and fronted with black velvet; whilst her bodice was one glittering mass of precious stones. When swift messengers brought news that the King was coming, Anne mounted at the door of the tent a beautiful white palfrey; and surrounded by her servitors, each bearing upon his golden coat the black lion of Cleves, and followed by her train, she set forth to meet her husband.

Henry, unwieldy and lame as he was with a running ulcer in the leg, was as vain and fond of pomp as ever, and outdid his bride in splendour. His coat was of purple velvet cut like a frock, embroidered all over with a flat gold pattern interlined with narrow gold braid, and with gold lace laid crosswise over it all. A velvet overcoat surmounted the gorgeous garment, lined also with gold tissue, the sleeves and breast held together with great buttons of diamonds, rubies, and pearls. His sword and belt were covered with emeralds, and his bonnet and undercap were "so rich in jewels that few men could value them"; whilst across his shoulders he wore a baldrick, composed of precious stones and pearls, that was the wonder of all beholders. The fat giant thus bedizened bestrode a great war-horse to match, and almost equally magnificent; and, preceded by heralds and trumpeters, followed by the great officers, the royal household and the bishops, and accompanied by the Duke Philip of Bavaria, just betrothed to the Princess Mary, Henry rode through the long lane of his velvet-clad admirers to meet Anne, hard by the cross upon Blackheath. When she approached him, he doffed his jewelled bonnet and bowed low; and then embraced her, whilst she, with every appearance of delight and duty, expressed her pleasure at meeting him. Thus, together, with their great cavalcades united, over five thousand horsemen strong, they rode in the waning light of a midwinter afternoon to Greenwich; and, as one who saw it but knew not the tragedy that lurked behind the splendour, exclaimed, "Oh! what a sight was this to see, so goodly a Prince and so noble a King to ride with so fair a lady of so goodly a stature, and so womanly a countenance, and especial of so good qualities. I think that no creature could see them but his heart rejoiced."

ANNE OF CLEVES
From a portrait by a German artist in St. John's College, Oxford

There was one heart, at all events, that did not rejoice, and that was Henry's. He went heavily through the ceremony of welcoming home his bride in the great hall at Greenwich, and then led her to her chamber; but no sooner had he got quit of her, than retiring to his own room he summoned Cromwell. "Well!" he said, "is it not as I told you? Say what they will, she is nothing like so fair as she was reported to be. She is well and seemly, but nothing else." Cromwell, confused, could only mumble something about her having a queenly manner. But Henry wanted a way out of his bargain rather than reconciliation to it; and he ordered Cromwell to summon the Council at once— Norfolk, Suffolk, Cromwell, Cranmer, Fitzwilliam, and Tunstal— to consider the prior engagement made between Anne and the Duke of Lorraine's son. The question had already been discussed and disposed of, and the revival of it thus at the eleventh hour shows how desperate Henry was. The Council assembled immediately, and summoned the German envoys who had negotiated the marriage and were now in attendance on Anne. The poor men were thunderstruck at the point of an impediment to the marriage being raised then, and begged to be allowed to think the matter over till the next morning, Sunday. When they met the Council again in the morning, they could only protest that the prior covenant had only been a betrothal, which had never taken effect, and had been formally annulled. If there was any question about it, however, they offered to remain as prisoners in England until the original deed of revocation was sent from Cleves.

When this answer was carried to Henry he broke out angrily that he was not being well treated, and upbraided Cromwell for not finding a loophole for escape. He did not wish to marry the woman, he said. "If she had not come so far, and such great preparations made, and for fear of making a ruffle in the world— of driving her brother into the hands of the Emperor and the French King— he never would marry her." Cromwell was apparently afraid to encourage him in the idea of repudiation, and said nothing; and after dinner the King again summoned the Council to his presence. To them he bitterly complained of having been deceived. Would the lady, he asked, make a formal protestation before notaries that she was free from all contracts? Of course she would, and did, as soon as she was asked; but Henry's idea in demanding this is evident. If she had refused it would give a pretext for delay, but if she did as desired, and by any quibble the prior engagement was found to be valid, her protestation to the contrary would be good grounds for a divorce. But still Henry would much rather not have married her at all. "Oh! is there no other remedy?" he asked despairingly on Monday, after Anne had made her protestation. "Must I needs against my will put my neck into the yoke?" Cromwell could give him no comfort, and left him gloomy at the prospect of going through the ceremony on the morrow. On Tuesday morning, when he was apparelled for the wedding, as usual in a blaze of magnificence of crimson satin and cloth of gold, Cromwell entered his chamber on business. "My lord," said Henry, "if it were not to satisfy the world and my realm, I would not do what I must do this day for any earthly thing." But withal he went through it as best he might, though with heavy heart and gloomy countenance, and the unfortunate bride, we are told, was remarked to be "demure and sad," as well she might be, when her husband and Cranmer placed upon her finger the wedding-ring with the ominous inscription, "God send me well to keep."

Early the next morning Cromwell entered the King's chamber between hope and fear, and found Henry frowning and sulky. "How does your Grace like the Queen?" he asked. Henry grumblingly, and not quite relevantly, replied that he, Cromwell, was not everybody; and then he broke out, "Surely, my lord, as you know, I liked her not well before, but now I like her much worse." With an incredible grossness, and want of common decency, he then went into certain details of his wife's physical qualities that had disgusted him and turned him against her. He did not believe, from certain peculiarities that he described, that she was a maid, he said; but so far as he was concerned, he was so "struck to the heart" that he had left her as good a maid as he had found her. Nor was the King more reticent with others. He was free with his details to the gentlemen of his chamber, Denny, Heneage, and others, as to the signs which it pleased him to consider suspicious as touching his wife's previous virtue, and protested that he never could, or would, consummate the marriage; though he professed later that for months after the wedding he did his best to overcome his repugnance, and lived constantly in contact with his wife. But he never lost sight of the hope of getting free. If he did not find means soon to do so, he said, he should have no more issue. His conscience told him— that tender conscience of his— that Anne was not his legal wife; and he turned to Cromwell for a remedy, and found none: for Cromwell knew that the breaking up of the Protestant union, upon which he had staked his future, would inevitably mean now the rise of his rivals and his own ruin.

He fought stoutly for his position, though Norfolk and Gardiner were often now at the King's ear. His henchman, Dr. Barnes, who had gone to Germany as envoy during the marriage negotiations, was a Protestant, and in a sermon on justification by faith he violently attacked Gardiner. The latter, in spite of Cromwell and Cranmer, secured from the King an order that Barnes should humbly and publicly recant. He did so at Easter at the Spital, but at once repeated the offence, and he and two other clergymen who thought like him were burnt for heresy. Men began to shake their heads and look grave now as they spoke of Cromwell and Cranmer; but the Secretary stood sturdily, and in May seemed as if he would turn the tables upon his enemies. Once, indeed, he threatened the Duke of Norfolk roughly with the King's displeasure, and at the opening of Parliament he took the lead as usual, expressing the King's sorrow at the religious bitterness in the country, and demanding large supplies for the purposes of national defence.

But, though still apparently as powerful as ever, and more than ever overbearing, he dared not yet propose to the King a way out of the matrimonial tangle. Going home to Austin Friars from the sitting of Parliament on the 7th June, he told his new colleague, Wriothesley, that the thing that principally troubled him was that the King did not like the Queen, and that his marriage had never been consummated. Wriothesley, whose sympathies were then Catholic, suggested that "some way might be devised for the relief of the King." "Ah!" sighed Cromwell, who knew what such a remedy would mean to him, "but it is a great matter." The next day Wriothesley returned to the subject, and begged Cromwell to devise some means of relief for the King: "for if he remained in this grief and trouble they should all smart for it some day." "Yes," replied Cromwell, "it is true; but it is a great matter." "Marry!" exclaimed Wriothesley, out of patience, "I grant that, but let a remedy be searched for." But Cromwell had no remedy yet but one that would ruin himself, and that he dared not propose, so he shook his head sadly and changed the subject.

The repudiation of Anne was, as Cromwell said, a far greater matter than at first sight appeared. The plan to draw into one confederation for the objects of England the German Protestants, the King of Denmark, and the Duke of Cleves, whose seizure of Guelderland had brought him in opposition to the Emperor, was the most threatening that had faced Charles for years. His own city of Ghent was in open revolt, and Francis after all was but a fickle ally. If once more the French King turned from him and made friends with the Turk and the Lutherans, then indeed would the imperial power have cause to tremble and Henry to rejoice. Cromwell had striven hard to cement the Protestant combination; but again and again he had been thwarted by his rivals. The passage of the Six Articles against his wish, although the execution of the Act was suspended at Cromwell's instance, had caused the gravest distrust on the part of Hans Frederick and the Landgrave of Hesse; and if Henry were encouraged to repudiate his German wife, not only would her brother— already in negotiation with the imperial agents for the investiture of Gueldres, and his marriage with the Emperor's niece, the Duchess of Milan— be at once driven into opposition to England, but Hans Frederick and Hesse would also abandon Henry to the tender mercies of his enemies.

The only way to avoid such a disaster following upon the repudiation of Anne was first to drive a wedge of distrust between Charles and Francis, now in close confederacy. In January the Emperor had surprised the world by his boldness in traversing France to his Flemish dominions. He was feasted splendidly by Francis, and escaped unbetrayed; but during his stay in France desperate attempts were made by Wyatt, Henry's ambassador with Charles, Bonner, the ambassador in France, and by the Duke of Norfolk, who went in February on a special mission, to sow discord between the allied sovereigns, and not without some degree of success. Charles during his stay in France was badgered by Wyatt into saying some hasty words, which were deliberately twisted by Norfolk into a menace to France and England alike. Francis was reminded with irritating iteration that Charles had plenty of smiles and soft words for his French friends, but avoided keeping his promises about the cession of Milan or anything else. So in France those who were in favour of the imperial alliance, the Montmorencies and the Queen, declined in their hold over Francis, and their opponents, the Birons, the Queen of Navarre, Francis' sister, and the Duchess of Etampes, his mistress, planned with Henry's agents for an understanding with England. This, as may be supposed, was not primarily Cromwell's policy, but that of Norfolk and his friends, because its success would inevitably mean the conciliation of the German princes and Cleves by the Emperor, and the break-up of the Protestant confederacy and England, by which Cromwell must now stand or fall.

As early as April, Marillac, the French ambassador in England, foretold the great change that was coming. The arrest of Barnes, Garrard, and Jerome, for anti-Catholic teaching, and the persecutions everywhere for those who offended ever so slightly in the same way, presaged Cromwell's fall. "Cranmer and Cromwell," writes Marillac, "do not know where they are. Within a few days there will be seen in this country a great change in many things, which this King begins to make in his ministers, recalling those he had disgraced, and degrading those he had raised. Cromwell is tottering: for all those now recalled were dismissed at his request, and bear him no little grudge— amongst others, the Bishops of Winchester (*i.e.* Gardiner), Durham, and Bath, men of great learning and experience, who are now summoned to the Privy Council. It is said that Tunstal (*i.e.* Durham) will be Vicar-General, and Bath Privy Seal, which are Cromwell's principal offices.... If he holds his own (*i.e.* Cromwell), it will only be because of his close assiduity in business, though he is very rude in his demeanour. He does nothing without consulting the King, and is desirous of doing justice, especially to foreigners."

This was somewhat premature, but it gives a good idea of the process that was going on. There is no doubt that Cromwell believed in his ability to keep his footing politically; for he was anything but rigid in his principles, and if the friendship with France initiated by his rivals had, as it showed signs of doing, developed into an alliance that would enable Henry both to dismiss his fears of the Emperor and throw over the Protestants, he would probably have accepted the situation, and have proposed a means for Henry to get rid of his distasteful wife. But this opportunism did not suit his opponents in Henry's Council. They wanted to get rid of the man quite as much as they did his policy; for his insolence had stung them to the quick, great nobles as most of them were, and he the son of a blacksmith. Some other means, therefore, than a mere change of policy was necessary to dislodge the strong man who guided the King. Parliament had met on the 12th April, and it was managed with Cromwell's usual boldness and success. As if to mark that his great ability was still paramount, he was made Earl of Essex and Great Chamberlain of England in the following week.

But the struggle in the Council, and around the King, continued unabated. Henry was warned by Cromwell's enemies of the danger of allowing religious freedom to be carried too far, and of thus giving the Catholic powers an excuse for executing the Pope's decree of deprivation against him. He was reminded that the Emperor and Francis were still friends, that the latter was suspiciously preparing for war, and that Henry's brother-in-law the Duke of Cleves' quarrel with the Emperor might drag England into war for the sake of a beggarly German dukedom of no importance or value to her. On the other hand, Cromwell would point out to Henry the disobedience and insolence of the Catholics who questioned his spiritual supremacy, and cause Churchmen who advocated a reconciliation with Rome to be imprisoned. Clearly such a position could not continue indefinitely, and Norfolk anticipated Cromwell by playing the final trump card— that of arousing Henry's personal fears. The word treason and a hint that anything could be intended against his person always brought Henry to heel. What the exact accusation against Cromwell was no one knows, though it was whispered at the time that the nobles had told Henry that Cromwell had amassed great stores of money and arms, and maintained a vast number of dependants (1500 men, it was asserted, wore his livery), with a sinister object; some said to marry the Princess Mary and make himself King; and that he had received a great bribe from the Duke of

Cleves and the Protestants to bring about the marriage of Anne. Others said that he had boasted that he was to receive a crown abroad from a foreign potentate (*i.e.*, the Emperor), and that he had talked of defending the new doctrines at the sword's point. No such accusations, however, are on official record; and there is no doubt that the real reason for his arrest was the animosity of the aristocratic and Catholic party against him, acting upon the King's fears and his desire to get rid of Anne of Cleves.

On the 9th June Parliament was still sitting, discussing the religious question with a view to the settlement of some uniform doctrine. The Lords of the Council left the Chamber to go across to Whitehall to dinner before midday; and as they wended their way across the great courtyard of Westminster a high wind carried away Cromwell's flat cap from his head. It was the custom when one gentleman was even accidentally uncovered for those who were with him also to doff their bonnets. But, as an attendant ran and recovered Cromwell's flying headgear on that occasion, the haughty minister looked grimly round and saw all his colleagues, once so humble, holding their own caps upon their heads. "A high wind indeed must this be," sneered Cromwell, "to blow my cap off, and for you to need hold yours on." He must have known that ill foreboded; for during dinner no one spoke to him. The meal finished, Cromwell went to the Council Chamber with the rest, and, as was his custom, stood at a window apart to hear appeals and applications to him, and when these were disposed of he turned to the table to take his usual seat with the rest. On this occasion Norfolk stopped him, and told him that it was not meet that traitors should sit amongst loyal gentlemen. "I am no traitor!" shouted Cromwell, dashing his cap upon the ground; but the captain of the guard was at the door, and still protesting the wretched man was hurried to the Water Gate and rowed swiftly to the Tower, surrounded by halberdiers, Norfolk as he left the Council Chamber tearing off the fallen minister's badge of the Garter as a last stroke of ignominy.

Cromwell knew he was doomed, for by the iniquitous Act that he himself had forged for the ruin of others, he might be attainted and condemned legally without his presence or defence. "Mercy! Mercy! Mercy!" he wrote to the King in his agony; but for him there was as little mercy as he had shown to others. His death was a foregone conclusion, for Henry's fears had been aroused: but Cromwell had to be kept alive long enough for him to furnish such information as would provide a plausible pretext for the repudiation of Anne. He was ready to do all that was asked of him— to swear to anything the King wished.

He testified that he knew the marriage had never been consummated, and never would be; that the King was dissatisfied from the first, and had complained that the evidence of the nullification of the prior contract with the heir of Lorraine was insufficient; that the King had never given full consent to the marriage, but had gone through the ceremony under compulsion of circumstances, and with mental reservation. When all this was sworn to, Cromwell's hold upon the world was done. Upon evidence now unknown he was condemned for treason and heresy without being heard in his own defence, and on the 28th July 1540 he stood, a sorry figure, upon the scaffold in the Tower. He had been a sinner, he confessed, and had travailed after the things of this world; but he fervently avowed that he was a good Catholic and no heretic, and had harboured no thought of evil towards his sovereign. But protestations availed not; and his head, the cleverest head in England, was pitiably hacked off by a bungling headsman. Before that happened, the repudiation of Anne of Cleves was complete, and a revival of the aristocratic and Catholic influence in England was an accomplished fact.

CHAPTER VIII

1540-1542

THE KING'S "GOOD SISTER" AND THE KING'S BAD WIFE—THE LUTHERANS AND ENGLISH CATHOLICS

During her few months of incomplete wedlock with the King, Anne had felt uneasily the strange anomaly of her position. She accompanied Henry in his daily life at bed and board, and shared with him the various festivities held in celebration of the marriage; the last of which was a splendid tournament given by the bachelor courtiers at Durham House on May-day. She had studied English diligently, and tried to please her husband in a hundred well-meant but ungainly ways. She had by her jovial manner and real kindness of heart become very popular with those around her; but yet she got no nearer to the glum, bloated man by her side. In truth she was no fit companion for him, either physically or mentally. Her lack of the softer feminine charms, her homely manners, her lack of learning and of musical talent, on which Henry set so much store, were not counterbalanced by strong will or commanding ability which might have enabled her to dominate him, or by feminine craft by which he might have been captivated.

She was a woman, however, and could not fail to know that her repudiation in some form was in the air. It was one of the accusations against Cromwell that he had divulged to her what the King had said about the marriage; but, so far from doing so, he had steadily avoided compliance with her oft-repeated requests for an interview with him. Shortly before Cromwell's fall, Henry had complained to him that Anne's temper was becoming tart; and then Cromwell thought well to warn her through her Chamberlain that she should try to please the King more. The poor woman, desirous of doing right, tactlessly flew to the other extreme, and her cloying fondness aroused Henry's suspicion that Cromwell had informed her of his intention to get rid of her. Anne's Lutheranism, moreover, had begun to grate upon the tender conscience of her husband under the prompting of the Catholic party;

although she scrupulously followed the English ritual, and later became a professed Catholic; and to all these reasons which now made Henry doubly anxious for prompt release, was added another more powerful than any. One of Anne's maids of honour was a very beautiful girl of about eighteen, Katharine, the orphan daughter of Lord Edmund Howard, brother of the Duke of Norfolk, and consequently first cousin of Anne Boleyn. During the first months of his unsatisfying union with Anne, Henry's eyes must have been cast covetously upon Katharine; for in April 1540 she received a grant from him of a certain felon's property, and in the following month twenty-three quilts of quilted sarsnet were given to her out of the royal wardrobe. When Cromwell was still awaiting his fate in the Tower, and whispers were rife of what was intended against the Queen, Marillac the observant French ambassador wrote in cipher to his master, telling him that there was another lady in the case; and a week afterwards (6th July) he amplified his hints by saying that, either for that reason or some other, Anne had been sent to Richmond, on the false pretence that plague had appeared in London, and that Henry, very far from joining her there, as he had promised, had not left London, and was about to make a progress in another direction. Marillac rightly says that "if there had been any suspicion of plague, the King would not stay for any affair, however great, as he is the most timid person that could be in such a case."

The true reason why Anne was sent away was Henry's invariable cowardice, that made him afraid to face a person whom he was wronging. Gardiner had promptly done what Cromwell had been ruined for not doing, and had submitted to the King within a few days of the arrest of his rival a complete plan by which Anne might be repudiated. First certain ecclesiastics, under oath of secrecy, were to be asked for their opinion as to the best way to proceed, and the Council was thereupon to discuss and settle the procedure in accordance: the question of the previous contract and its repudiation was to be examined; the manner in which the Queen herself was to be approached was to be arranged, and evidence from every one to whom the King had spoken at the time as to his lack of consent and consummation was to be collected. All this had been done by the 7th July, when the clergy met at Westminster, summoned by writ under the great seal, dated the 6th, to decide whether the King's marriage was valid or not in the circumstances detailed. The obedient Parliament, sitting with closed doors, a few days previously had, by Norfolk's orders, petitioned the King to solve certain doubts that had been raised about the marriage, and Henry, ever desirous of pleasing his faithful lieges, and to set at rest conscientious scruples, referred the question to his prelates in Synod for decision.

Anne, two days before this, summoned to Richmond the ambassador of her brother, who came to her at four o'clock in the morning; and she then sent for the Earl of Rutland, the chief of her household, to be present at the interview. The King, she said, had sent her a message and asked for a reply. The effect of the message was to express doubts as to the validity of their marriage, and to ask her if she was content to leave the decision of it to the English clergy. The poor woman, much perturbed, had refused to send an answer without consideration, and she had then desired that her brother's envoy should give, or at all events carry, the answer to the King, but this he refused to do; and she in her trouble could only appeal to Rutland for advice. He prated about the "graciousness and virtue" of the King, and assured her that he would "do nothing but that should stand by the law of God, and for the discharge of his conscience and hers, and the quietness of the realm, and at the suit of all his lords and commons." The King was content to refer the question to the learned and virtuous bishops, so that she had cause to be glad rather than sorry. Anne was confused and doubtful; for she did not know what was intended towards her. But, considering the helplessness of her position and the danger of resistance, she met the deputation of the Council that came to her next day (6th July) in a spirit of complete surrender. She was, she said in German, always content to obey the King, and would abide by the decision of the prelates; and with this answer Gardiner posted back to London that night, to appear at the Synod the next morning.

Neither Anne, nor any one for her, appeared. The whole evidence, which was that already mentioned, was to show the existence of a prior contract, of the annulling of which no sufficient proofs had been produced, the avowals of the King and the Queen to their confidants that the marriage had never been consummated, and never would be; and, lastly, the absence of "inner consent" on the part of the King from the first. Under the pressure of Gardiner— for Cranmer, overshadowed by a cloud and in hourly fear of Cromwell's fate, was ready to sign anything— the union was declared to be invalid, and both parties were pronounced capable of remarriage. A Bill was then hurriedly rushed through Parliament confirming the decision of Convocation, and Cranmer, for the third time, as Primate, annulled his master's marriage. Anne was still profoundly disturbed at the fate that might be in store for her; and when Suffolk, Southampton, and Wriothesley went to Richmond on the 10th July to obtain her acceptance of the decision, she fainted at the sight of them. They did their best to reassure her, giving her from the King a large present of money and a specially affectionate letter. She was assured that if she would acquiesce and remain in the realm she should be the King's adopted sister, with precedence before all other ladies but the King's wife and daughters; a large appanage should be secured to her, and jewels, furniture, and the household of a royal princess provided for her. She was still doubtful; and some persuasion had to be used before she would consent to sign the letter dictated to her as the King's "sister"; but at last she did so, and was made to say that "though the case was hard and sorrowful, for the great love she bears to his noble person, yet, having more regard for God and His truth than for any worldly affection, she accepts the judgment, praying that the King will take her as one of his most humble servants, and so determine of her that she may sometimes enjoy his presence."

This seemed almost too good to be true when Henry read it, and he insisted upon its being written and signed again in German, that Anne might not subsequently profess ignorance of its wording. When Anne, however, was asked to write to her brother, saying that she was fully satisfied, she at first refused. Why should she write to him before he wrote to her? she asked. If he sent a complaint, she would answer it as the King wished; but after a few days she gave way on this point when further pressed. So delighted was Henry at so much submission to his will, that he was kindness and generosity itself. On the 14th July he sent the Councillors again to Richmond, with another handsome present and a letter to his "Right dear, and right entirely beloved sister," thanking her gratefully for her "wise and honourable proceedings." "As it is done in respect of God and His truth; and, continuing your conformity, you shall find us a perfect friend content to repute you as our dearest sister." He promised her £4000 a year, with the two royal residences of Richmond and Bletchingly, and a welcome at Court when she pleased to come. In return she sent him another amiable letter, and the wedding-ring; expressing herself fully satisfied. She certainly carried out her part of the arrangement to perfection, whether from fear or complaisance; assuring the envoys of her brother the Duke that she was well treated, as in a material sense indeed she was, and thenceforward made the best of her life in England.

Her brother and the German Protestants were of course furiously indignant; but, as the injured lady expressed herself not only satisfied but delighted with her position, no ground could be found for open quarrel. She was probably a person of little refinement of feeling, and highly appreciated the luxury and abundance with which she thenceforward was surrounded, enjoying, as she always did, recreation and fine dress, in which she was distinguished above any of Henry's wives. On the day after the Synod had met in Westminster to decide the invalidity of the marriage (7th July), Pate, the English ambassador, saw the Emperor at Bruges, with a message from Henry which foreshadowed an entire change in the foreign policy of England. Charles received Pate at midnight, and was agreeably surprised to learn that conscientious scruples had made Henry doubt the validity of his union with Anne. The Emperor's stiff demeanour changed at once, and, as the news came day by day of the progress of the separation of Henry from his Protestant wife, the cordiality of the Emperor grew towards him, whilst England itself was in full Catholic reaction.

The fall of Cromwell had, as it was intended to do, provided Henry with a scapegoat. The spoliation and destruction of the religious houses, by which the King and many of the Catholic nobles had profited enormously, was laid to the dead man's door; the policy of plundering the Church, of union with Lutherans, and the favouring of heresy, had been the work of the wicked minister, and not of the good King— that ill-served and ungratefully-used King, who was always innocent, and never in the wrong, who simply differed from other good Catholics in his independence of the Bishop of Rome: merely a domestic disagreement. With such suave hypocrisy as this difficulties were soon smoothed over; and to prove the perfect sincerity with which Henry proceeded, Protestants like Barnes, Garrard, and Jerome were burnt impartially side by side with Catholics who did not accept the spiritual supremacy of Henry over the Church in England, such as Abell, Powell, Fetherstone, and Cook. The Catholic and aristocratic party in England had thus triumphed all along the line, by the aid of anti-Protestant Churchmen like Gardiner and Tunstal. Their heavy-handed enemy, Cromwell, had gone, bearing the whole responsibility for the past; the King had been flattered by exoneration from blame, and pleased by the release from his wife, so deftly and pleasantly effected. No one but Cromwell was to blame for anything: they were all good Catholics, whom the other Catholic powers surely could not attack for a paltry quarrel with the Pope; and, best of all, the ecclesiastical spoil was secured to them and their heirs for ever, for they all maintained the supremacy of the King in England, good Catholics though they were.

But, withal, they knew that Henry must have some one close to him to keep him in the straight way. The nobles were not afraid of Cranmer, for he kept in the background, and was a man of poor spirit; and, moreover, for the moment the danger was hardly from the reformers. The nobles had triumphed by the aid of Gardiner, and Gardiner was now the strong spirit near the King; but the aims of the nobles were somewhat different from those of Churchmen; and a Catholic bishop as the sole director of the national policy might carry them farther than they wished to go. Henry's concupiscence must therefore once more be utilised, and the woman upon whom he cast his eyes, if possible, made into a political instrument to forward the faction that favoured her. Gardiner was nothing loath, for he was sure of himself; but how eager Norfolk and his party were to take advantage of Henry's fancy for Katharine Howard, to effect her lodgment by his side as Queen, is seen by the almost indecent haste with which they began to spread the news of her rise, even before the final decision was given as to the validity of the marriage with Anne. On the 12th July a humble dependant of the Howards, Mistress Joan Bulmer (of whom more will be heard), wrote to Katharine, congratulating her upon her coming greatness, and begging for an office about her person: "for I trost the Quyne of Bretane wyll not forget her secretary."

Less than a fortnight later (21st July) the French ambassador gives as a piece of gossip that Katharine Howard was already pregnant by the King, and that the marriage was therefore being hurried on. Exactly when or where the wedding took place is not known, but it was a private one, and by the 11th August Katharine was called Queen, and acknowledged as such by all the Court. On the 15th Marillac wrote that her name had been added to the prayers in the Church service, and that the King had gone on a hunting expedition, presumably accompanied by his new wife; whilst "Madame de Cleves, so far from claiming to be married, is more joyous than ever, and wears new dresses every day." Everybody thus was well satisfied except the Protestants. Henry, indeed, was delighted with his tiny, sparkling girl-wife, and did his best to be a gallant bridegroom to her, though there was none of the pomp and splendour that accompanied his previous nuptials. The autumn of 1540 was passed in a leisurely progress through the shires to Grafton, where most of the honeymoon was spent. The rose crowned was chosen by Henry as his bride's personal cognisance, and the most was made of her royal descent and connections by the enamoured King. "The King is so amorous of her," wrote Marillac in September, "that he cannot treat her well enough, and caresses her more than he did the others." Even thus early, however, whispers were heard of the King's fickleness. Once it was said that Anne of Cleves was pregnant by him, and he would cast aside Katharine in her favour, and shortly afterwards he refrained from seeing his new wife for ten days together, because of something she had done to offend him.

The moral deterioration of Henry's character, which had progressed in proportion with the growing conviction of his own infallibility and immunity, had now reached its lowest depth. He was rapidly becoming more and more bulky; and his temper, never angelic, was now irascible in the extreme. His health was bad, and increasing age had made him more than ever impatient of contradiction or restraint, and no consideration but that of his own interest and safety influenced him. The policy which he adopted under the guidance of Gardiner and Norfolk was one of rigorous enforcement of the Six Articles, and, at the same time, of his own spiritual supremacy in England. All chance of a coalition of Henry with the Lutherans was now out of the question ("Squire Harry means to be God, and to do as pleases himself," said Luther at the time); and the Emperor, freed from that danger, and faced with the greater peril of a coalition of the French and Turks, industriously endeavoured to come to some *modus vivendi* with his German electors. The rift between Charles and Francis was daily widening; and Henry himself was aiding the process to his full ability; for he knew that whilst they were disunited he was safe. But for the first time in his reign, except when he defied the Pope, he adopted a policy— probably his own and not that of his ministers— calculated to offend both the Catholic powers, whilst he was alienated from the reforming element on the Continent.

By an Act of Parliament the ancient penal laws against foreign denizens were re-enacted, and all foreigners but established merchants were to be expelled the country; whilst alien merchants resident were to pay double taxation. The taxation of Englishmen, enormous under Cromwell, was now recklessly increased, with the set purpose of keeping the lieges poor, just as the atrocious religious executions were mainly to keep them submissive, and incapable of questioning the despot's will. But, though Englishmen might be stricken dumb by persecution, the expulsion or oppression of foreigners led to much acrimony and reprisals on the part both of the Emperor and Francis. An entirely gratuitous policy of irritation towards France on the frontier of Calais and elsewhere was also adopted, apparently to impress the Emperor, and for the satisfaction of Henry's arrogance, when he thought it might be safe to exercise it. The general drift of English policy at the time was undoubtedly to draw closer to the Emperor, not entirely to the satisfaction of the Duke of Norfolk, who was usually pro-French; but even here the oppressive Act against foreigners by which Henry hoped to show Charles that his friendship was worth buying made cordiality in the interim extremely difficult. When Chapuys in the Emperor's name remonstrated with the Council about the new decree forbidding the export of goods from England except in English bottoms, the English ministers rudely said that the King could pass what laws he liked in his own country, just as the Emperor could in his. Charles and his sister, the Regent of the Netherlands, took the hint, and utterly astounded Henry by forbidding goods being shipped in the Netherlands in English vessels.

The danger was understood at once. Not only did this strike a heavy blow at English trade, but it upset the laboriously constructed pretence of close communion with the Emperor which had been used to hoodwink the French. Henry himself bullied and hectored, as if he was the first injured party; and then took Chapuys aside in a window-bay and hinted at an alliance. He said that the French were plotting against the Emperor, and trying to gain his (Henry's) support, which, however, he would prefer to give to the Emperor if he wished for it. Henry saw, indeed, that he had drawn the bow too tight, and was ready to shuffle out of the position into which his own arrogance had led him. So Gardiner was sent in the winter to see the Emperor with the King's friend Knyvett, who was to be the new resident ambassador; the object of the visit being partly to impress the French, and partly to persuade Charles of Henry's strict Catholicism, and so to render more difficult any such agreement being made as that aimed at by the meeting at Worms between the Lutheran princes and their suzerain. Gardiner's mission was not very successful, for Charles understood the move perfectly; but it was not his policy then to alienate Henry, for he was slowly maturing his plans for crushing France utterly, and hoped whilst Catholic influence was paramount in England to obtain the help or at least the neutrality of Henry.

The fall of Cromwell had been hailed by Catholics in England as the salvation of their faith, and high hopes had attended the elevation of Gardiner. But the crushing taxation, the arbitrary measures, and, above all, the cruel persecution of those who, however slightly, questioned the King's spiritual supremacy, caused renewed discontent amongst the extreme Catholics, who still looked yearningly towards Cardinal Pole and his house. It is not probable that any Yorkist conspiracy existed in England at the time; the people were too much terrified for that; but Henry's ambassadors and agents in Catholic countries had been forced sometimes to dally with the foreign view of the King's supremacy, and Gardiner, whose methods were even more unscrupulous than those of Cromwell, suddenly pounced upon those of Henry's ministers who might be supposed to have come into contact with the friends of the House of York. Pate, the English ambassador with the Emperor, was suspicious, and escaped to Rome; but Sir Thomas Wyatt, who had been the ambassador in Spain, was led to the Tower handcuffed with ignominy; Dr. Mason, another ambassador, was also lodged in the fortress, at the suggestion of Bonner. Even Sir Ralph Sadler, one of the Secretaries of State, was imprisoned for a short time, whilst Sir John Wallop, the ambassador in France, was recalled and consigned to a dungeon, as was Sir Thomas Palmer, Knight Porter of Calais, and others; though most of them were soon afterwards pardoned at the instance of Katharine Howard. In the early spring of 1541 an unsuccessful attempt was made at a Catholic rising in Yorkshire, where the feeling was very bitter; and though the revolt was quickly suppressed, it was considered a good opportunity for striking terror into those who still doubted the spiritual supremacy of Henry, and resented the plunder of the monasteries. The atrocious crime was perpetrated of bringing out the mother of Pole, the aged Countess of Salisbury, last of the Plantagenets, from her prison in the Tower to the headsman's block. Lord Leonard Gray was a another blameless victim, whilst Lord Dacre of the South was, on a trumped-up charge of murder, hanged like a common malefactor at Tyburn. Lord Lisle, Henry's illegitimate uncle, was also kept in the Tower till his death.

When the reign of terror had humbled all men to the dust, the King could venture to travel northward with the purpose of provoking and subjecting his nephew, the King of Scots, the ally of France. All this seems to point to the probability that at this time (1541) Henry had decided to take a share on the side of the Emperor in the war which was evidently looming between Charles and Francis. He was broken and fretful, but his vanity and ambition were still boundless; and Gardiner, whose policy, and not Norfolk's, it undoubtedly was, would easily persuade him that an alliance in war with Charles could not fail to secure for him increased consideration and readmission into the circle of Catholic nations, whilst retaining his own supremacy unimpaired. Henry's pompous progress in the North, accompanied by Katharine, occupied nearly five months, till the end of October. How far the young wife was influential in keeping Henry to the policy just described it is impossible to say, but beyond acquiescence in an occasional petition or hint, it is difficult to believe that the elderly, self-willed man would be moved by the thoughtless, giddy girl whom he had married.

If the opposite had been the case, Norfolk's traditions and leanings would have been more conspicuous than they are in Henry's actions at the time. It is true that, during the whole period, a pretence of cordial negotiation was made for a marriage between Princess Mary and a French prince, but it is certain now, whatever Norfolk may have thought at the time, that the negotiation was solely in order to stimulate Charles to nearer approach, and to mislead Francis whilst the English preparations for war and the strengthening of the garrisons towards France and Scotland went steadily on.

An alliance with the Emperor in a war with France was evidently the policy upon which Henry, instigated by his new adviser, now depended to bring him back with flying colours into the comity of Catholic sovereigns, whilst bating no jot of his claims to do as he chose in his own realm. Such a policy was one after Henry's own heart. It was showy and tricky, and might, if successful, cover him with glory, as well as redound greatly to his profit in the case of the dismemberment of France. But it would have been impossible whilst the union symbolised by the Cleves marriage existed; and, seen by this light, the eagerness of Gardiner to find a way for the King to dismiss the wife who had personally repelled him is easily understood, as well as Cromwell's disinclination to do so. The encouragement of the marriage with Katharine Howard, part of the same intrigue, was still further to attach the King to its promoters, and the match was doubtless intended at the same time to conciliate Norfolk and the nobles whilst Gardiner carried through his policy. We shall see that, either by strange chance or deep design, those who were opposed to this policy were the men who were instrumental in shattering the marriage that was its concomitant.

Henry and his consort arrived at Hampton Court from the North on the 30th October 1541, and to his distress he found his only son, Edward, seriously ill of quartan fever. All the physicians within reach were summoned, and reported to the anxious father that the child was so fat and unhealthy as to be unlikely to live long. The King had now been married to Katharine for fifteen months, and there were no signs of probable issue. Strange whispers were going about on back stairs and ante-chambers with regard to the Queen's proceedings. She was known to have been a giddy, neglected girl before her marriage, having been brought up by her grandmother, the Dowager-Duchess of Norfolk, without the slightest regard for her welfare or the high rank of her family; and her confidants in a particularly dissolute Court were many and untrustworthy. The King, naturally, was the last person to hear the malicious tittle-tattle of jealous waiting-maids and idle pages about the Queen; and though his wife's want of reserve and dignity often displeased him, he lived usually upon affectionate terms with her. There was other loose talk, also, going on to the effect that on one of the visits of Anne of Cleves to Hampton Court after Henry's marriage with Katharine, the King and his repudiated wife had made up their differences, with the consequence that Anne was pregnant by him. It was not true; though later it gave much trouble both to Henry and Anne, but it lent further support to the suggestions that were already being made that the King would dismiss Katharine and take Anne back again. The air was full of such rumours, some prompted, as we shall see, by personal malice, others evidently by the opponents of Gardiner's policy, which was leading England to a war with France and a close alliance with the imperial champion of Catholicism.

On the 2nd November, Henry, still in distress about the health of his son, attended Mass, as usual, in the chapel at Hampton Court, and as he came out Cranmer prayed for a private interview with him. The archbishop had for many months been in the background, for Gardiner would brook no competition; but Cranmer was personally a favourite with the King,— Cromwell said once that Henry would forgive him anything,— and when they were alone Cranmer put him in possession of a shameful story that a few days before had been told to him, which he had carefully put into writing; and, after grave discussion with the Earl of Hertford (Seymour) and the Lord Chancellor (Audley), had determined to hand to the King. The conjunction of Cranmer, Seymour, and Audley, as the trio that thought it their duty to open Henry's eyes to the suspicions cast upon his wife, is significant. They were all of them in sympathy with the reformed religion, and against the Norfolk and Gardiner policy; and it is difficult to escape from the conclusion that, however true may have been the statements as to Katharine's behaviour, and there is no doubt that she was guilty of much that was laid to her charge, the enlightenment of Henry as to her life before and after marriage was intended to serve the political and religious ends of those who were instrumental in it.

The story as set forth by Cranmer was a dreadful one. It appears that a man named John Lascelles, who was a strong Protestant, and had already foretold the overthrow of Norfolk and Gardiner, went to Cranmer and said that he had been visiting in Sussex a sister of his, whose married name was Hall. She had formerly been in the service of the Howard family and of the Dowager-Duchess of Norfolk, in whose houses Katharine Howard had passed her neglected childhood; and Lascelles, recalling the fact, had, he said, recommended his sister to apply to the young Queen, whom she had known so intimately as a girl, for a place in the household. "No," replied the sister, "I will not do that; but I am very sorry for her." "Why are you sorry for her?" asked Lascelles. "Marry," quoth she, "because she is light, both in living and conditions" (*i.e.* behaviour). The brother asked for further particulars, and, thus pressed, Mary Hall related that "one Francis Derham had lain in bed with her, and between the sheets in his doublet and hose, a hundred nights; and a maid in the house had said that she would lie no longer with her (Katharine) because she knew not what matrimony was. Moreover, one Mannock, a servant of the Dowager-Duchess, knew and spoke of a private mark upon the Queen's body." This was the document which Cranmer handed to the King, "not having the heart to say it by word of mouth": and it must be admitted that as it was only a bit of second-hand scandal, without corroboration, and could not refer to any period subsequent to Katharine's marriage, it did not amount to much. Henry is represented as having been inclined to make light of it, which was natural, but he nevertheless summoned Fitzwilliam (Southampton), Lord Russell (Lord Admiral), Sir Anthony Browne, and Wriothesley, and deputed to them the inquiry into the whole matter. Fitzwilliam hurried to London and then to Sussex to examine Lascelles and his sister, whilst the others were sent to take the depositions of Derham, who was now in Katharine's service, and was ordered to be apprehended on a charge of piracy in Ireland sometime previously, and Mannock, who was a musician in the household of the Duchess.

On the 5th November the ministers came to Hampton Court with the shocking admissions which they had extracted from the persons examined. Up to that time Henry had been gay, and had thought little of the affair, but now, when he heard the statements presented to him, he was overcome with grief: "his heart was pierced with pensiveness," we are told, "so that it was long before he could utter his sorrow, and finally with copious tears, which was strange in his courage, opened the same." The next day, Sunday, he met Norfolk and the Lord Chancellor secretly in the fields, and then with the closest privacy took boat to London without bidding farewell to Katharine, leaving in the hands of his Council the unravelling of the disgraceful business.

The story, pieced together from the many different depositions, and divested of its repetitions and grossness of phraseology, may be summarised as follows. Katharine, whose mother had died early, had grown up uncared for in the house of her grandmother at Horsham in Norfolk, and later at Lambeth; apparently living her life in common with the women-servants. Whilst she was yet quite a child, certainly not more than thirteen, probably younger, Henry Mannock, one of the Duchess's musicians, had taught her to play the virginals; and, as he himself professed, had fallen in love with her. The age was a licentious one; and the maids, probably to disguise their own amours, appear to have taken a sport in promoting immoral liberties between the orphan girl and the musician, carrying backwards and forwards between the ill-matched pair tokens and messages, and facilitating secret meetings at untimely hours: and Mannock deposed unblushingly to have corrupted the girl systematically and shamefully, though not criminally. On one occasion the old Duchess found this scamp hugging her granddaughter, and in great anger she beat the girl, upbraided the musician, and forbade such meetings for the future. Mary Hall, who first gave the information, represents herself as having remonstrated indignantly with Mannock for his presumption in pledging his troth, as one of the other women told her he had, with Katharine. He replied impudently that all he wanted of the girl was to seduce her, and he had no doubt he should succeed in doing so, seeing the liberties she had already permitted him to take with her. Mary Hall said that she had warned him that the Howards would kill or ruin him if he did not take care. Katharine, according to Mary Hall's tale, when told of Mannock's impudent speech, had angrily said that she cared nothing for him; but he managed the next time he saw her, by her own contrivance, to persuade her that he was so much in love as not to know what he said.

Before long, however, a more dangerous lover, because one of better rank, appeared in the field, and spoilt Mannock's game. This was Francis Derham, a young gentleman of some means in the household of the Duke of Norfolk, of whom he seems to have been a distant connection. In his own confession he boldly admitted that he was in love with Katharine, and had promised her marriage. The old Duchess always had the keys of the maids' dormitory, where Katharine also slept, brought to her chamber after the doors were locked; but means were found by the women to laugh at locksmiths, and the most unbridled licence prevailed amongst them. Derham, with the lovers of two of the women, used to obtain access almost nightly to the dormitory, where they remained feasting and rioting until two or three in the morning: and there can remain little doubt that, on the promise of marriage, Derham practically lived with Katharine as his wife thus clandestinely, for a considerable period, whilst she was yet very young. Mannock, who found himself supplanted, thereupon wrote an anonymous letter to the Duchess and left it in her pew at chapel, saying that if her

Grace would rise again an hour after she had retired and visit the gentlewomen's chamber she would see something that would surprise her. The old lady, who was not free from reproach in the matter herself, railed and stormed at the women; and Katharine, who was deeply in love with Derham, stole the anonymous letter from her grandmother's room and showed it to him, charging Mannock with having written it. The result, of course, was a quarrel, and the further enlightenment of the Duchess with regard to her granddaughter's connection with Derham. The old lady herself was afterwards accused of having introduced Derham into her own household for the purpose of forwarding a match between him and Katharine; and finally got into great trouble and danger by seizing and destroying Derham's papers before the King's Council could impound them: but when she learnt the lengths to which the immoral connection had been carried, and the shameful licentiousness that had accompanied it, she made a clean sweep of the servants inculpated, and brought her granddaughter to live in Lambeth amongst a fresh set of people.

There is no doubt that Katharine and Derham were secretly engaged to be married, and, apart from the immoral features of the engagement, no very great objection could have been taken to it. She was a member of a very large family, an orphan with no dower or prospects, and her marriage with Derham, who was a sort of relative, would have been not a glaringly unequal one. With lover-like alacrity he provided her with the feminine treasures which she coveted, but which her lack of means prevented her from buying. Artificial flowers, articles of dress, or materials for them, trinkets and adornments, not to speak of the delicacies which he brought to furnish forth the tables during the nightly orgy. He had made no great secret of his engagement to, and intention of marrying Katharine, and had shown various little tokens of her troth that she had given him. On one of his piratical raids, moreover, he had handed to her the whole of his money, as to his affianced wife, and told her she might keep it if he came not back, whilst on other occasions he had exercised his authority, as her betrothed, to chide her for her attentions to others. When at last the old Duchess learnt fully of the immoral proceedings that had been going on, Katharine got another severe beating, and Derham fled from the vengeance of the Howards. After the matter had blown over, and Katharine was living usually at Lambeth, Derham found his way back, and attempted clandestinely to renew the connection. But Katharine by this time was older and more experienced, as beseemed a lady at Court. It was said that she was affianced to her cousin, Thomas Culpeper; but in any case she indignantly refused to have anything to do with Derham, and hotly resented his claim to interfere in her affairs.

So far the disclosures referred solely to misconduct previous to Katharine's marriage with the King, and, however reprehensible this may have been, it only constructively became treason *post facto*, by reason of the concealment from the King of his wife's previous immoral life; whereby the royal blood was "tainted," and he himself injured. Cranmer was therefore sent to visit Katharine with orders to set before her the iniquity of her conduct and the penalty prescribed by the law; and then to promise her the King's mercy on certain conditions. The poor girl was frantic with grief and fear when the Primate entered; and he in compassion spared her the first parts of his mission, and began by telling her of her husband's pity and clemency. The reaction from her deadly fear sent her into greater paroxysms than ever of remorse and regret. "This sudden mercy made her offences seem the more heinous." "This was about the hour" (6 o'clock), she sobbed, "that Master Heneage was wont to bring me knowledge of his Grace." The promise of mercy may or may not have been sincere; but it is evident that the real object of Cranmer's visit was to learn from Katharine whether the betrothal with Derham was a binding contract. If that were alleged in her defence the marriage with the King was voidable, as that of Anne of Cleves was for a similar cause; and if, by reason of such prior contract, Katharine had never legally been Henry's wife, her guilt was much attenuated, and she and her accomplices could only be punished for concealment of fact to the King's detriment, a sufficiently grave crime, it is true, in those days, but much less grave if Katharine was never legally Henry's wife. It may therefore have seemed good policy to offer her clemency on such conditions as would have relieved him of her presence for ever, with as little obloquy as possible, but other counsels eventually prevailed. Orders were given that she was to be sent to Sion House, with a small suite and no canopy of state, pending further inquiry; whilst the Lord Chancellor, Councillors, peers, bishops, and judges were convened on the 12th November, and the evidence touching the Queen laid before them. It was decided, however, that Derham should not be called, and that all reference to a previous contract of marriage should be suppressed. On the following Sunday the whole of the Queen's household was to be similarly informed of the offences and their gravity, and to them also no reference to a prior engagement that might serve to lighten the accusations or their own responsibility was to be made.

Katharine Howard's fate if the matter had ended here would probably have been divorce on the ground of her previous immorality "tainting the royal blood," and lifelong seclusion; but in their confessions the men and women involved had mentioned other names; and on the 13th November, the day before Katharine was to be taken to Sion, the scope of the inquiry widened. Mannock in his first examination on the 5th November had said that Mistress Katharine Tylney, the Queen's chamberwoman, a relative of the old Duchess, could speak as to Katharine's early immoral life; and when this lady found herself in the hands of Wriothesley she told some startling tales. "Did the Queen leave her chamber any night at Lincoln or elsewhere during her recent progress with the King?" "Yes, her Majesty had gone on two occasions to Lady Rochford's room, which could be reached by a little pair of back stairs near the Queen's apartment." Mrs. Tylney and the Queen's other attendant, Margery Morton, had attempted to accompany their mistress, but had been sent back. Mrs. Tylney had obeyed, and had gone to bed; but Margery had crept back up the stairs again to Lady Rochford's room. About two o'clock in the morning Margery came to bed in the same dormitory as the other maids. "Jesu! is not the Queen abed yet?" asked the surprised Tylney, as she awoke. "Yes," in effect, replied Margery, "she has just retired." On the second occasion Katharine sent the rest of her attendants to bed and took Tylney with her to Lady Rochford's room, but the maid, with Lady Rochford's servant, were shut up in a small closet, and not allowed to see who came into the principal apartments. But, nevertheless, her suspicions were aroused by the strange messages with which she was sent by Katharine to Lady Rochford: "so strange that she knew not how to utter them." Even at Hampton Court lately, as well as at Grimsthorpe during the progress, she had been bidden by the Queen to ask Lady Rochford "when she should have the thing she promised her," the answer being that she (Lady Rochford) was sitting up for it, and would bring the Queen word herself.

Then Margery Morton was tackled by Sir Anthony Browne. She had never mistrusted the Queen until the other day, at Hatfield, "when she saw her Majesty look out of the window to Mr. Culpeper in such sort that she thought there was love between them." Whilst at Hatfield the Queen had given orders that none of her attendants were to enter her bedroom unless they were summoned. Margery, too, had been sent on mysterious secret errands to Lady Rochford, which she could not understand, and, with others of the maids, had considered herself slighted by the Queen's preference for Katharine Tylney and for those who owed their position to Lady Rochford; which lady, she said, she considered the principal cause of the Queen's folly. Thus far there was nothing beyond the suspicions of jealous women, but Lady Rochford was frightened into telling a much more damning story, though she tried to make her own share in it as light as possible. The Queen, she confessed, had had many interviews in her rooms with Culpeper— at Greenwich, Lincoln, Pontefract, York, and elsewhere— for many months past; but as Culpeper stood at the farther end of the room with his foot upon the top of the back stairs, so as to be ready to slip down in case of alarm, and the Queen talked to him at the door, Lady Rochford professed to be ignorant of what passed between them. One night, she recalled, the Queen and herself were standing at the back door at eleven at night, when a watchman came with a lantern and locked the door. Shortly afterwards, however, Culpeper entered the room, saying that he and his servant had picked the lock. Since the first suspicion had been cast upon the Queen by Lascelles, Katharine, according to Lady Rochford, had continually asked after Culpeper. "If that matter came not out she feared nothing," and finally, Lady Rochford, although professing to have been asleep during some of Culpeper's compromising visits, declared her belief that criminal relations had existed between him and the Queen:

Culpeper, according to the depositions, made quite a clean breast of it, though what means were adopted for making him so frank is not clear. Probably torture, or the threat of it, was resorted to, since Hertford, Riche, and Audley had much to do with the examinations; whilst even the Duke of Norfolk and Wriothesley, not to appear backward in the King's service, were as anxious as their rivals to make the case complete. Culpeper was a gentleman of great estate in Kent and elsewhere, holding many houses and offices; a gentleman of the chamber, clerk of the armoury, steward and keeper of several royal manors; and he had received many favours from the King, with whom he ordinarily slept. He deposed to and described many stolen interviews with Katharine, all apparently after the previous Passion Week (1541), when the Queen, he said, had sent for him and given him a velvet cap. Lady Rochford, according to his statement, was the go-between, and arranged all the assignations in her apartments, whilst the Queen, whenever she reached a house during the progress, would make herself acquainted with the back doors and back stairs, in order to facilitate the meetings. At Pontefract she thought the back door was being watched by the King's orders, and Lady Rochford caused her servant to keep a counter watch. On one occasion, he said, the Queen had hinted that she could favour him as a certain lady of the Court had favoured Lord Parr; and when Culpeper said he did not think that the Queen was such a lady as the one mentioned, she had replied, "Well, if I had tarried still in the maidens' chamber I would have tried you;" and on another occasion she had warned him that if he confessed, even when he was shriven, what had passed between them, the King would be sure to know, as he was the head of the Church. Culpeper's animus against Lady Rochford is evident. She had provoked him much, he said, to love the Queen, and he intended to do ill with her. Evidence began to grow, too, that not only was Derham admittedly guilty with the Queen before marriage, but that suspicious familiarity had been resumed afterwards. He himself confessed that he had been more than once in the Queen's private apartment, and she had given him various sums of money, warning him to heed what he said; which, truth to tell, he had not done, according to other deponents.

Everybody implicated in the scandals was imprisoned, mostly in the Tower, several members of the house of Howard being put under guard; and Norfolk, trembling for his own position, showed as much zeal as any one to condemn his unfortunate niece. He knew, indeed, at this time that he had been used simply as a catspaw in the advances towards France, and complained bitterly that the match he had secretly suggested between the Princess Mary and the Duke of Orleans was now common talk, which gave ground for his enemies who were jealous of him to denounce him to the King as wishing to embrace all great affairs of State. It is clear that at this period it was not only the Protestants who were against Norfolk, but his own colleagues who were planning the alliance with the Emperor; which to some extent explains why such men as Wriothesley, Fitzwilliam, and Browne were so anxious to make the case of Katharine and her family look as black as possible, and why Norfolk aided them so as not to be left behind. When, on the 15th December, the old Dowager-Duchess of Norfolk, his stepmother, his half-brother, Lord William Howard and his wife, and his sister, Lady Bridgewater, were imprisoned on the charge of having been privy to Katharine's doings before marriage, the Duke wrote as follows to the King: "I learnt yesterday that mine ungracious mother-in-law, mine unhappy brother and his wife, and my lewd sister of Bridgewater were committed to the Tower; and am sure it was not done but for some false proceeding against your Majesty. Weighing this with the abominable deeds done by my two nieces (*i.e.* Katharine Howard and Anne Boleyn), and the repeated treasons of many of my kin, I fear your Majesty will abhor to hear speak of me or my kin again.

Prostrate at your Majesty's feet, I remind your Majesty that much of this has come to light through my own report of my mother-in-law's words to me, when I was sent to Lambeth to search Derham's coffers. My own truth, and the small love my mother-in-law and nieces bear me, make me hope; and I pray your Majesty for some comfortable assurance of your royal favour, without which I will never desire to live. Kenninghall Lodge, 15th December 1541."

On the 1st December, Culpeper and Derham had been arraigned before a special Commission in Guildhall, accused of treason. The indictment set forth that before her marriage Katharine had "led an abominable, base, carnal, voluptuous, and vicious life, like a common harlot ... whilst, at other times, maintaining an appearance of chastity and honesty. That she led the King to love her, believing her to be pure, and arrogantly coupled with him in marriage." That upon her and Derham being charged with their former vicious life, they had excused themselves by saying that they were betrothed before the marriage with the King; which betrothal they falsely and traitorously concealed from the King when he married her. After the marriage they attempted to renew their former vicious courses at Pontefract and elsewhere, the Queen having procured Derham's admission into her service, and entrusted secret affairs to him. Against Culpeper it was alleged that he had held secret and illicit meetings with the Queen, who had "incited him to have intercourse with her, and insinuated to him that she loved him better than the King and all others. Similarly Culpeper incited the Queen, and they had retained Lady Rochford as their go-between, she having traitorously aided and abetted them."

It will be noticed that actual adultery is not alleged, and the indictment follows very closely the deposition of the witnesses. The *liaison* with Derham before the marriage was not denied; nor were the meetings with Culpeper after the marriage. This and the concealment were sufficient for the King's purpose, without adding to his ignominy by labouring to prove the charge of adultery. After pleading not guilty, the two men, in face of the evidence and their own admissions, changed their plea to guilty, and were promptly condemned to be drawn through London to Tyburn, "and there hanged, cut down alive, disembowelled, and, they still living, their bowels burnt, the bodies then to be beheaded and quartered:" a brutal sentence that was carried out to the letter in Derham's case only, on the 10th December, Culpeper being beheaded.

KATHARINE HOWARD
From a portrait by an unknown artist in the National Portrait Gallery

Although the procedure had saved the King as much humiliation as possible, the affair was a terrible blow to his self-esteem as well as to his affections; for he seems to have been really fond of his young wife. Chapuys, writing on the 3rd December, says that he shows greater sorrow at her loss than at any of his previous matrimonial misfortunes. "It is like the case of the woman who cried more bitterly at the loss of her tenth husband than for all the rest put together, though they had all been good men; but it was because she had never buried one before without being sure of the next. As yet, it does not seem that he has any one else in view." The French ambassador, a few days later, wrote that "the grief of the King was so great that it was believed that it had sent him mad; for he had called suddenly for a sword with which to kill the

Queen whom he had loved so much. Sometimes sitting in Council he suddenly calls for horses, without saying whither he would go. Sometimes he will say irrelevantly that that wicked woman had never had such delight in her incontinency as she should have torture in her death; and then, finally, he bursts into tears, bewailing his misfortune in meeting such ill-conditioned wives, and blaming his Council for this last mischief."

In the meanwhile Henry sought such distraction as he might at Oatlands and other country places, solaced by music and mummers, whilst Norfolk, in grief and apprehension, lurked on his own lands, and Gardiner kept a firm hand upon affairs. The discomfiture of the Howards, who had brought about the Catholic reaction, gave new hope to the Protestants that the wheel of fate was turning in their favour. Anne of Cleves, they began to whisper, had been confined of a "fair boy"; "and whose should it be but the King's Majesty's, begotten when she was at Hampton Court?" This rumour, which the King, apparently, was inclined to believe, gave great offence and annoyance to him and his Council, as did the severely repressed but frequent statements that he intended to take back his repudiated wife. It was not irresponsible gossip alone that took this turn, for on the 12th December the ambassador from the Duke of Cleves brought letters to Cranmer at Lambeth from Chancellor Olsiliger, who had negotiated the marriage, commending to him the reconciliation of Henry with Anne. Cranmer, who understood perfectly well that with Gardiner as the King's factotum such a thing was impossible, was frightened out of his wits by such a suggestion, and promptly assured Henry that he had declined to discuss it without the Sovereign's orders.

But the envoy of Cleves was not lightly shaken off, and at once sought audience of Henry himself to press the cause of "Madam Anne." He was assured that the King's grief at his present troubles would prevent his giving audience; and the Protestant envoy then tackled the Council on the subject. As may be supposed, he met with a rebuff. The lady would be better treated than ever, he was told, but the separation was just and final, and the Duke of Cleves must never again request that his sister should be restored to the position of the King's wife. The envoy begged that the answer might be repeated formally to him, whereupon Gardiner flew into a rage, and said that the King would never take Anne back, whatever happened. The envoy was afraid to retort for fear of evil consequences to Anne, but the Duke of Cleves, who was now in close league with the French, endeavoured to obtain the aid of his new allies to forward his sister's cause in England.

Francis, however, saw, like every one else, that war between him and the Emperor was now inevitable, and was anxious not to drive Henry into alliance with Charles against him. Cleves by himself was powerless, and the trend of politics in England under Gardiner, and with Henry in his present mood, was entirely unfavourable to a union with the Lutherans on the Continent; so Anne of Cleves continued her placid and jovial existence as "the King's good sister," rather than his wife, whilst the Protestants of England soon found that they had misjudged the situation produced by Katharine Howard's fall. All that the latter really had done was to place Norfolk and the French sympathisers under a cloud, and make Gardiner entirely master of the situation whilst he carried out the King's own policy.

Henry returned to Greenwich for Christmas 1541, and at once began his bargaining to sell his alliance with the Emperor at as high a price as possible. He had already in hand the stoppage of trade with Flanders, which his ministers were still laboriously and stiffly discussing with the Emperor's representatives. Any concession in that respect would have to be paid for. The French, too, were very anxious, according to his showing, for his friendship, and were offering him all manner of tempting matrimonial alliances, and when Henry, on the day after Christmas Day, received Chapuys at Greenwich, he was all smiles, but determined to make the best of his opportunities. The Emperor had just met with a terrible disaster at sea during his operations against Algiers, and had returned to Spain depressed at his losses, and the more ready to make terms with Henry if possible. Chapuys was a hard bargainer, and it was a fair game of brag that ensued between him and Henry. Chapuys began by flattering the King: "and got him into very high spirits by such words, which the Lord Privy Seal (*i.e.* Fitzwilliam) says are never thrown away upon him," and then told him that he would give him in strict confidence some important information about French intrigues.

After dinner the ball opened in earnest, Chapuys and Henry being alone and seated, with Fitzwilliam, Russell, and Browne at some distance away. The imperial ambassador began by saying that the King of France had made a determined bid to marry his second son, Orleans, with the Infanta of Portugal. This was a shock to Henry, and he changed colour; for one of his own trump cards was the sham negotiation in which Norfolk had been the tool, to marry the Princess Mary to Orleans. For a time he could only sputter and exclaim; but when he had collected his senses he countered by saying that Francis only wished to get the Infanta into his power, not for marriage, "but for objects of greater consequence than people imagined." Besides, the French wanted the Princess Mary for Orleans, and were anxious to send an embassy to him about it: indeed, the French ambassador was coming to see him about it with fresh powers next day. Chapuys protested that he spoke as one devoted to Henry's service; but he was sure the French did not mean business. They would never let Orleans marry a Princess of illegitimate birth. "Ah!" replied Henry, "but though she may be a bastard, I have power from Parliament to appoint her my successor if I like;" but Chapuys gave several other reasons why the match with Mary would never suit the French. "Why," cried Henry, "Francis is even now soliciting an interview with me with a view to alliances." "Yes, I know they say that," replied the ambassador, "but at the same time Francis has sent an ambassador to Scotland, with orders not to touch at an English port." This was a sore point with Henry, and he again winced at the blow.

Then he began to boast. He was prepared to face any one, and James of Scotland was in mortal fear of him. Chapuys then mentioned that France had made a secret treaty with Sweden and Denmark to obtain control of the North Sea, and divert all the Anglo-German trade to France, which Henry parried, by saying that Francis was in league with the German Protestants, and, notwithstanding the new decree of the Diet of Ratisbon, could draw as many mercenary soldiers as he liked from the Emperor's vassals. He felt sure that Francis would invade Flanders next spring; and if he, Henry, had cared to marry a daughter of France, as her father wished him to do, he might have had a share of his conquests. This made Chapuys angry, and he said that perhaps Holstein and Cleves had also been offered shares. Henry then went on another tack, and said that he knew quite well that Francis and Charles together intended, if they could, to make war on England. Considering, however, the Emperor's disaster at Algiers, and the state of Europe, he was astonished that Charles had not tried to make a close friendship with him. Chapuys jumped at the hint, and begged Henry to state his intentions, that they might be conveyed to the Emperor. But the King was not to be drawn too rapidly, and would not say whether he was willing to form an alliance with the Emperor until some one with full and special powers was sent to him. He had been cheated too often and left in the lurch before, he said. "He was quite independent. If people wanted him they might come forward with offers." This sparring went on for hours on that day and the next, interspersed with little wrangles about the commercial question, and innuendoes as to the French intrigues. But Chapuys, who knew his man, quite understood that Henry was for sale; and, as usual, might, if dexterously handled, be bought by flattery and feigned submission to his will, hurriedly wrote to his master that: "If the Emperor wishes to gain the King, he must send hither at once an able person, with full powers, to take charge of the negotiation:" since he, Chapuys, was in ill health and unequal to it.

Thus the English Catholic reaction that had been symbolised by the repudiation of Anne of Cleves, and the marriage with Katharine Howard, was triumphantly producing the results which Henry and Gardiner had intended. The excommunicated King, the man who had flung aside his proud Spanish wife and bade defiance to the vicegerent of Christ, was to be flattered and sought in alliance by the head of the house of Aragon and the appointed champion of Roman orthodoxy. He was to come back into the fold unrepentant, with no submission or reparation made, a good Catholic, but his own Pope. It was a prospect that appealed strongly to a man of Henry's vain and ostentatious character, for it gave apparent sanction to his favourite pose that everything he did was warranted by the strictest right and justice; it promised the possibility of an extension of his Continental territory, and the establishment of his own fame as a warrior and a king. We shall see how his pompous self-conceit enabled his ally to trick him out of his reward, and how the consequent reaction against those who had beguiled him drew his country farther along the road of the Reformation than Henry ever meant to go. But at present all looked rose-coloured, for the imperial connection and the miserable scandal of Katharine Howard rather benefited than injured the chances of its successful negotiation. Cranmer, Hertford, and Audley had shot their bolt in vain so far as political or religious aims were attained.

In the meanwhile the evidence against Katharine and her abettors was being laboriously wrung out of all those who had come into contact with her. The poor old Duchess of Norfolk and her son and daughters and several underlings were condemned for misprison of treason to perpetual imprisonment and confiscation, and in Parliament on the 21st January a Bill of Attainder against Katharine and three lady accomplices was presented to the Lords. The evidence presented against Katharine was adjudged to be insufficient in the absence of direct allegations of adultery after her marriage, or of specific admissions from herself. This and other objections seem to have delayed the passage of the Bill until the 11th of February, when it received the royal assent by commission, condemning Katharine and Lady Rochford to death for treason. During the passage of the Bill, as soon, indeed, as the procedure of Katharine's condemnation had been settled, Henry plucked up spirits again, and with characteristic heartlessness once more began to play the gallant. "The King," writes Chapuys, "had never been merry since first hearing of the Queen's misconduct, but he has been so since (the attainder was arranged), especially on the 29th, when he gave a supper and banquet with twenty-six ladies at the table, besides gentlemen, and thirty-five at another table adjoining. The lady for whom he showed the greatest regard was a sister of Lord Cobham, whom Wyatt, some time ago, divorced for adultery. She is a pretty young creature, with wit enough to do as badly as the others if she were to try. The King is also said to fancy a daughter of Mistress Albart(?) and niece of Sir Anthony Browne; and also for a daughter, by her first marriage, of the wife of Lord Lisle, late Deputy of Calais."

Up to this time Katharine had remained at Sion House, as Chapuys reported, "making good cheer, fatter and more beautiful than ever; taking great care to be well apparelled, and more imperious and exacting to serve than even when she was with the King, although she believes she will be put to death, and admits that she deserves it. Perhaps if the King does not wish to marry again he may show her some compassion." No sooner, however, had the Act of Attainder passed its third reading in the Commons (10th January) than Fitzwilliam was sent to Isleworth to convey her to the Tower. She resisted at first, but was of course overpowered, and the sad procession swept along the wintry river Londonward. First came Fitzwilliam's barge with himself and several Privy Councillors, then, in a small covered barge, followed the doomed woman, and the rear was guarded by a great barge full of soldiers under the aged Duke of Suffolk, whose matrimonial adventures had been almost as numerous as those of his royal brother-in-law. Under the frowning portcullis of the Traitors' Gate in the gathering twilight of the afternoon, the beautiful girl in black velvet landed amidst a crowd of Councillors, who treated her with as much ceremony as if she still sat by the King's side. She proudly and calmly gloried in her love for her betrothed Culpeper, whom she knew she soon would join in death. There was no hysterical babbling like that of her cousin, Anne Boleyn; no regret in her mien or her words now. Even as he, with his last breath, had confessed his love for her, and mourned that the King's passion for her had stood in the way of their honest union, so did she, with flashing eyes and blazing cheeks, proclaim that love was victorious over death; and that since there had been no mercy for the man she loved she asked no mercy for herself from the King whose plaything of a year she had been.

On Sunday evening, 12th February, she was told that she must be prepared for death on the morrow, and she asked that the block should be brought to her room, that she might learn how to dispose her head upon it. This was done, and she calmly and smilingly rehearsed her part in the tragedy of the morrow. Early in the morning, before it was fully light, she was led out across the green, upon which the hoar-frost glistened, to the scaffold erected on the same spot that had seen the sacrifice of Anne Boleyn. Around it stood all the Councillors except Norfolk and Suffolk: even her first cousin, the poet Surrey, with his own doom not far off, witnessed the scene. Upon the scaffold, half crazy with fear, stood the wretched Lady Rochford, the ministress of the Queen's amours, who was to share her fate. Katharine spoke shortly. She died, she said, in full confidence in God's goodness. She had grievously sinned and deserved death, though she had not wronged the King in the particular way that she had been accused of. If she had married the man she loved, instead of being dazzled by ambition, all would have been well; and when the headsman knelt to ask her forgiveness, she pardoned him, but exclaimed, "I die a Queen, but I would rather have died the wife of Culpeper;" and then, kneeling in prayer, her head was struck off whilst she was unaware. Lady Rochford followed her to the block as soon as the head and trunk of the Queen had been piteously gathered up in black cloth by the ladies who attended her at last, and conveyed to the adjoining chapel for sepulture close to the grave of Anne Boleyn.

Katharine Howard had erred much for love, and had erred more for ambition, but taking a human view of the whole circumstances of her life, and of the personality of the man she married, she is surely more worthy of pity than condemnation. Only a few days after her death we learn from Chapuys (25th February) that "the King has been in better spirits since the execution, and during the last three days before Lent there has been much feasting. Sunday was devoted to the lords of his Council and courtiers, Monday to the men of the law, Tuesday to the ladies, who all slept at the Court. The King himself did nothing but go from room to room ordering and arranging the lodgings to be prepared for these ladies, and he made them great and hearty cheer, without showing special affection for any particular one. Indeed, unless Parliament prays him to take another wife, he will not be in a hurry to do so, I think. Besides, there are few, if any, ladies now at Court who would aspire to such an honour; for by a new Act just passed, any lady that the King may marry, if she be a subject, is bound, on pain of death, to declare any charge of misconduct that can be brought against her;

and all who know or suspect anything against her must declare it within twenty days, on pain of perpetual imprisonment and confiscation." Henry, with five unsuccessful matrimonial adventures to his account, might well pause before taking another plunge; though, from the extract printed above, it was evident that he had no desire to put himself out of the way of temptation. The only course upon which he seemed quite determined was to resist all the blandishments of the Protestants, the German Lutherans, and the French to take back Anne of Cleves, who, we are told, had waxed half as beautiful again as she was since she had begun her jolly life of liberty and beneficence, away from so difficult a husband as Henry.

CHAPTER IX

1542-1547

KATHARINE PARR—THE PROTESTANTS WIN THE LAST TRICK

The disappearance of Katharine Howard and the temporary eclipse of Norfolk caused no check to the progress of the Catholic cause in England. When Gardiner was with the Emperor in the summer of 1541 he had been able to make in Henry's name an agreement by which neither monarch should treat anything to the other's disadvantage for the next ten months; and as war loomed nearer between Charles and Francis, the chances of a more durable and binding treaty being made between the former and Henry improved. When Gardiner had hinted at it in Germany, both Charles and Granvelle had suggested that the submission of Henry to the Pope would be a necessary preliminary. But the Emperor's brother, Ferdinand, was in close grips with the Turk in Hungary, and getting the worst of it; Francis was again in negotiation with the infidel, and French intrigue in Italy was busy. Henry therefore found that the Emperor's tone softened considerably on the report of Chapuys' conversation at Windsor in February, whilst the English terms became stiffer, as Francis endeavoured to turn his feigned negotiations with Henry into real ones. The whole policy of Henry at the period was really to effect an armed league with the Emperor, by means of which France might be humiliated, perhaps dismembered, whilst Henry was welcomed back with open arms by the great Catholic power, in spite of his contumacy, and the hegemony of England established over Scotland. In order the better to incline Charles to essential concessions, it was good policy for Henry to give several more turns of the screw upon his own subjects, to prove to his future ally how devout a Catholic he was, and how entirely Cromwell's later action was being reversed.

The great Bibles were withdrawn from the churches, the dissemination of the Scriptures restricted, and the Six Articles were enforced more severely than ever; but yet when, after some months of fencing and waiting, Chapuys came to somewhat closer quarters with the English Council, he still talked, though with bated breath now, about Henry's submission to the Pope and the legitimation of the Princess Mary. But the Emperor's growing need for support gradually broke down the wall of reserve that Henry's defection from Rome had raised, and Gardiner and Chapuys, during the spring of 1542, were in almost daily confabulation in a quiet house in the fields at Stepney. In June the imperial ambassador made a hasty visit to Flanders to submit the English terms for an alliance to the Queen Regent. Henry's conditions in appearance were hard, for by going to war with France he would, he said, lose the great yearly tribute he received from that country; but Charles and his sister knew how to manage him, and were not troubled with scruples as to keeping promises. So, to begin with, the commercial question that had so long been rankling, was now rapidly settled, and the relations daily grew more cordial. Henry had agents in Germany and Flanders ordering munitions of war and making secret compacts with mercenary captains; he was actively reinforcing his own garrisons and castles, organising a fine fleet, collecting vast fresh sums of money from his groaning subjects, and in every way preparing himself to be an ally worth purchase by the Emperor at a high price.

In July 1542 the French simultaneously attacked the imperial territory in four distinct directions; and Henry summoned the ambassadors of Charles and Francis to Windsor to tell them that, as war was so near him, he must raise men for his defence, especially towards Scotland, but meant no menace to either of the Continental powers. Chapuys had already been assured that the comedy was only to blind the French, and cheerfully acquiesced, but the Frenchmen took a more gloomy view and knew it meant war. With Scotland and Henry it was a case of the lamb and the wolf. Henry knew that he dared not send his army across the Channel to attack France without first crushing his northern neighbour. The pretended negotiations with, and allegations against, the unfortunate Stuart were never sincere. James was surrounded by traitors: for English money and religious rancour had profoundly divided the Scottish gentry; Cardinal Beaton, the Scots King's principal minister, was hated; the powerful Douglas family were disaffected and in English pay; and the forces with which James V. rashly attempted to raid the English marches in reprisal for Henry's unprovoked attacks upon him were wild and undisciplined. The battle of Solway Moss (November 1542) was a disgraceful rout for the Scots, and James, heartbroken, fled from the ruin of his cause to Tantallon and Edinburgh, and thence to Falkland to die. Then, with Scotland rent in twain, with a new-born baby for a Queen, and a foreign woman as regent, Henry could face a war with France by the side of the Emperor, with assurance of safety on his northern border, especially if he could force upon the rulers of Scotland a marriage between his only son and the infant Mary Stuart, as he intended to do.

KATHARINE PARR
From a painting in the collection of the EARL OF ASHBURNHAM

There was infinite haggling with Chapuys with regard to the style to be given to Henry in the secret treaty, even after the heads of the treaty itself had been agreed upon. He must be called sovereign head of the English Church, said Gardiner, or there would be no alliance with the Emperor at all, and the difficulty was only overcome by varying the style in the two copies of the document, that signed by Chapuys bearing the style of; "King of England, France, and Ireland, etc.," and that signed by the English ministers adding the King's ecclesiastical claims. If the territories of either monarch were invaded the other was bound to come to his aid. The French King was to be summoned to forbear intelligence with the Turk, to satisfy the demands of the Emperor and the King of England in the many old claims they had against him, and no peace was to be made with France by either ally, unless the other's claims were satisfied. The claims of Henry included the town and county of Boulogne, with Montreuil and Therouenne, his arrears of pension, and assurance of future payment: and the two allies agreed within two years to invade France together, each with 20,000 foot and 5000 horse. This secret compact was signed on the 11th February 1543; and the diplomatic relations with France were at once broken off. At last the repudiation of Katharine of Aragon was condoned, and Henry was once more the Emperor's "good brother";— a fit ally for the Catholic king, the champion of orthodox Christianity. As if to put the finishing touch upon Henry's victory, Charles held an interview with the Pope in June 1543 on his way through Italy, and succeeded in persuading him that the inclusion of the King who defied the Church in the league of militant Catholics was a fit complement to the alliance of France and enemies of all Christianity; and would secure the triumph of the Papacy and the return of England into the fold.

Whilst the preparations for war thus went busily forward on all sides, with Chantonnay in England and Thomas Seymour in Germany and Flanders arranging military details of arms, levies, and stores, and the Emperor already clamouring constantly for prompt English subsidies and contingents against his enemies, Henry, full of importance and self-satisfaction at his position, contracted the only one of his marriages which was not promoted by a political intrigue, although at the time it was effected it was doubtless looked upon as favouring the Catholic party. Certainly no lady of the Court enjoyed a more blameless reputation than Katharine Lady Latimer, upon whom the King now cast his eyes. A daughter of the great and wealthy house of Parr of Kendal, allied to the royal blood in no very distant degree, and related to most of the higher nobility of England, she was, so far as descent was concerned, quite as worthy to be the wife of a king as the unfortunate daughters of the house of Howard. Her brother, Lord Parr, soon to be created Earl of Essex and Marquis of Northampton, a favourite courtier of the King and a very splendid magnate, had been one of the chief enemies of Cromwell; who had in his last days usurped the ancient earldom which Parr had claimed in right of his Bourchier wife, whilst Katharine's second husband, Neville Lord Latimer, had been so strong a Catholic as to have risked his great possessions, as well as his head, by joining the rising in the North that had assumed the name of the Pilgrimage of Grace and had been mainly directed against Cromwell's measures. She was, moreover, closely related to the Throckmortons, the stoutly Catholic family whose chief, Sir George, Cromwell had despoiled and imprisoned until the intrigue already related drove the minister from power in June 1540, with the mysterious support, so it is asserted, of Katharine Lady Latimer herself, though the evidence of it is not very convincing.

Katharine had been brought up mostly in the north country with extreme care and wisdom by a hard-headed mother, and had been married almost as a child to an elderly widower, Lord Borough, who had died soon afterwards, leaving her a large jointure. Her second husband, Lord Latimer, had also been many years older than herself; and accompanying him, as she did, in his periodical visits to London, where they had a house in the precincts of the Charterhouse, she had for several years been remarkable in Henry's Court, not only for her wide culture and love of learning, but also for her friendship with the Princess Mary, whose tastes were exactly similar to her own. Lord Latimer died in London at the beginning of 1543, leaving to Katharine considerable property; and certainly not many weeks can have passed before the King began to pay his court to the wealthy and dignified widow of thirty-two. His attentions were probably not very welcome to her, for he was a terribly dangerous husband, and any unrevealed peccadillo in the previous life of a woman he married might mean the loss of her head.

There was another reason than this, however, that made the King's addresses especially embarrassing to Katharine. The younger of the two magnificent Seymour brothers, Sir Thomas, had thus early also approached her with offers of love. He was one of the handsomest men at Court, and of similar age to Katharine. He was already very rich with the church plunder, and was the King's brother-in-law; so that he was in all respects a good match for her. He must have arrived from his mission to Germany immediately after Lord Latimer's death, and remained at Court until early in May, about three months; during which time, from the evidence of Katharine's subsequent letters, she seems to have made up her mind to marry him. It may be that the King noticed signs of their courtship, for Sir Thomas Seymour was promptly sent on an embassy to Flanders in company with Dr. Wotton, and subsequently with the English contingent to the Emperor's army to France, where he remained until long after Henry's sixth marriage.

That Henry himself lost no time in approaching the widow after her husband's death is seen by a tailor's bill for dresses for Lady Latimer being paid out of the Exchequer by the King's orders as early as the

16th February 1543, when it would seem that her husband cannot have been dead much more than a month. This bill includes linen and buckram, the making of Italian gowns, "pleats and sleeves," a slope hood and tippet, kirtles, French, Dutch, and Venetian gowns, Venetian sleeves, French hoods, and other feminine fripperies; the amount of the total being £8, 9s. 5d.; and, as showing that even before the marriage considerable intimacy existed between Katharine and the Princess Mary, it is curious to note that some of the garments appear to have been destined for the use of the latter. By the middle of June the King's attentions to Lady Latimer were public; and already the lot of the sickly, disinherited Princess Mary was rendered happier by the prospective elevation of her friend. Mary came to Court at Greenwich, as did her sister Elizabeth; and Katharine is specially mentioned as being with them in a letter from Dudley, the new Lord Lisle, to Katharine's brother, Lord Parr, the Warden of the Scottish Marches. The King had then (20th June) just returned from a tour of inspection of his coast defences, and three weeks later Cranmer as Primate issued a licence for his marriage with Katharine Lady Latimer, without the publication of banns.

On the 12th July 1543 the marriage took place in the upper oratory "called the Quynes Preyevey Closet" at Hampton Court. When Gardiner the celebrant put the canonical question to the bridegroom, his Majesty answered "with a smiling face," yea, and, taking his bride's hand, firmly recited the usual pledge. Katharine, whatever her inner feelings may have been, made a bright and buxom bride, and from the first endeavoured, as none of the other wives had done, to bring together into some semblance of family life with her the three children of her husband. Her reward was that she was beloved and respected by all of them; and Princess Mary, who was nearly her own age, continued her constant companion and friend.

As she began so she remained; amiable, tactful, and clever. Throughout her life with Henry her influence was exerted wherever possible in favour of concord, and I have not met with a single disparaging remark with regard to her, even from those who in the last days of the King's life became her political opponents. Her character must have been an exceedingly lovable one, and she evidently knew to perfection how to manage men by humouring their weak points. She could be firm, too, on occasions where an injustice had to be remedied. A story is told of her in connection with her brother Parr, Earl of Essex, in the *Chronicle of Henry VIII.*, which, so far as I know, has not been related by any other historian of the reign.

Parr fell in love with Lord Cobham's daughter, a very beautiful girl, who, as told in our text, was mentioned as one of the King's flames after Katharine Howard's fall. Parr had married the great Bourchier heiress, but had grown tired of her, and by suborned evidence charged her with adultery, and she was found guilty and sentenced to death. "The good Queen, his sister, threw herself at the feet of the King and would not rise until he had promised to grant her the boon she craved, which was the life of the Countess (of Essex). When the King heard what it was, he said, But, Madam, you know that the law enacts that a woman of rank who so forgets herself shall die unless her husband pardon her. To this the Queen answered, Your Majesty is above the law, and I will try to get my brother to pardon. Well, said the King, if your brother be content I will pardon her." The Queen then sends for her brother and upbraids him for bringing perjured witnesses against his wife, which he denies and says he has only acted in accordance with the legal evidence. "I can promise you, brother, that it shall not be as you expect: I will have the witnesses put to the torture, and then by God's help we shall know the truth." Before this could be done Parr sent his witnesses to Cornwall, out of the way: and again Katharine insisted upon the Countess' pardon, by virtue of the promise that the King had given her. This somewhat alarmed Parr, and Katharine managed to effect a mutual renunciation, after which Parr married Lord Cobham's daughter.

Gardiner had been not only the prelate who performed the ceremony but had himself given the bride away; so that it may fairly be concluded that he, at least, was not discontented with the match. Wriothesley, his obedient creature, moreover, must have been voicing the general feeling of Catholics when he wrote to the Duke of Suffolk in the North his eulogy of the bride a few days after the wedding. "The King's Majesty was mareid onne Thursdaye last to my ladye Latimor, a woman, in my judgment, for vertewe, wisdomme and gentilnesse, most meite for his Highnesse: and sure I am his Mat^e had never a wife more agreable to his harte than she is. Our Lorde sende them long lyf and moche joy togethir." Both the King's daughters had been at the wedding, Mary receiving from Katharine a handsome present as bride's-maid; but Henry had the decency not to bid the presence of Anne of Cleves. She is represented as being somewhat disgusted at the turn of events. Her friends, and perhaps she herself, had never lost the hope that if the Protestant influence became paramount, Henry might take her back. But the imperial alliance had made England an enemy of her brother of Cleves, whose territory the Emperor's troops were harrying with fire and sword; and her position in England was a most difficult one. "She would," says Chapuys, "prefer to be with her mother, if with nothing but the clothes on her back, rather than be here now, having specially taken great grief and despair at the King's espousal of his new wife, who is not nearly so good-looking as she is, besides that there is no hope of her (Katharine) having issue, seeing that she had none by her two former husbands."

As we have seen, Katharine had all her life belonged to the Catholic party, of which the northern nobles were the leaders, and doubtless this fact had secured for her marriage the ready acquiescence of Gardiner and his friends, especially when coupled with the attachment known to exist between the bride and the Princess Mary. But Katharine had studied hard, and was devoted to the "new learning," which had suddenly become fashionable for high-born ladies. The Latin classics, the writings of Erasmus, of Juan Luis Vives, and others were the daily solace of the few ladies in England who had at this time been seized with the new craze of culture, Katharine, the King's daughters, his grand-nieces the Greys, and the daughters of Sir Anthony Cook, being especially versed in classics, languages, philosophy, and theology. The "new learning" had been, and was still to be, for the most part promoted by those who sympathised with the reformed doctrines, and Katharine's devotion to it brought her into intimate contact with the learned men at Court whose zeal for the spread of classical and controversial knowledge was coupled with the spirit of inquiry which frequently went with religious heterodoxy.

Not many days after the marriage, Gardiner scented danger in this foregathering of the Queen with such men as Cranmer and Latimer, and at the encouragement and help given by her to the young princesses in the translation of portions of the Scriptures, and of the writings of Erasmus. There is no reason to conclude that Katharine, as yet, had definitely attached herself to the reform party, but it is certain that very soon after her marriage her love of learning, or her distrust of Gardiner's policy and methods, caused her to look sympathetically towards those at Court who went beyond the King in his opposition to Rome. Gardiner dared not as yet directly attack either Katharine or Cranmer, for the King was personally much attached to both of them, whilst Gardiner himself was never a favourite with him. But indirectly these two persons in privileged places might be ruined by attacking others first; and the plan was patiently and cunningly laid to do it, before a new party of reformers led by Cranmer, reinforced by Katharine, could gain the King's ear and reverse the policy of his present adviser.

At the instance of Gardiner's creature Dr. London, a canon of Windsor, a prosecution under the Six Articles was commenced against a priest and some choristers of the royal chapel, and one other person, who were known to meet together for religious discussion. For weeks London's spies had been listening to the talk of those in the castle and town who might be suspected of reformed ideas; and with the evidence so accumulated in his hand, Gardiner moved the King in Council to issue a warrant authorising a search for unauthorised books and papers in the town and castle of Windsor. Henry, whilst allowing the imprisonment of the accused persons with the addition of Sir Philip Hoby and Dr. Haines, both resident in the castle, declined to allow his own residence to be searched for heretical books. This was a set back for Gardiner's plan; but it succeeded to the extent of securing the conviction and execution at the stake of three of the accused. This was merely a beginning; and already those at Court were saying that the Bishop of Winchester "aimed at higher deer" than those that had already fallen to his bow.

Hardly had the ashes of the three martyrs cooled, than a mass of fresh accusations was formulated by London against several members of the royal household. The reports of spies and informers were sent to Gardiner by the hand of Ockham, the clerk of the court that had condemned the martyrs, but one of the persons accused, a member of Katharine's household, received secret notice of what was intended and waylaid Ockham. Perusal of the documents he bore showed that much of the information had been suborned by Dr. London and his assistant Simons, and Katharine was appealed to for her aid. She exerted her influence with her husband to have them both arrested and examined. Unaware that their papers had been taken from Ockham, they foreswore themselves and broke down when confronted with the written proofs that the case against the accused had been trumped up on false evidence with ulterior objects. Disgrace and imprisonment for the two instruments, London and Simons, followed, but the prelate who had inspired their activity was too indispensable to the King to be attacked, and he, firm in his political predominance, bided his time for yet another blow at his enemies, amongst whom he now included the Queen, whose union with the King he and other Catholics had so recently blessed.

Cranmer, secure as he thought in the King's regard and in his great position as Primate, had certainly laid himself open to the attacks of his enemies, by his almost ostentatious favour to the clergy of his province who were known to be evading or violating the Six Articles. The chapter of his own cathedral was profoundly divided, and the majority of its members were opposed to what they considered the injustice of their Archbishop. Cranmer's commissary, his nephew Nevinson, whilst going out of his way to favour those who were accused before the chapter of false doctrine, offended deeply the majority of the clergy by his zeal— which really only reflected that of the Archbishop himself— in the displacing and destruction of images in the churches, even when the figures did not offend against the law by being made the objects of superstitious pilgrimages and offerings. For several years past the cathedral church of Canterbury had been a hotbed of discord, in consequence of Cranmer's having appointed, apparently on principle, men of extreme opinions on both sides as canons, prebendaries, and preachers; and so great had grown the opposition in his own chapter to the Primate's known views in the spring of 1543, that it was evident that a crisis could not be long delayed, especially as the clergy opposed to the prelate had the letter of the law on their side, and the countenance of Gardiner, Bishop of Winchester, all powerful as he was in the lay counsels of the King.

Some of the Kentish clergy who resented the Archbishop's action had laid their heads together in March 1543, and formulated a set of accusations against him. This the two most active movers in the protest had carried to the metropolis for submission to Gardiner. They first, however, approached the Dr. London already referred to, who rewrote the accusations with additions of his own, in order to bring the accused within the penal law. The two first movers, Willoughby and Searl, took fright at this, for it was a dangerous thing to attack the Archbishop, and hastily returned home; but Dr. London had enough for his present purpose, and handed his enlarged version of their depositions to Gardiner. London's disgrace, already related, stayed the matter for a time, but a few months afterwards a fresh set of articles, alleging illegal acts on the part of the Archbishop, was forwarded by the discontented clergy to Gardiner, and the accusers were then summoned before the Privy Council, where they were encouraged to make their testimony as strong as possible. When the depositions were complete they were sent to the King by Gardiner, in the hope that now the great stumblingblock of the Catholic party might be cleared from the path, and that the new Queen's ruin might promptly follow that of the Primate.

But they reckoned without Henry's love for Cranmer. Rowing on the Thames one evening in the late autumn soon after the depositions had been handed to him, the King called at the pier by Lambeth Palace and took Cranmer into his barge. "Ah, my chaplain," he said jocosely, as the Archbishop took his seat in the boat, "I have news for you. I know now who is the greatest heretic in Kent;" and with this he drew from his sleeve and handed to Cranmer the depositions of those who had sought to ruin him. The Archbishop insisted upon a regular Commission being issued to test the truth of the accusations; but Henry could be generous when it suited him, and he never knew how soon he might need Cranmer's pliable ingenuity again. So, although he issued the Commission, he made Cranmer its head, and gave to him the appointment of its members; with the natural result that the accusers and all their abettors were imprisoned and forced to beg the Primate's forgiveness for their action. But the man who gave life to the whole plot, Bishop Gardiner of Winchester, still led the King's political counsels, much as Henry disliked him personally; for the armed alliance with the Emperor could only bring its full harvest of profit and glory to the King of England if the Catholic powers on the Continent were convinced of Henry's essential orthodoxy, notwithstanding his quarrel with the Pope. So, though Cranmer might be favoured privately and Katharine's coquetting with the new learning and its professors winked at, Gardiner, whose Catholicism was stronger than that of his master, had to be the figure-head to impress foreigners.

In July 1543 the English contingent to aid the imperial troops to protect Flanders was sent from Guisnes and Calais under Sir John Wallop. By the strict terms of the treaty they were only to be employed for a limited period for the defence of territory invaded by the enemy; but soon after Wallop's arrival he was asked to take part in the regular siege of Landrecy in Hainault, that had been occupied by the French. Henry allowed him to do so under protest. It was waste of time, he said, and would divert the forces from what was to be their main object; but if he allowed it, he must have the same right when the war in France commenced to call upon the imperial contingent with him also to besiege a town if he wished to do so. Both the allies, even before the war really began, were playing for their own hands with the deliberate intention of making use of each other; and in the dismal comedy of chicanery that followed and lasted almost to Henry's death, this siege of Landrecy and that of St. Disier were made the peg upon which countless reclamations and recriminations were hung. The Emperor was ill, in dire need of money, and overwhelmed with anxiety as to the attitude of the Lutheran princes during the coming struggle. His eyes were turned towards Italy, and he depended much upon the diversion that Henry's forces might effect by land and sea; and conscious that the campaign must be prompt and rapid if he was to profit by it, he sent one of his most trusted lieutenants, Ferrante Gonzaga, Viceroy of Sicily, to England at the end of the year 1543 to settle with Henry the plan of the campaign to be undertaken in the spring.

His task was a difficult one; for Henry was as determined to use Charles for his advantage as Charles was to use him. After much dispute it was agreed that Henry, as early in the summer as possible, should lead his army of 35,000 foot and 7000 horse to invade France from Calais, whilst the imperial troops were to invade by Lorraine, form a junction with the English on the Somme, and push on towards Paris. Rapidity was the very essence of such a plan; but Henry would not promise celerity. He could not, he said, transport all his men across the sea before the end of June: the fact being that his own secret intention all along was to conquer the Boulognais country for himself, gain a free hand in Scotland, and leave the Emperor to shift as he might. Utter bad faith on both sides pervaded the affair from first to last. The engaging and payment of mercenaries by England, the purchase of horses, arms, and stores, the hire of transport, the interference with commerce— everything in which sharp dealing could be employed by one ally to get the better of the other was taken advantage of to the utmost. Henry, enfeebled as he was by disease and obesity, was determined to turn to his personal glory the victory he anticipated for his arms. His own courtiers dared not remonstrate with him; and, although Katharine prayed him to have regard for his safety, he brushed aside her remonstrances as becoming womanly fears for a dearly loved husband. Charles knew that if the King himself crossed the Channel the English army would not be at the imperial bidding. Envoys were consequently sent from Flanders to pray Henry, for his health's sake, not to risk the hardships of a sea voyage and a campaign. The subject was a sore one with him; and when the envoy began to dwell too emphatically upon his infirmities, he flew into a passion and said that the Emperor was suffering from gout, which was much worse than any malady he (Henry) had, and it would be more dangerous for the Emperor to go to the war.

Henry's decision to accompany his army at once increased the importance of Katharine; who, in accordance with precedent, would become regent in her husband's absence. A glimpse of her growing influence at this time is seen in a letter of hers, dated 3rd June 1544, to the Countess of Hertford, that termagant Ann Stanhope who afterwards was her jealous enemy. Hertford had been sent in March to the Scottish Border to invade again, and this time utterly crush Scotland, where Henry's pensioners had played him false, and betrothed their infant

Queen to the heir of France. The Countess, anxious that her husband should be at home during the King's absence— probably in order that if anything happened to Henry, Hertford might take prompt measures on behalf of the new King, his nephew, and safeguard his own influence— wrote to Katharine praying for her aid. The Queen's answer is written on the same sheet of paper as one from Princess Mary to the Countess, whose letters to Katharine had been sent through the Princess. "My lord your husband's comyng hyther is not altered, for he schall come home before the Kynge's Majesty take hys journey over the sees, as it pleaseth his Majesty to declare to me of late. You may be ryght assured I wold not have forgotten my promise to you in a matter of lesse effect than thys, and so I pray you most hartely to think....— KATERYN THE QUENE."

Since Henry insisted upon going to the war himself the next best thing, according to the Emperor's point of view, to keeping him away was to cause some Spanish officer of high rank and great experience to be constantly close to him during the campaign. Except the little skirmishes on the borders of Scotland, Englishmen had seen no active military service for many years, and it was urged upon Henry that a general well acquainted with modern Continental warfare would be useful to him. The Emperor's Spanish and Italian commanders were the best in the world, as were his men-at-arms; and a grandee, the Duke of Najera, who was on his way from Flanders to Spain by sea, was looked upon as being a suitable man for the purpose of advising the King of England. Henry was determined to impress him and entertained him splendidly, delaying him as long as possible, in order that he might be persuaded to accompany the English forces. The accounts of Najera's stay in England show that Katharine had now, the spring of 1544, quite settled down in her position as Queen and coming Regent. Chapuys mentions that when he first took Najera to Court he "visited the Queen and Princess (Mary), who asked very minutely for news of the Emperor ... and, although the Queen was a little indisposed, she wished to dance for the honour of the company. The Queen favours the Princess all she can; and since the Treaty with the Emperor was made, she has constantly urged the Princess' cause, insomuch as in this sitting of Parliament she (Mary) has been declared capable of succeeding in default of the Prince."

A Spaniard who attended Najera tells the story of the Duke's interview with Katharine somewhat more fully. "The Duke kissed the Queen's hand and was then conducted to another chamber, to which the Queen and ladies followed, and there was music and much beautiful dancing. The Queen danced first with her brother very gracefully, and then Princess Mary and the Princess of Scotland (*i.e.* Lady Margaret Douglas) danced with other gentlemen, and many other ladies also danced, a Venetian of the King's household dancing some gaillards with such extraordinary activity that he seemed to have wings upon his feet; surely never was a man seen so agile. After the dancing had lasted several hours the Queen returned to her chamber, first causing one of the noblemen who spoke Spanish to offer some presents to the Duke, who kissed her hand. He would likewise have kissed that of the Princess Mary, but she offered her lips; and so he saluted her and all the other ladies. The King is regarded as a very powerful and handsome man. The Queen is graceful and of cheerful countenance; and is praised for her virtue. She wore an underskirt, showing in front, of cloth of gold, and a sleeved over-dress of brocade lined with crimson satin, the sleeves themselves being lined with crimson velvet, and the train was two yards long. She wore hanging from the neck two crosses and a jewel of very magnificent diamonds, and she wore a great number of splendid diamonds in her headdress." The author of this curious contemporary document excels himself in praise of the Princess Mary, whose dress on the occasion described was even more splendid than that of the Queen, consisting as it did entirely of cloth of gold and purple velvet. The house and gardens of Whitehall also moved the witness to wonder and admiration. The green alleys with high hedges of the garden and the sculpture with which the walks were adorned especially attracted the attention of the visitors, and the greatness of London and the stately river Thames are declared to be incomparable.

The Duke of Najera, unwilling to stay, and, apparently, not impressing Henry very favourably, went on his way; and was immediately followed by another Spanish commander of equal rank and much greater experience in warfare, the Duke of Alburquerque, and he, too, was received with the splendour and ostentation that Henry loved, ultimately accompanying the King to the siege of Boulogne as military adviser; both the King and Queen, we are told, treating him with extraordinary favour.

By the time that Henry was ready to cross the Channel early in July to join his army, which several weeks before had preceded him under the command of Norfolk and Suffolk, the short-lived and insincere alliance with the Emperor, from which Henry and Gardiner had expected so much, was already strained almost to breaking point. The great imperialist defeat at Ceresole in Savoy earlier in the year had made Henry more disinclined than ever to sacrifice English men and treasure to fight indirectly the Emperor's battle in Italy. Even before that Henry had begun to show signs of an intention to break away from the plan of campaign agreed upon. How dangerous it would be, he said, for the Emperor to push forward into France without securing the ground behind him. "Far better to lay siege to two or three large towns on the road to Paris than to go to the capital and burn it down." Charles was indignant, and continued to send reminders and remonstrances that the plan agreed upon must be adhered to. Henry retorted that Charles himself had departed from it by laying siege to Landecy. The question of supplies from Flanders, the payment and passage of mercenaries through the Emperor's territories, the free concession of trading licences by the Queen Regent of the Netherlands, and a dozen other questions, kept the relations between the allies in a state of irritation and acrimony, even before the campaign well began, and it is clear thus early that Henry started with the fixed intention of conquering the territory of Boulogne, and then perhaps making friends with Francis, leaving the Emperor at war. With both the great rivals exhausted, he would be more sought after than ever. He at once laid siege to Montreuil and Boulogne, and personally took command, deaf to the prayers and remonstrances of Charles and his sister, that he would not go beyond Calais, "for his health's sake"; but would send the bulk of his forces to join the Emperor's army before St. Disier. The Emperor had himself broken the compact by besieging Landrecy and St. Disier; and so the bulk of Henry's army sat down before Boulogne, whilst the Emperor, short of provisions, far in an enemy's country, with weak lines of communication, unfriendly Lorraine on his flank and two French armies approaching him, could only curse almost in despair the hour that he trusted the word of "his good brother," the King of England.

Katharine bade farewell to her husband at Dover when he went on his pompous voyage, and returned forthwith to London, fully empowered to rule England as Regent during his absence. She was directed to use the advice and counsel of Cranmer, Wriothesley, the Earl of Hertford, who was to replace her if she became incapacitated, Thirlby, and Petre; Gardiner accompanying the King as minister. The letters written by Katharine to her husband during his short campaign show no such instances of want of tact as did those of the first Katharine, quoted in the earlier pages of this book. It is plain to read in them the clever, discreet woman, determined to please a vain man; content to take a subordinate place and to shine by a reflected light alone. "She thanks God for a prosperous beginning of his affairs;" "she rejoices at the joyful news of his good health," and in a business-like way shows that she and her council are actively forwarding the interests of the King with a single-hearted view to his honour and glory alone.

During this time the young Prince Edward and his sister Mary were at Hampton Court with the Queen; but the other daughter, Elizabeth, lived apart at St. James's. Though it is evident that the girl was generally regarded and treated as inferior to her sister, she appears to have felt a real regard for her stepmother, almost the only person who, since her infancy, had been kind to her. Elizabeth wrote to the Queen on the 31st July a curious letter in Italian. "Envious fortune," she writes, "for a whole year deprived me of your Highness's presence, and, not content therewith, has again despoiled me of that boon. I know, nevertheless, that I have your love; and that you have not forgotten me in writing to the King. I pray you in writing to his Majesty deign to recommend me to him; praying him for his ever-welcome blessing; praying at the same time to Almighty God to send him good fortune and victory over his enemies; so that your Highness and I together may the sooner rejoice at his happy return. I humbly pray to God to have your Highness in His keeping; and respectfully kissing your Highness' hand.— ELIZABETH."

Katharine indeed, in this trying time of responsibility, comes well out of her ordeal. The prayer composed by her for peace at this period is really a beautiful composition; and the letter from her to her husband, printed by Strype, breathes sentiment likely to please such a man as Henry, but in language at once womanly and dignified. "Although the distance of time and account of days," she writes, "neither is long nor many, of your Majesty's absence, yet the want of your presence, so much beloved and desired by me, maketh me that I cannot quietly pleasure in anything until I hear from your Majesty. The time therefore seemeth to me very long, with a great desire to know how your Highness hath done since your departing hence; whose prosperity and health I prefer and desire more than mine own. And, whereas I know your Majesty's absence is never without great need, yet love and affection compel me to desire your presence. Again the same zeal and affection forceth me to be best content with that which is your will and pleasure. Thus, love maketh me in all things set apart mine own convenience and pleasure, and to embrace most joyfully his will and pleasure whom I love. God, the knower of secrets, can judge these words to be not only written with ink but most truly impressed upon the heart. Much more I omit, less it be thought I go about to praise myself or crave a thank. Which thing to do I mind nothing less, but a plain simple relation of the love and zeal I bear your Majesty, proceeding from the abundance of the heart.... I make like account with your Majesty, as I do with God, for His benefits and gifts heaped upon me daily; acknowledging myself to be a great debtor to Him, not being able to recompense the least of His benefit. In which state I am certain and sure to die, yet I hope for His gracious acceptance of my goodwill. Even such confidence have I in your Majesty's gentleness, knowing myself never to have done my duty as were requisite and meet for such a noble Prince, at whose hands I have received so much love and goodness that with words I cannot express it."

It will be seen by this, and nearly every other letter that Katharine wrote to her husband, that she had taken the measure of his prodigious vanity, and indulged him to the top of his bent. In a letter written to him on the 9th August, referring to the success of the Earl of Lennox, who had just married Henry's niece, Margaret Douglas, and had gone to Scotland to seize the government in English interest, Katharine says: "The good speed which Lennox has had, is to be imputed to his serving a master whom God aids. He might have served the French king, his old master, many years without attaining such a victory." This is the attitude in which Henry loved to be approached, and with such letters from his wife in England confirming the Jove-like qualities attributed to him in consequence of his presence with his army in France, Henry's short campaign before Boulogne was doubtless one of the pleasantest experiences in his life.

To add to his satisfaction, he had not been at Calais a week before Francis began to make secret overtures for peace. It was too early for that, however, just yet, for Henry coveted Boulogne, and the sole use made of the French approaches to him was to impress the imperial agents with his supreme importance. The warning was not lost upon Charles and his sister the Queen Regent of the Netherlands, who themselves began to listen to the unofficial suggestions for peace made by the agents of the Duchess d'Etampes, the mistress of Francis, in order, if possible, to benefit herself and the Duke of Orleans in the conditions, to the detriment of the Dauphin Henry. Thenceforward it was a close game of diplomatic finesse between Henry and Charles as to which should make terms first and arbitrate on the claims of the other.

St. Disier capitulated to the Emperor on the 8th August; and Charles at once sent another envoy to Henry at Boulogne, praying him urgently to fulfil the plan of campaign decided with Gonzaga, or the whole French army would be concentrated upon the imperial forces and crush them. But Henry would not budge from before Boulogne, and Charles, whilst rapidly pushing forward into France, and in serious danger of being cut off by the Dauphin, listened intently for sounds of peace. They soon came, through the Duke of Lorraine; and before the end of August the Emperor was in close negotiation with the French, determined, come what might, that the final settlement of terms should not be left in the hands of the King of England. Henry's action at this juncture was pompous, inflated, and stupid, whilst that of Charles was statesmanlike, though unscrupulous. Even during the negotiations Charles pushed forward and captured Epernay and Château Thierry, where the Dauphin's stores were. This was on the 7th September, and then having struck his blow he knew that he must make peace at once. He therefore sent the young Bishop of Arras, Granvelle, with a message to Henry which he knew would have the effect desired. The King of England was again to be urged formally but insincerely to advance and join the Emperor, but if he would not the Emperor must make peace, always providing that the English claims were satisfactorily settled.

Arras arrived in the English camp on the 11th September. He found Henry in his most vaunting mood; for only three days before the ancient tower on the harbour side opposite Boulogne had been captured by his men. He could not move forward, he said; it was too late in the season to begin a new campaign, and he was only bound by the treaty to keep the field four months in a year. If the Emperor was in a fix, that was his look-out. The terms, moreover, suggested for the peace between his ally and France were out of the question, especially the clause about English claims. The French had already offered him much better conditions than those. Arras pushed his point. The Emperor must know definitely, he urged, whether the King of England would make peace or not, as affairs could not be left pending. Then Henry lost his temper, as the clever imperial ministers knew he would do, and blurted out in a rage: "Let the Emperor make peace for himself if he likes, but nothing must be done to prejudice my claims." It was enough for the purpose desired, for in good truth the Emperor had already agreed with the French, and Arras posted back to his master with Henry's hasty words giving permission for him to make a separate peace. In vain for the next two years Henry strove to unsay, to palliate, to disclaim these words. Quarrels, bursts of violent passion, incoherent rage, indignant denials, were all of no avail; the words were said, and vouched for by those who heard them; and Charles hurriedly ratified the peace already practically made with France on terms that surprised the world, and made Henry wild with indignation.

The Emperor, victor though he was, in appearance gave away everything. His daughter or niece was to marry Orleans, with Milan or Flanders as a dowry; Savoy was to be restored to the Duke, and the French were to join the Emperor in alliance against the Turk. None knew yet— though Henry may have suspected it— that behind the public treaty there was a secret compact by which the two Catholic sovereigns agreed to concentrate their joint powers and extirpate a greater enemy than the Turk, namely, the rising power of Protestantism in Europe. Henry was thus betrayed and was at war alone with France, all of whose forces were now directed against him. Boulogne fell to the English on the 14th September, three days after Arras arrived in Henry's camp, and the King hurried back to England in blazing wrath with the Emperor and inflated with the glorification of his own victory, eager for the applause of his subjects before his laurels faded and the French beleagured the captured town. Gardiner and Paget, soon to be joined temporarily by Hertford, remained in Calais in order to continue, if possible, the abortive peace negotiations with France. But it was a hopeless task now; for Francis, free from fear on his north-east frontier, was determined to win back Boulogne at any cost. The Dauphin swore that he would have no peace whilst Boulogne remained in English hands, and Henry boastfully declared that he would hold it for ever now that he had won it.

Thenceforward the relations between Henry and the Emperor became daily more unamiable. Henry claimed under the treaty that Charles should still help him in the war, but that was out of the question. When in 1546 the French made a descent upon the Isle of Wight, once more the treaty was invoked violently by the King of England: almost daily claims, complaints, and denunciations were made on both sides with regard to the vexed question of contraband of war for the French, mostly Dutch herrings; and the right of capture by the English. The Emperor was seriously intent upon keeping Henry on fairly good terms, and certainly did not wish to go to war with him; but he had submitted to the hard terms of the peace of Crespy with a distinct object, and dared not jeopardise it by renewing his quarrel with France for the sake of Henry.

Slowly it had forced itself upon the mind of Charles that his own Protestant vassals, the Princes of the Schmalkaldic league, must be crushed into obedience, or his own power would become a shadow; and his aim was to keep all Christendom friendly until he had choked Lutheranism at its fountain-head. From the period of Henry's return to England in these circumstances, growing sympathy for those whom a Papal and imperial coalition were attacking caused the influence of the Catholic party in his Councils gradually but spasmodically to decline. Chapuys, who himself was hastening to the grave, accompanied his successor Van Der Delft as ambassador to England at Christmas (1544), and describes Henry as looking very old and broken, but more boastful of his victory over the French than ever. He professed, no doubt sincerely, a desire to remain friendly with the Emperor; and after their interview with him the ambassadors, without any desire being expressed on their part, were conducted to the Queen's oratory during divine service. In reply to their greetings and thanks for her good offices for the preservation of friendship and her kindness to Princess Mary, Katharine "replied, very graciously, that she did not deserve so much courtesy from your Majesty (the Emperor). What she did for Lady Mary was less than she would like to do, and was only her duty in every respect. With regard to the maintenance of friendship, she said she had done, and would do, nothing to prevent its growing still firmer, and she hoped that God would avert the slightest dissension; as the friendship was so necessary, and both sovereigns were so good."

HENRY VIII.
From a portrait by HOLBEIN *in the possession of the Earl of War-wick*

Katharine was equally amiable, though evidently now playing a political part, when four months later the aged and crippled Chapuys bade his last farewell to England. He was being carried in a chair to take leave of Henry at Whitehall one morning in May at nine o'clock. He was an hour earlier than the time fixed for his audience, and was passing through the green alleys of the garden towards the King's apartments, when notice was brought to him that the Queen and Princess Mary were hastening after him. He stopped at once, and had just time to hobble out of his chair before the two ladies reached him. "It seemed from the small suite she had with her, and the haste with which she came, as if her purpose in coming was specially to speak to me. She was attended only by four or five ladies of the chamber, and opened the conversation by saying that the King had told her the previous evening that I was coming that morning to say good-bye. She was very sorry, on the one hand, for my departure, as she had been told that I had always performed my duties well, and the King trusted me; but on the other hand she doubted not that my health would be better on the other side of the sea. I could, however, she said, do as much on the other side as here, for the maintenance of the friendship, of which I had been one of the chief promoters. For this reason she was glad I was going; although she had no doubt that so wise and good a sovereign as your Majesty (*i.e.* the Emperor) would see the need and importance of upholding the friendship, of which the King, on his side, had given so many proofs in the past. Yet it seemed to her that your Majesty had not been so thoroughly informed hitherto, either by my letters or otherwise, of the King's sincere affection and goodwill, as I should be able to report verbally. She therefore begged me earnestly, after I had presented to your Majesty her humble service, to express explicitly to you, all that I had learned here of the good wishes of the King."

There was much more high-flown compliment both from Katharine and her step-daughter before the gouty ambassador went on his way; but it is evident that Katharine, like her husband, was at this time (May 1545) apprehensive as to the intentions of Charles and his French allies towards England, and was still desirous to obtain some aid in the war under the treaty, in order, if possible, to weaken the new friendship with France and the Catholic alliance. In the meanwhile the failure of Gardiner's policy, and the irritation felt at the Emperor's abandonment of England, placed the minister somewhat under a cloud. He had failed, too, to persuade the Emperor personally to fulfil the treaty, as well as in his negotiations for peace with the French; and, as his sun gradually sank before the King's annoyance, that of Secretary Paget, of Hertford, of Dudley, and of Wriothesley, now Lord Chancellor, a mere time-serving courtier, rose. The Protestant element around Katharine, too, became bolder, and her own participation in politics was now frankly on the anti-Catholic side. The alliance— insincere and temporary though it was— between the Emperor and France, once more produced its inevitable effect of drawing together England and the German Lutherans. It is true that Charles' great plan for crushing dissent by the aid of the Pope was not yet publicly known; but the Council of Trent was slowly gathering, and it was clear to the German princes of the Schmalkaldic league that great events touching religion and their independence were in the air; for Cardinal Farnese and the Papal agents were running backward and forward to the Emperor on secret missions, and all the Catholic world rang with denunciation of heresy.

In June the new imperial ambassador, Van Der Delft, sounded the first note of alarm from England. Katharine Parr's secretary, Buckler, he said, had been in Germany for weeks, trying to arrange a league between the Protestant princes and England. This was a matter of the highest importance, and Charles when he heard of it was doubly desirous of keeping his English brother from quite breaking away; whilst in September there arrived in England from France a regular embassy from the Duke of Saxony, the Landgrave of Hesse, the Duke of Würtemburg, and the King of Denmark, ostensibly to promote peace between England and France, but really bent upon effecting a Protestant alliance. Henry, indeed, was seriously alarmed. He was exhausted by his long war in France, harassed in the victualling of Boulogne and even of Calais, and fully alive to the fact that he was practically defenceless against an armed coalition of the Emperor and France. In the circumstances it was natural that the influence over him of his wife, and of his brother-in-law Hertford, both inclined to a reconciliation with France and an understanding with the German Protestants, should increase.

Katharine, now undisguisedly in favour of such a policy, was full of tact; during the King's frequent attacks of illness she was tender and useful to him, and the attachment to her of the young Prince Edward, testified by many charming little letters of the boy, too well known to need quotation here, seemed to promise a growth of her State importance. The tendency was one to be strenuously opposed by Gardiner and his friends in the Council, and once more attempts were made to strike at the Queen through Cranmer, almost simultaneously with a movement, flattering to Henry and hopeful for the Catholic party, to negotiate a meeting at Calais or in Flanders between him and the Emperor, to settle all questions and make France distrustful. For any such approach to be productive of the full effects desired by Gardiner, it was necessary to couple with it severe measures against the Protestants. Henry was reminded that the coming attack upon the German Lutherans by the Emperor, with the acquiescence of France, would certainly portend an attack upon himself later; and he was told by the Catholic majority of his Council that any tenderness on his part towards heresy now would be specially perilous. The first blow was struck at Cranmer, and was struck in vain. The story in full is told by Strype from Morice and Foxe, and has been repeated by every historian of the reign. Gardiner and his colleagues represented to Henry that, although the Archbishop was spreading heresy, no one dared to give evidence against a Privy Councillor whilst he was free. The King promised that they might send Cranmer to the Tower, if on examination of him they found reason to do so. Late that night Henry sent across the river to Lambeth to summon the Archbishop from his bed to see him, told him of the accusation, and his consent that the accused should be judged and, if advisable, committed to the Tower by his own colleagues on the Council. Cranmer humbly thanked the King, sure, as he said, that no injustice would be permitted. Henry, however, knew better, and indignantly said so; giving to his favourite prelate his ring for a token that summoned the Council to the royal presence.

The next morning early Cranmer was summoned to the Council, and was kept long waiting in an ante-room amongst suitors and serving-men. Dr. Butts, Henry's privileged physician, saw this and told the King that the Archbishop of Canterbury had turned lackey; for he had stood humbly waiting outside the Council door for an hour. Henry, in a towering rage, growled, "I shall talk to them by-and-by." When Cranmer was charged with encouraging heresy he demanded of his colleagues that he should be confronted with his accusers. They refused him rudely, and told him he should be sent to the Tower. Then Cranmer's turn came, and he produced the King's ring, to the dismay of the Council, who, when they tremblingly faced their irate sovereign, were taken to task with a violence that promised them ill, if ever they dared to touch again the King's friend. But though Cranmer was unassailable, the preachers who followed his creed were not. In the spring of 1546 the persecutions under the Six Articles commenced afresh, and for a short time the Catholic party in the Council had much their own way, having frightened Henry into abandoning the Lutheran connection, in order that the vengeance of the Catholic league might not fall upon him, when the Emperor had crushed the Schmalkaldic princes.

Henry's health was visibly failing, and the two factions in his Court knew that time was short in which to establish the predominance of either at the critical moment. On the Protestant side were Hertford, Dudley, Cranmer, and the Queen, and on the other Gardiner, Paget, Paulet, and Wriothesley; and as Katharine's influence grew with her husband's increasing infirmity, it became necessary for the opposite party if possible to get rid of her before the King died. In February 1546 the imperial ambassador reported: "I am confused and apprehensive to have to inform your Majesty that there are rumours here of a new Queen, although I do not know why or how true they may be. Some people attribute them to the sterility of the Queen, whilst others say that there will be no change whilst the present war lasts. The Duchess of Suffolk is much talked about, and is in great favour; but the King shows no alteration in his behaviour towards the Queen, though she is, I am informed, annoyed at the rumours." Hints of this sort continued for some time, and evidently took their rise from a deliberate attack upon Katharine by the Catholic councillors. She herself, for once, failed in her tact, and laid herself open to the designs of her enemies. She was betrayed into a religious discussion with Henry during one of his attacks of illness, in the presence of Gardiner, much to the King's annoyance. When she had retired the Bishop flattered Henry by saying that he wondered how any one could have the temerity to differ from him on theology, and carried his suggestions further by saying that such a person might well oppose him in other things than opinions. Moved by the hints at his danger, always a safe card to play with him, the King allowed an indictment to be drawn up against Katharine, and certain ladies of her family, under the Six Articles. Everything was arranged for the Queen's arrest and examination, when Wriothesley, the Lord Chancellor, a servile creature who always clung to the strongest side, seems to have taken fright and divulged the plot to one of her friends. Katharine was at once informed and fell ill with fright, which for a short time deferred the arrest. Being partially recovered she sought the King, and when he began to talk about religion, she by her submission and refusal to contradict his views, as those of one far too learned for her to controvert, easily flattered him back into a good humour with her. The next day was fixed for carrying her to the Tower, and again Henry determined to play a trick upon his ministers. Sending for his wife in the garden, he kept her in conversation until the hour appointed for her arrest. When Wriothesley and the guard approached, the King turned upon him in a fury, calling him knave, fool, beast, and other opprobrious names, to the Lord Chancellor's utter surprise and confusion.

The failure of the attack upon Katharine in the summer of 1546 marks the decline of the Catholic party in the Council. Peace was made with France in the autumn; and Katharine did her part in the splendid reception of the Admiral of France and the great rejoicings over the new peace treaty (September 1546). Almost simultaneously came the news of fresh dissensions between the Emperor and Francis; for the terms of the peace of Crespy were flagrantly evaded, and it began to be seen now that the treaty had for its sole object the keeping of France quiet and England at war whilst the German Protestants were crushed. Not in France alone, but in England too, the revulsion of feeling against the Emperor's aims was great. The treacherous attack upon his own vassals in order to force orthodoxy upon them at the sword's point had been successful, and it was seen to constitute a menace to all the world. Again Protestant envoys came to England and obtained a loan from Henry: again the Duke Philip of Bavaria, who said that he had never heard mass in his life until he arrived in England, came to claim the hand of the Princess Mary; and the Catholics in the King's Council, forced to stand upon the defensive, became, not the conspirators but those conspired against. Hertford and Dudley, now Lord Admiral, were the King's principal companions, both in his pastimes and his business; and the imperial ambassador expressed his fears for the future to a caucus of the Council consisting of Gardiner, Wriothesley, and Paulet, deploring, as he said, that "not only had the Protestants their openly declared champions ... but I had even heard that some of them had gained great favour with the King, though I wished they were as far away from Court as they were last year. I did not mention names, but the persons I referred to were the Earl of Hertford and the Lord Admiral. The councillors made no reply, but they clearly showed that they understood me, and continued in their great devotion to your Majesty."

Late in September the King fell seriously ill, and his life for a time was despaired of. Dr. Butts had died some months before, and the Queen was indefatigable in her attendance; and the Seymours, as uncles of the heir, rose in importance as the danger to the King increased. The only strong men on the Council on the Catholic side were Gardiner, who was extremely unpopular and already beaten, and Norfolk. Paulet was as obedient to the prevailing wind as a weathercock; Wriothesley was an obsequious, greedy sycophant; Paget a humble official with little influence, and the rest were nonentities. The enmity of the Seymours against the Howards was of long standing, and was as much personal as political; especially between the younger brother, Sir Thomas Seymour, and the Earl of Surrey, the heir of Norfolk, whose quarrels and affrays had several times caused scandal at Court. There was much ill-will also between Surrey and his sister, the widowed Duchess of Richmond, who after the death of her young husband had been almost betrothed to Sir Thomas Seymour. With these elements of enmity a story was trumped up which frightened the sick King into the absurd idea that Surrey aimed at succeeding to the crown, to the exclusion of Henry's children. It was sufficient to send him to the Tower, and afterwards to the block as one of Henry's most popular victims. His father, the aged Duke of Norfolk, was got rid of by charges of complicity with him. Stripped of his garter, the first of English nobles was carried to the Tower by water, whilst his brilliant poet son was led through the streets of London like a pickpurse, cheered to the echo by the crowd that loved him. The story hatched to explain the arrests to the public, besides the silly gossip about Surrey's coat-of-arms and claims to the crown, was, that whilst the King was thought to be dying in November at Windsor, the Duke and his son had plotted to obtain possession of the Prince for their own ends on the death of his father. Having regard for the plots and counterplots that we know divided the Council at the time, this is very probable, and was exactly what Hertford and Dudley were doing, the Prince, indeed, being then in his uncle's keeping at Hertford Castle.

At the end of December the King suffered from a fresh attack, which promised to be fatal. He was at Whitehall at the time, whilst Katharine was at Greenwich, an unusual thing which attracted much comment; but whether she was purposely excluded by Hertford from access to him or not, it is certain that the Protestant party of which she, the Duchess of Suffolk, and the Countess of Hertford were the principal lady members, and the Earl of Hertford and Lord Admiral Dudley the active leaders, alone had control of affairs. Gardiner had been threatened with the Tower months before, and had then only been saved by Norfolk's bold protest. Now Norfolk was safe under bolts and bars, whilst Wriothesley and Paulet were openly insulted by Hertford and Dudley, and, like their chief Gardiner, lay low in fear of what was to come when the King died. They were soon to learn. The King had been growing worse daily during January. His legs, covered with running ulcers, were useless to him and in terrible torture. His bulk was so unwieldy that mechanical means had to be employed to lift him. Surrey had been done to death in the Tower for high treason, whilst yet the King's stiffened hand could sign the death-warrant; but when the time came for killing Norfolk, Henry was too far gone to place his signature to the fatal paper. Wriothesley, always ready to oblige the strong, produced a commission, stated to be authorised by the King, empowering him as Chancellor to sign for him, which he did upon the warrant ordering the death of Norfolk, whose head was to fall on the following morning. But it was too late, for on the morrow before the hour fixed for the execution the soul of King Henry had gone to its account, and none dared carry out the vicarious command to sacrifice the proudest noble in the realm for the convenience of the political party for the moment predominant.

On the afternoon of 26th January 1547 the end of the King was seen to be approaching. The events of Henry's deathbed have been told with so much religious passion on both sides that it is somewhat difficult to arrive at the truth. Between the soul in despair and mortal anguish, as described by Rivadeneyra, and the devout Protestant death-bed portrayed by some of the ardent religious reformers, there is a world of difference. The accepted English version says that, fearing the dying man's anger, none of the courtiers dared to tell him of his coming dissolution, until his old friend Sir Anthony Denny, leaning over him, gently broke the news. Henry was calm and resigned, and when asked if he wished to see a priest, he answered: "Only Cranmer, and him not yet." It was to be never, for Henry was speechless and sightless when the Primate came, and the King could answer only by a pressure of his numbed fingers the question if he died in the faith of Christ. Another contemporary, whom I have several times quoted, though always with some reservation, says that Henry, some days before he died, took a tender farewell of the Princess Mary, to whose motherly care he commended her young brother; and that he then sent for the Queen and said to her, "'It is God's will that we should part, and I order all these gentlemen to honour and treat you as if I were living still; and, if it should be your pleasure to marry again, I order that you shall have seven thousand pounds for your service as long as you live, and all your jewels and ornaments.' The good Queen could not answer for weeping, and he ordered her to leave him. The next day he confessed, took the sacrament, and commended his soul to God."

Henry died, in fact, as he had lived, a Catholic. The Reformation in England, of which we have traced the beginnings in this book, did not spring mature from the mind and will of the King, but was gradually thrust upon him by the force of circumstances, arising out of the steps he took to satisfy his passion and gratify his imperious vanity. Freedom of thought in religion was the last thing to commend itself to such a mind as his, and his treatment of those who disobeyed either the Act of Supremacy or the Bloody Statute (the Six Articles) shows that neither on the one side or the other would he tolerate dissent from his own views, which he characteristically caused to be embodied in the law of the land, either in politics or religion. The concession to subjects of the right of private judgment in matters of conscience seemed to the potentates of the sixteenth century to strike at the very base of all authority, and the very last to concede such a revolutionary claim was Henry Tudor. His separation from the Papal obedience, whilst retaining what, in his view, were the essentials of the Papal creed, was directed rather to the increase than to the diminution of his own authority over his subjects, and it was this fact that doubtless made it more than ever attractive to him. To ascribe to him a complete plan for the aggrandisement of England and her emancipation from foreign control, by means of religious schism, has always appeared to me to endow him with a political sagacity and prescience which, in my opinion, he did not possess, and to estimate imperfectly the forces by which he was impelled.

We have seen how, entirely in consequence of the unexpected difficulties raised by the Papacy to the first divorce, he adopted the bold advice of Cranmer and Cromwell to defy the Pope on that particular point. The opposition of the Pope was a purely political one, forced upon him by the Emperor for reasons of State, in order to prevent a coalition between England and France; and there were several occasions when, if the Pope had been left to himself, he would have found a solution that would have kept England in the orthodox fold. But for the persistence of the opposition Henry would never have taken the first step that led to the Reformation. Having taken it, each other step onward was the almost inevitable consequence of the first, having regard to the peculiar character of the King. It has been the main business of this book to trace in what respect the policy that ended in the great religious schism was reflected or influenced by the matrimonial adventures of the King, who has gone down to history as the most married monarch of modern times. We have seen that, although, with the exception of Katharine of Aragon and Anne Boleyn, each for a short time, the direct influence of Henry's wives upon events was small, each one represented, and coincided in point of time with, a change in the ruling forces around the King. We have seen that the libidinous tendency of the monarch was utilised by the rival parties, as were all other elements that might help them, to forward the opportunity by which a person to some extent dependent upon them might be placed at the side of the King as his wife; and when for the purpose it was necessary to remove the wife in possession first, we have witnessed the process by which it was effected.

The story from this point of view has not been told before in its entirety, and as the whole panorama unrolls before us, we mark curiously the regular degeneration of Henry's character, as the only checks upon his action were removed, and he progressively defied traditional authority and established standards of conduct without disaster to himself. The power of the Church to censure or punish him, and the fear of personal reprobation by the world, were the influences that, had they retained their force over him to the end, would probably have kept Henry to all appearance a good man. But when he found, probably to his own surprise, that the jealous divisions of the Catholic powers on the Continent made defiance of the Church in his case unpunishable, and that crafty advisers and servile Parliaments could give to his deeds, however violent and cruel, the sanction of Holy Writ and the law of the land, there was no power on earth to hold in check the devil in the breast of Henry Tudor; and the man who began a vain, brilliant sensualist, with the feelings of a gentleman, ended a repulsive, bloodstained monster, the more dangerous because his evil was always held to be good by himself and those around him.

In his own eyes he was a deeply wronged and ill-used man when Katharine of Aragon refused to surrender her position as his wife after twenty years of wedlock, and appealed to forces outside England to aid her in supporting her claim. It was a rebellious, a cruel, and a wicked thing for her and her friends to stand in the way of his tender conscience, and of his laudable and natural desire to be succeeded on the throne by a son of his own. Similarly, it seemed very hard upon him that all Europe, and most of his own country, should be threateningly against him for the sake of Anne Boleyn, for whom he had already sacrificed and suffered so much, and particularly as she was shrewish and had brought him no son. He really was a most ill-used man, and it was a providential instance of divine justice that Cromwell, in the nick of time, when the situation had become unendurable and Jane Seymour's prudish charms were most elusive, should fortunately discover that Anne was unworthy to be Henry's wife, and Cranmer should decide that she never *had* been his wife. It was not his fault, moreover, that Anne of Cleves' physical qualities had repelled him. A wicked and ungenerous trick had been played upon him. His trustful ingenuousness had been betrayed by flatterers at the instance of a knavish minister, who, not content with bringing him a large unsympathetic Dutch vrow for a wife, had pledged him to an alliance with a lot of insignificant vassal princes in rebellion against the greater sovereigns who were his own peers. It was a just decree of heaven that the righteous wisdom of Gardiner and Norfolk should enable it to be demonstrated clearly that the good King had once more been deceived, and that Anne, and the policy she stood for, could be repudiated at the same time without opprobrium or wrongdoing. Again, how relentless was the persecution of the powers of evil against the obese invalid of fifty who married in ignorance of her immoral past a light-lived beauty of seventeen, and was undeceived when her frivolity began to pall upon him by those whose political and religious views might benefit by the disgrace of the party that had placed Katharine Howard by the King's side as his wife. That the girl Queen should lose her head for lack of virtue before her marriage and lack of prudence after it, was, of course, quite just, and in accordance with the law of the land— for all that Henry did was strictly legal— but it was a heartrending thing that the good husband should suffer the distress of having once believed in so unworthy a wife. Still Katharine Howard was not sacrificed in vain, for, although the Catholic policy she represented suffered no check, for reasons set forth in earlier pages, the King's sad bereavement left him in the matrimonial market and enhanced his price as an ally, for much of the future depended upon the wife and the party that should be in possession when the King died. As we have seen, the Protestants, or rather the anti-Catholics, won the last trick; and Somerset's predominance meant that the Reformation in England should not be one of form alone but of substance.

The life of Katharine Parr after Henry's death hardly enters into the plan of this book; but a few lines may be devoted to it, and to her pitiable end. The instant rise of the Protector Somerset on the death of Henry brought with it a corresponding increase in the importance of his brother Sir Thomas, then Lord Seymour of Sudeley, who was certainly no less ambitious than his brother, and probably of much stronger character. For a time all went well between the brothers, Thomas being created Lord Admiral, to the annoyance of Dudley— now Earl of Warwick— who had held the office, and receiving great grants of forfeited estates and other wealth. But soon the evident attempts of Lord Seymour to rival his elder brother, and perhaps to supplant him, aroused the jealousy of Somerset, or more likely of his quarrelsome and haughty wife.

Some love passages, we have seen, took place between Seymour and Katharine Parr before her marriage with the King, so that it need not be ascribed to ambition that the lover should once more cast his eyes upon the royal widow before the weeds for the King had been cast aside. Katharine, with a large dower that has already been mentioned, lived alternately in her two mansion-houses at Chelsea and Hanworth; and to her care was consigned the Lady Elizabeth, then a girl of fourteen. As early as the beginning of May 1547, Seymour had visited the widowed Queen at Chelsea with his tale of love. Katharine was now thirty-four years of age, and having married in succession three old men, might fairly be entitled to contract a fourth marriage to please herself. There was no more manly or handsome figure in England than that of Seymour, with his stately stature, his sonorous voice, and his fine brown beard; and in his quiet meetings with the Queen in her pretty riverside garden at Chelsea, he appears to have found no difficulty in persuading Katharine of the sincerity of his love.

For a time the engagement was kept secret; but watchful eyes were around the Queen, especially those of her own kin, and the following letter, written by Seymour to her on the 17th May, shows that her sister, Lady Herbert, at least, had wind from Katharine of what was going on: "After my humble commendations of your Highness. Yester night I supped at my brother Herbert's, of whom, for your sake besydes my nown, I receved good cheyre. And after the same I received from your Highness by my sister Herbert your commendations, which were more welcome than they were sent. And after the same she (Lady Herbert) waded further with me touching my being with your Highness at Chelsey, which I denied; but that, indeed, I went by the garden as I went to the Bishop of London's howse; and at this point I stood with her for a time, till at last she told me further tokens that made me change colour; and she, like a false wench, took me with the maner. Then, remembering what she was, and knowing how well ye trusted her, I examined her whether these things came from your Highness and by that knew it to be true; for the which I render unto your Highness my most umbell and harty thanks: for by her company (in default of yours) I shall shorten the weeks in these parts, which heretofore were three days longer in every of them than they were under the planets at Chelsey. Besydes this commoditye I may ascertain (*i.e.* inform) your Highness by her how I do proceed in my matter...." Seymour goes on to say that he has not yet dared to try his strength until he is fully in favour, this having reference apparently to his intention of begging his brother to permit the marriage, and then he proceeds: "If I knew by what means I might gratify your Highness for your goodness to me at our last being together, I should not be slack to declare mine to you again, and the intent that I will be more bound to your Highness, I do make my request that, yf it be nott painfull to your Highness, that once in three days I may receve three lynes in a letter from you; and as many lynes and letters more as shall seem good to your Highness. Also I shall ombeley desyr your Highness to geve me one of your small pictures yf ye hav one left, who with his silence shall give me occasion to think on the friendly cheere I shall have when my sawght (suit?) shall be at an end. 12 o'clock in the night this Tewsday the 17th May 1547. From him whom ye have bound to honour, love, and in all lawful thynges obbey.— T. SEYMOUR."

The Queen had evidently pledged her troth to her lover at the previous meeting; and it would appear that when Katharine had promised to write to him but once a fortnight her impatience, as much as his, could ill suffer so long a silence. Either in answer to the above letter, or another similar one, Katharine wrote: "My Lord, I send you my most humble and hearty commendations, being desirous to know how ye have done since I saw you. I pray ye be not offended with me in that I send sooner to you than I said I would, for my promise was but once a fortnight. Howbeit, the time is well abbreviated, by what means I know not, except weeks be shorter at Chelsey than in other places. My Lord, your brother hath deferred answering such requests as I made to him till his coming hither, which he sayeth shall be immediately after the term. This is not the first promise I have received of his coming, and yet unperformed. I think my lady (*i.e.* the Duchess of Somerset) hath taught him that lesson, for it is her custom to promise many comings to her friends and to perform none. I trust in greater matters she is more circumspect." Then follows a curious loving postscript, which shows that Katharine's fancy for Seymour was no new passion. "I would not have you think that this, mine honest good will toward you, proceeds from any sudden motion of passion; for, as truly as God is God, my mind was fully bent the other time I was at liberty to marry you before any man I know. Howbeit, God withstood my will therein most vehemently for a time, and through His grace and goodness made that possible which seemed to me most impossible: that was, made me renounce utterly mine own will, and follow His most willingly. It were long to write all the process of this matter. If I live I shall declare it to you myself. I can say nothing; but as my lady of Suffolk saith: 'God is a marvellous man.'— KATHERYN THE QUENE."

The course of true love did not run smoothly. Somerset, and especially his wife, did not like the idea of his younger brother's elevation to higher influence by his marrying the Queen-Dowager; and the Protector proved unwilling to grant his consent to the marriage. Katharine evidently resented this, and was inclined to use her great influence with the young King himself over his elder uncle's head. When Seymour was in doubt how to approach his brother about it, Katharine wrote spiritedly: "The denial of your request shall make his folly more manifest to the world, which will more grieve me than the want of his speaking. I would not wish you to importune for his goodwill if it come not frankly at first. It shall be sufficient once to require it, and then to cease. I would desire you might obtain the King's letters in your favour, and also the aid and furtherance of the most notable of the Council, such as ye shall think convenient, which thing being obtained shall be no small shame to your brother and sister in case they do not the like." In the same letter Katharine rather playfully dallies with her lover's request that she will abridge the period of waiting from two years to two months, and then she concludes in a way which proves if nothing else did how deeply she was in love with Seymour. "When it shall pleasure you to repair hither (Chelsea) ye must take some pains to come early in the morning, so that ye may be gone again by seven o'clock; and thus I suppose ye may come without being suspect. I pray ye let me have knowledge overnight at what hour ye will come, that your portress (*i.e.* Katharine herself) may wait at the gate to the fields for you."

It was not two years, or even two months, that the impatient lovers waited: for they must have been married before the last day in May 1547, four months after Henry's death. Katharine's suggestion that the boy King himself should be enlisted on their side, was adopted; and he was induced to press Seymour's suit to his father's widow, as if he were the promoter of it. When the secret marriage was known to Somerset, he expressed the greatest indignation and anger at it; and a system of petty persecution of Katharine began. Her jewels, of which the King had left her the use during her life, were withheld from her; her jointure estates were dealt with by Somerset regardless of her wishes and protests; and her every appearance at Court led to a squabble with the Protector's wife as to the precedence to be accorded to her. On one occasion it is stated that this question of precedence led in the Chapel Royal to a personal encounter between Katharine and proud Ann Stanhope.

Nor was Katharine's life at home with her gallant, empty-headed, turbulent husband, cloudless. The Princess Elizabeth lived with them; and though she was but a girl, Seymour began before many months of married life to act suspiciously with her. The manners of the time were free; and Seymour might perhaps innocently romp suggestively, as he did, sometimes alone and sometimes in his wife's presence, with the young Princess as she lay in bed; but when Katharine, entering a chamber suddenly once, found young Elizabeth embraced in her husband's arms, there was a domestic explosion which led to the departure of the girl from the Chelsea household. Katharine was pregnant at the time; and Elizabeth's letter to her on her leaving Chelsea shows that although, for the sake of prudence, the girl was sent away, there was no great unkindness between her and her stepmother in consequence. She says that she was chary of her thanks when leaving, because "I was replete with sorrow to depart from your Highness, especially leaving you undoubtful of health, and, albeit I answered little, I weighed more deeper when you said you would warn me of all the evils that you should hear of me."

When the poor lady's time drew near, she wrote a hopeful yet pathetic letter to her husband, who was already involving himself in the ambitious schemes that brought his head to the block. Both she and her husband in their letters anticipated the birth of their child with a frankness of detail which make the documents unfitted for reproduction here; and it is evident that, though they were now often separated, this looked-for son was to be a new pledge to bind them together for the future. In June 1548 Seymour took his wife to Sudeley Castle for her confinement; and from there carried on, through his agents with the King, his secret plots to supersede his brother Somerset as Protector of the realm. He and his wife were surrounded by a retinue so large, as of itself to constitute a menace to the Protector; but Katharine's royal title gave a pretext for so large a household, and this and her personal influence secured whilst she lived her husband's safety from attack by his brother.

At length, on the 30th August, Katharine's child was born, a daughter, and at first all went well. Even Somerset, angry and distrustful as he was, was infected by his brother's joy, and sent congratulations. But on the fourth day the mother became excited, and wandered somewhat; saying that she thought she would die, and that she was not being well treated. "Those who are about me do not care for me, but stand laughing at my grief," she complained to her friend Lady Tyrwhitt. This was evidently directed against Seymour, who stood by. "Why, sweetheart," he said, "I would you no hurt." "No, my Lord," replied Katharine, "I think so; but," she whispered, "you have given me many shrewd taunts." This seems to have troubled Seymour, and he suggested to Lady Tyrwhitt that he should lie on the bed by the Queen's side and try to calm her; but his efforts were without effect, for she continued excitedly to say that she had not been properly dealt with. These facts, related and magnified by attendants, and coupled with Seymour's desire to marry Elizabeth as soon as his wife died, gave rise to a pretty general opinion that Katharine was either poisoned or otherwise ill treated. But there are many circumstances that point in the contrary direction, and there can be no reasonable doubt now, that although in her inmost mind she had begun to distrust her husband, and the anxiety so caused may have contributed to her illness, she died (on the 5th September) of ordinary puerperal fever.

She was buried in great state in the chapel at Sudeley Castle, and her remains, which have been examined and described several times, add their testimony to the belief that the unfortunate Queen died a natural death. The death of Katharine Parr, the last, and least politically important, of Henry's six wives, took place, so far as English history is concerned, on the day that heralded the death of her royal husband. From the moment that Somerset and his wife sat in the seats of the mighty there was no room for the exercise of political influence by the Queen-Dowager; and these latter pages telling of her fourth marriage, this time for love, form but a human postscript to a political history.

HISTORICAL CONTEXT

During the period the contents of this book took place, the world was a very different place. The events of the time produced an impact on world events. In order for you the reader to better appreciate and connect with this book, it is therefore important to have some context on world events during this timeframe. To this end, we have included a detailed events calendar for the *16th* century for your reference.

Disclaimer: Some scenes throughout history may not be suitable for children, for example, in relation to war or violence. Please use your own discretion before reading this section to your child or allowing your child to read it.

1501 The world's population was estimated to be 435 million, or one-fourth of the 6.4 billion people on the planet today.
Timur's (Tamerlane's) survivors had converted to the Shia branch of Islam. They were willing to resort to violence in order to spread Shi'ism. They seize Tabriz and establish it as their capital. A long-standing tradition existed of fathers passing down power and religious virtue to their sons.
1502 Columbus embarks on his fourth and final voyage to the Caribbean. He remained adamant that the islands were located off the coast of India.
1504 Machiavelli travels to France for his thesis, examining the power of a single ruler over numerous authorities.
1506 Columbus died in Spain.
1509 Erasmus, a Dutch humanist, wrote *In Praise of Folly*. He was a devout Catholic who was troubled by the majority of Christians', what he believed to be, erroneous beliefs at the time. He argued for the translation of the Bible from Latin to indigenous languages, believing that laypeople could comprehend Christianity just as well as priests.
1510 Portuguese cannon-armed ships dominate the Indian Ocean. Indian ships are constructed using coconut fiber ropes rather than iron nails. Portuguese Catholics establish themselves in Goa, India's westernmost port, which was frequented by Muslims on their way to Arabia. Goa became the Asian port and capital of Portugal. India now has a population of 105 million people, or one-twelfth of Pakistan's.
1512 the Sistine Chapel was completed.

1514 the first spice traders arrived in what is now Indonesia.

1517 A Portuguese ship docked in Guangzhou (Canton).

1517 Martin Luther, an Augustinian theologian, lists his 95 theses.

1519 Hispaniola's gold mining industry waned. Spaniards retained a high regard for gold, prompting a quest for gold in the New World. Hernando Cortez was sent to Mexico by Spain's Americas authority.

1520 The Danes flee Sweden.

1521 The Ottoman Empire expanded. Suleiman (Sulayman) succeeds their sultan, Selim.

1531 Martin Luther informed the sodomites.

1532 Machiavelli's *The Prince* (1513) was published.

1532 The Portuguese begin transporting African slaves to Brazil.

1535 Henry VIII proclaimed himself King of England.

1536 Toyotomi Hideyoshi was born in Japan, the son of a poor farmer.

1536 Henry VIII accuses Anne Boleyn of adultery, has her beheaded and marries Jane Seymour.

1538 Barbarossa, an Ottoman Barbary pirate, defeats the Pope's, Venice's, and Spain's combined Christian ships at Preveza (on the coast of western Greece, 124 miles south-east of the Italian peninsula). The Ottoman Empire possesses dominion over the Mediterranean Sea.

1539 Japan abolishes trading monopolies and institutes a free market.

1540 Humayun, Babur's eldest son, rules India, but his inherited empire is in shambles. Humayan was deposed by Islamic nobility and Afghans. Humayun flees to Iran, where he becomes a member of the Safavid court.

Calvin, 32, was expelled from France.

1541 Spanish conquistadors arrived.

1541, Suleiman conquered Buda.

1542 A storm blew a Chinese ship carrying Siam hides and three Portuguese to a small Japanese island 20 miles south of Kyushu. The Japanese learned to use muskets from the Portuguese.

1543 Copernicus was assassinated. By delaying publication of his treatise "*On the Revolution of Heavenly Bodies*," he was able to challenge Church orthodoxy until his death.

1545, attacks on Catholic clergy occurred in France. Troops were assigned to a collection of towns in order to combat Protestant heresy. 3,000 Protestants were slaughtered, and twenty towns were leveled.

Humayun leads a force of 14,000 Safavid warriors east from exile in Iran. Humayun ascended to the throne of Kabul.

1547 King Henry VIII dies.

1549 missionary Francis Xavier arrives in Japan.

1550 Ambrose Pare invented prosthetic limbs.

1551 In France, heretics such as Martin Luther and John Calvin were banned. Paris, Toulouse, Grenoble, Rouen, Bordeaux, and Agners have all executed heretics and book peddlers. A new Protestant bloodbath is underway. Approximately 3,000 Protestants were murdered, and 763 homes, 89 stables, and 31 warehouses were set on fire.

1553 Tsar Ivan IV was born.

1554 Queen Mary I married Philip of Spain, becoming queen consort of Habsburg Spain on his accession in January 1556. Spain gains influence over English affairs through the marriage.

1555 Charles V, King of the Habsburgs, King of Spain, and Holy Roman Emperor, signs the Peace of Augsburg with a group of Protestant German princes (the Schmalkaldic League). The Peace of Augsburg established each prince's right to choose between Lutheranism and Roman Catholicism in order to impose his religion on his subjects.

1556 Humayun collapses and dies on his way to prayer. Muhammad Akbar, his thirteen-year-old son born to an Iranian lady, succeeds him. He declared himself neutral between Islam and Hinduism, deposing Islam as the national religion. The promotion of religious and cultural tolerance will take place. His kingdom will be built on the strength of his military might.

1558, Elizabeth succeeds Queen Mary. Elizabeth restored the state religion to Anglican Protestantism.

1559 Ice cream is invented by an Italian.

1560 Europe was still sick and hungry. Half of all live births die before reaching the age of 12 months (as in the poorest countries today). The wealthy can expect to live to be between 48 and 56 years old, while the poor may only reach the age of 40.

1562 John Hawkins, an English sailor, attacked a slave ship bound for Brazil. He establishes the slave trade in Hispaniola by trading captives for ginger, pearls, and sugar, amassing wealth and attracting other Englishmen.

1563 Trent Council, which began in 1545, concluded in 1563. Tradition was considered equal to text as a source of spiritual knowledge, and the Bible can only be interpreted by the Church. The clergy have been instructed to improve their discipline and education. Concubines must be given up. Bishops are required to reside within their diocese. Additionally, they must make at least one visit every two years to each religious house within their jurisdiction. Each diocese is required to establish a seminary for the education and training of clergy, with priority given to the poor. The laity, particularly the illiterate, will be educated, and sermons will be delivered in the common vernacular. Selling indulgences and Church positions, as well as nepotism, were prohibited. Additionally, a new era of choir music and composition was required to reflect the solemnity of the occasion.

1566 Selim II, Suleiman's son, became Ottoman Sultan. He was neither a politician nor a soldier, in contrast to his two elder brothers who betrayed Suleiman. He was the first in a line of sultans who lacked ambition. He was completely devoted to the harem and alcohol.

1568 Japan has been ravaged by civil wars. Oda Nobunaga, the ruler of Nagoya Castle, was a wealthy feudal lord. Japan has been anticipating the arrival of a unifying force. Nobunaga seizes control of the area surrounding Kyoto, which had been ruled by the Ashikaga dynasty as shoguns for centuries. The Ashikaga era in Japan has come to an end. In Kyoto, Shinto heavenly connections elevate the emperor.

From Holland to Jutland, a tidal wave destroyed the sea fortifications. More than a thousand people are killed.

1571 Tatars plunder and destroy Moscow's suburbs. They are driven back by the Russians.

1572 3,000 Protestants were assassinated in Paris on August 24, St. Bartholomew's Day. 20,000 Huguenots were executed across France in three days. Protestants were heartbroken and enraged, while Catholics were overjoyed.

1575 Japan was engulfed in major wars. With 3,000 musketeers, the Battle of Nagashino was won, consolidating the power in Japan. To facilitate trade and military movement, highways, long pikes, and iron-clad ships were constructed.

1575-76 Juan Ferdandez, a Spanish explorer, reportedly saw Tahiti but sailed past it.

1577 Jost Burgi, a Swiss clockmaker, invented the first minute hand clock.

1579 China has a population of 60 million. (That number will be 22 times that in 2005.)

Spain's King Philip II declared Prince William of Orange to be an outlaw.

1580 Oda Nobunga became lord of central Japan, following the surrender of Osaka's final Buddhist fortress-monastery.

1581 Philip II's seven northern Dutch provinces declared their independence. The Netherlands' United Provinces. The Eighty Years'

War is still ongoing.

1582 Oda Nobunaga is assassinated. Following this, Toyotomi Hideyoshi, one of Oda Nobunaga's most devoted military commanders, defeats Oda Nobunaga's descendants.

1584 Ivan IV appointed Boris Godunov as one of the guardians of his 27-year-old son, Feodor, on his deathbed.

King Philip II has compensated the estate of Prince William of Orange with 25,000 crowns. According to William, he was a "pest on all of Christianity" and an "enemy of humanity." William becomes a victim of assassination. The Dutch mourn the loss of their nation's father, William.

1585 Spain besieges Antwerp. The Dutch invented time bombs in the form of floating clocks.

1586, Bernardino Telesio, an Italian philosopher, published nine Aristotelian critiques. He is opposed to science, not metaphysics.

1587 some Japanese began dressing in European garb, and Christianity began to spread throughout the country. This is a trait that Hiseyoshi and others despise. Japanese Christians were denied entry to Japan during Hideyoshi's reign.

1588 The Spanish Armada was a Habsburg Spanish fleet of 130 ships that sailed from Lisbon in late May 1588 under the command of the Duke of Medina Sidonia, with the purpose of escorting an army from Flanders to invade England. Queen Elizabeth I defeats the fleet keeping England safe.

1590 Scientific advancements were being made through mechanical advancements. When testing lenses in a tube, an eyeglasses manufacturer in the Netherlands notices that nearby objects appear magnified. The microscope as we know it today was born.

1591 Despite his incompetence, Feodor retained the title of Tsar. Dmitri, Ivan's nine-year-old son and heir apparent, also dies after having his neck slashed. According to officials, the boy cut himself during an epileptic seizure. Fearful of Dmitri's demise, a mob attacks and assassinates his guards.

1592 Toyotomi Hideyoshi concentrates on foreign conquests. His military victories have convinced him that his soldiers are unstoppable, and he intends to conquer the rest of the world via China and Korea.

Clement VIII, Pope, declared "The world was afflicted by the Jews' usury, monopolies, and deception. They impoverished a large number of unfortunate people, particularly farmers, workers, and the very poor."

1593 Galileo invented the thermometer.

1594 Henry, the Protestant Bourbon King of Navarre, converted to Catholicism in order to gain power in Paris. The coronation of France's King Henry IV.

1595 Shakespeare, 30, was a busy actor and playwright. He was a Renaissance man whose work focused on human vanity rather than God.

1598 The Peace of Vervins ends the war between France and Spain.

1600 Giordano Bruno, an Italian philosopher, was staked.

The British East India Company was founded in 1600 by Queen Elizabeth of England to compete with the Dutch nutmeg trade from the Banda Islands.

This concludes the historical context.

Thank you for your interest in our publications. Please don't forget to check out our other books and leave a review if you enjoyed this book.